THE REFORM OF CIVIL

THE REFORM OF CIVIL LITIGATION

THE RT HON LORD JUSTICE JACKSON

Published in 2016 by
Thomson Reuters (Professional) UK Limited trading as
Sweet & Maxwell, Friars House, 160 Blackfriars Road, London SE1 8EZ
(Registered in England & Wales, Company No. 1679046.
Registered Office and address for service:
2nd floor, 1 Mark Square, Leonard Street, London EC2A 4EG)

For further information on our products and services, visit
www.sweetandmaxwell.co.uk

Typeset by Servis Filmsetting Ltd, Stockport, Cheshire, SK2 5AJ
Printed and bound by CPI Group (UK) Ltd, Croydon, CR0 4YY

No natural forests were destroyed to make this product;
only farmed timber was used and re-planted.

A CIP catalogue record for this book is available from the British Library.

ISBN 978-0-414-05686-2

CONTENTS

Part 2: Funding

Part 3: Consensual Settlement

Part 4: The Management of Litigation

Part 5: Particular Categories of Litigation

Part 6: Quantifying Costs

Contents

[x]

FOREWORD

All of us who are concerned about access to civil justice owe an enormous debt of gratitude to Sir Rupert Jackson. He has spent a great many years seeking to improve the administration of civil justice, from his time as a barrister assessor for Lord Woolf's Inquiry into Access to Justice in 1995 and 1996, via his monumental Review of Civil Litigation Costs between 2008 and 2010 at the request of Sir Anthony Clarke MR, to a series of important lectures which he has given during 2015–2016, and now the publication of this book.

Sir Rupert says that the book is intended to be a simple and clear explanation of the principal reforms which bear his name as a result of the Jackson Review, and that his target audience is law students and young practitioners. So speaks his customary modesty. The book is much more than that. It describes in detail not only the numerous reforms which have sprung from his Review, but the rationale for each of them, the way in which they have been implemented or why they have not, the success or otherwise they have enjoyed, what remains to be achieved and what further action should be taken. The matters on which he touches affect every person involved in the administration of civil justice—every litigant, professional representative and judicial office holder. The topics covered include (but are not limited to) amendments to the overriding objective and the introduction of proportionality as a guiding principle, conditional fee agreements, after-the-event-insurance, damages based agreements, case management, disclosure, costs management, qualified one-way costs shifting, referral fees, fixed recoverable costs, CPR Pt 36 offers, bills of costs, and assessment of costs.

Most of the recommendations of the Jackson Review have been implemented. Many have been obviously successful. There remain critics of some, including, for example, certain consequences of costs budgeting. Sir Rupert does not duck the criticism but robustly and cogently seeks to rebut it where appropriate, concedes that some things have not turned out precisely as anticipated and describes further work that is needed in some areas. This is why the book deserves and will have a far wider audience than students and young practitioners. It speaks to all those (including the incoming Master of the Rolls) who, like Sir Rupert, are concerned for civil justice and to those who are in a position to influence the administration of civil justice.

Sir Rupert recognises that some of the outstanding work to bring his recommendations to full effect dovetails into the review of the civil courts structure currently being undertaken by Lord Justice Briggs, which is itself being conducted in parallel with the wider four-year reform programme of the entire court system. Such outstanding work includes the greater and more effective use of alternative dispute resolution and of IT, better third party funding, including by means of a contingent legal aid fund or a supplementary legal aid scheme, and the extension of the fixed recoverable costs regime. Other areas, where the book is right up to date with continuing civil procedure developments, are the Working Party on

Disclosure set up by the Rolls Building jurisdictions, the devising of a new format bill of costs, and reforms to the procedures in the Court of Appeal to address the increased workload of that Court.

As Sir Rupert emphasises, the Jackson reforms are interconnecting and form a coherent package. They were all intended, one way or another, to promote access to justice at proportionate cost within the constraints of an adversarial common law system. The ability to access justice is an essential aspect of the Rule of Law, but there are inevitably practical constraints in achieving access. At the heart of the Jackson reforms lies the touchstone of proportionality. The introduction of that guiding principle and many of the other Jackson reforms, described and explained so admirably in this book, will provide an enduring testament to the vision and hard work of Sir Rupert for the benefit of all members of our society.

Sir Terence Etherton[1]

---

[1] Sir Terence Etherton will be Master of the Rolls from 4 October 2016.

NOTE ON THE PARLIAMENTARY PROCESS BY LORD FAULKS QC

I have had the interesting experience of seeing the Jackson reforms from different perspectives. I took part in debates from the government backbenches in the House of Lords when the reforms were first discussed, drawing on my experience as a civil barrister. I am now privileged to have oversight of those reforms as Minister of State for civil justice.

Although Sir Rupert Jackson's final report was published over six years ago now, there has been an almost constant process since then of consideration, consultation, Parliamentary debates, implementation and adaptation.

Sir Rupert's final report was published in January 2010. The then Labour Justice Secretary reacted warmly to the report, but matters had not progressed by the time of the general election in May of that year.

In July 2010, a written statement by the Parliamentary Under Secretary of State announced the new Coalition Government's intention to consult on the implementation of Sir Rupert's recommendations.

In November 2010, the Government published its consultation paper on "Proposals for reform of civil litigation funding and costs in England and Wales: implementation of Lord Justice Jackson's recommendations".

The consultation closed on 14 February 2011. The Government published its response on 29 March 2011.

The Legal Aid, Sentencing and Punishment of Offenders Bill (LASPO) was introduced in the House of Commons in June 2011 and in the House of Lords in November 2011.

Part 1 of the Bill contained changes to the scope of legal aid. Part 2 contained the legislative reflection of the Jackson reforms and Pt 3 was concerned with sentencing. Although it was a major piece of legislation, it went through the Commons without much difficulty. Perhaps this was unsurprising given the size of the Government's majority and that it was so early in the session.

Its progress in the Lords was much more difficult. By this time, considerable opposition to the Bill had emerged from the many stakeholders affected by its provisions. The opposition was primarily focused on Pt 1 of the Bill, but there were also critics of Pt 2.

It was said that difficult cases would not be pursued in the absence of success fees and recoverable after-the-event insurance premiums. Examples were given in relation to clinical negligence, environmental claims, defamation, claims arising out of industrial disease, and insolvency. There were also broader criticisms to the effect that the reforms would unbalance civil litigation in favour of defendants.

Perhaps the most cogent criticism of the Government's proposals was that the reforms presupposed the continuation of legal aid rather than its reduction or removal as provided for by Pt 1 of the Bill. As Sir Rupert explains in Ch. 5, in relation to clinical negligence cases, the legal aid authorities were accustomed to administering a scheme which entitled those who were eligible (after a means test) to have legal aid if their claims had merit. Expert reports could be obtained and appropriately experienced lawyers instructed.

The reality was, however, that many clinical negligence lawyers did not in fact use legal aid even in cases where it might have been obtained, preferring the more profitable conditional fee route.

In any event, the Government was committed to widespread cuts in public expenditure and decided that the £2 billion plus spent on legal aid needed to be significantly reduced.

This was not the first time a government had linked cuts in legal aid with a change in funding arrangements for civil litigation. The introduction in April 2000 of recoverable success fees and ATE premiums which gave rise to the so-called "costs war" was also accompanied by a substantial reduction in legal aid. These earlier reforms are described by Sir Rupert as "disastrous" and were the underlying cause of the need for a thorough overhaul of civil litigation.

Although I have something of a vested interest, I think it is fair to say that par-liamentary scrutiny in the House of Lords can be more thorough than it is in the Commons. Specific issues in the Bill received close attention, and the Government lost a large number of votes there and had to make some significant concessions. Despite many votes and the expression of strong concerns from some quarters about the likely impact of the measures, the Government suffered only one actual defeat in relation to Pt 2. That related to claims arising out of mesothelioma. For the reasons given by Sir Rupert, this exception makes little sense but the arguments in favour of making special provision for the victims of this dreadful disease had a great deal of appeal to Peers and Members of Parliament generally.

But what was particularly significant was that there was very little challenge to the overall structure of Pt 2. Although much was said about the need to maintain access to justice, there was—in the end—an acceptance of the need for reform.

The Bill received Royal Assent in May 2012. It came into force on 1 April 2013. A year for a major Bill to get through Parliament is by no means unusual. It was fol-lowed by a year for implementation (Rules and Regulations in reasonable time for people to adjust). It was a considerable challenge to get the detail right. In light of past experience, it was clear that the structure of the legislation needed to be sound.

Although there continued to be opposition to the effects of LASPO running up to the election in 2015, most of it was concentrated on the reduction in legal aid. It is significant that neither of the major opposition parties suggested that they would repeal LASPO.

A post-implementation review of Pt 2 is due to take place in April 2018. I would not, of course, wish to pre-empt the findings of any review, but I would be surprised if the principles of Sir Rupert's recommendations were found to be unsound. Whether the absence of legal aid in some areas is causing injustice may be the subject of debate, but I would not expect a call for a major overhaul of Pt 2 of LASPO.

Parliament rarely gets involved with the details of civil procedure, although it remains central to a satisfactory justice system. I agree with Sir Rupert that reform is a continuous process. I do not, however, agree with his description of the reforms as "a modest contribution for others to build upon". The only modesty about them is his.

PREFACE

Why was this book written? The idea for this book came after I had given a few lectures about the recent civil justice reforms to law students. Their reaction was one of gratitude for a simple explanation of voluminous material which they had not found easy (or particularly enjoyable) to digest. Law students and young practitioners do not have the time or inclination to plough through the Costs Review Preliminary Report (660 pages), its appendices (300 pages on CD), the Costs Review Final Report (550 pages), a series of implementation lectures, a series of post-implementation lectures, a raft of statutory provisions and the amended Civil Procedure Rules.

The aim of this book and the target audience. This book is intended to be a simple and clear explanation of the principal reforms which bear my name. It does not go through every one of those reforms. That would be tedious and make it difficult to see the wood for the trees. The book quotes only very small parts of the Costs Review Preliminary Report and the Final Report. The target audience is law students and young practitioners. These are the people who hold the future of civil justice in their hands.

It is also hoped that that the explanation in this book of how the reforms interlink and of the underlying intention may be of assistance to others.

Compression of material. Because the book is short, it has been necessary to compress material and to simplify. For example, the increase in general damages (explained in the tenth implementation lecture "Why Ten per cent?") has been squeezed into Ch. 5. That chapter also accommodates the reforms to conditional fee agreements and after-the-event insurance. For those seeking more detail, the Preliminary Report, its appendices, the Final Report, the implementation lectures and the post-implementation lectures await. They are all available on the Judiciary website.

Bearing in mind the target audience, very occasionally a note of levity creeps into the text. No offence to anyone is thereby intended.

The two other functions of this book. This book also has two other functions. First, it contributes to the ongoing debate about one or two contentious issues, such as J codes, hybrid damages-based-agreements and fixed costs. Secondly, it provides an account of the reform process which has dominated eight years of my life. This may be of interest to some, because it has brought me into the area of political debate to an extent that is unusual for a serving judge.

What this book is not. This book is not a detailed commentary on the rules implementing the reforms. Nor is it an attempt to resolve the thorny issues of interpretation to which some those rules have given rise. Other authors have produced excellent books for that purpose. See, for example, *Costs & Funding following the Civil Justice Reforms: Questions & Answers* by Hurst, Middleton and Mallalieu; *Andrews on Civil Proceedings* (Vol. 1 on court proceedings) by Neil Andrews; *Costs Law: An Expert Guide*, edited by Laura Slater; *Zuckerman on Civil Procedure* by Adrian Zuckerman; *Blackstone's Guide to the Civil Justice Reforms* 2013 by Sime and French; and, last but not least, the *White Book*.

Rupert Jackson
15 June 2016

ACKNOWLEDGEMENTS

The Review of Civil Litigation Costs
I am most grateful to:

- The assessors during the Costs Review, namely Mr Justice Cranston, Professor Paul Fenn, Senior Costs Judge Peter Hurst, Jeremy Morgan QC, Michael Napier CBE QC, Andrew Parker and Colin Stutt.

- The judicial assistants during the Costs Review, namely Pete Given, Ilona Groark, Hannah Piper and Julian Bailey.

- The accountant judicial assistants during the Costs Review, namely Lucy Harrison and Chris Tune.

- The countless people who served on working groups during the Costs Review and during the implementation period.

- Sir Vivian Ramsey, who took over my role in implementing the reforms between 30 April 2012 and late 2013.

This book
I am most grateful to:

- My present judicial assistant, Stephen Clark, for his considerable help in the preparation of this book.

- Nicholas Bacon QC, Alexander Hutton QC, Andrew Post QC, Robert Gaitskell QC, Roger Mallalieu, Karl Mackie, and Vince Neicho of Allen & Overy for their advice on various chapters.

- Numerous judges who have generously responded to my requests for advice or information. These include the London TCC judges, Mr Justice Blair, District Judge Burn, HH Judge Gore QC, Mr Registrar Clive Jones, District Judge Simon Middleton, HH Judge Platts, and HH Judge Waksman QC.

- Jason Rix of Allen & Overy for preparing the excellent diagram contained in Appendix A.

- Professor Paul Fenn of Nottingham University for providing the excellent graphs which appear at the end of Appendix B.

I thank Professor Hazel Genn, Professor Rachael Mulheron and Professor Neil Andrews for their advice on parts of the draft. I am also grateful to Professor Adrian Zuckerman and Professor Andrew Higgins, with whom I have discussed some of the issues in this book.

I thank Sir Terence Etherton for writing the foreword and Lord Faulks for providing a note on the parliamentary process.

I am grateful to the publishers for the speed and efficiency with which they have converted my ill-formatted text into a presentable book.

Finally and more generally, I thank my successive clerks, namely Abi Pilkington, Clare Smith and Olivia Jay, for their indefatigable efforts over the years in connection with the Costs Review, the implementation process and the preparation of this book.

Responsibility for all errors is mine alone.

RJ

LIST OF ABBREVIATIONS AND TERMS

Abbreviations

ABI:	Association of British Insurers
ACL:	Association of Costs Lawyers
ADR:	Alternative dispute resolution
ALF:	Association of Litigation Funders
APIL:	Association of Personal Injury Lawyers
ATE:	After-the-event insurance
BA:	British Airways
BSB:	Bar Standards Board
BTE:	Before-the-event insurance
CCMC:	Costs and case management conference
CEDR:	Centre for Effective Dispute Resolution
CFA:	Conditional fee agreement
CILEx:	Chartered Institute of Legal Executives
CJC:	Civil Justice Council
CLAF:	Contingent legal aid fund
CMC:	Case management conference
CM Council:	Civil Mediation Council
CPR:	Civil Procedure Rules (the procedural rules applying to the County Court, High Court and Court of Appeal since 26 April 1999)
DBA:	Damages-based agreement
EAT:	Employment Appeal Tribunal
ECHR:	European Convention on Human Rights
EFDM:	Electronic filing and document management
ET:	Employment Tribunal
FCA:	Financial Conduct Authority (successor to the FSA)
FOIL:	Forum of Insurance Lawyers
FR:	Review of Civil Litigation Costs Final Report ("Final Report")
FSA:	Financial Services Authority (a body which was abolished in 2013)
FSB:	Federation of Small Businesses
GHR:	Guideline hourly rate
IP:	Intellectual property
IPA:	Insolvency Practitioners Association
JSG:	Judicial Steering Group
LASPO:	Legal Aid, Sentencing and Punishment of Offenders Act 2012
LEDES:	Legal Electronic Data Exchange Standard
LIP:	Litigant in person
LSLA:	London Solicitors Litigation Association
MDU:	Medical Defence Union

MLA:	Media Lawyers Association
MoJ:	Ministry of Justice
MPS:	Medical Protection Society
NHSLA:	National Health Service Litigation Authority
NMH:	National Mediation Helpline
ODR:	Online dispute resolution
OFT:	Office of Fair Trading (a body which was abolished in 2014)
PCC:	Patents County Court (this became the Intellectual Property Enterprise Court in October 2013)
PD:	Practice Direction
PDPAC:	Practice Direction – Pre-Action Conduct
PI:	Personal injury
PIBA:	Personal Injury Bar Association
PPD:	Public Participation Directive
PR:	Review of Civil Litigation Costs Preliminary Report ("Preliminary Report")
PTR:	Pre-trial review
QOCS:	Qualified one-way costs shifting
RCJ:	Royal Courts of Justice
RSC:	Rules of the Supreme Court (the procedural rules applying to the High Court and Court of Appeal before 26 April 1999)
RTA:	Road traffic accident
SABIP:	Strategic Advisory Board for Intellectual Property Policy
SCL:	Society of Construction Law
SLAS:	Supplementary legal aid scheme
SME:	Small or medium enterprise
SRA:	Solicitors Regulation Authority
TAR:	Technology Assisted Review
TCC:	Technology and Construction Court
TeCSA:	Technology and Construction Solicitors Association
TECBAR:	Technology and Construction Bar Association
TPF:	Third party funding
UTBMS:	Uniform Task-Based Management System

Terms

Harbour Lecture:	The Harbour Lecture on 13 May 2015 entitled "Confronting costs management"
He:	He or she (sincere apologies for this; sometimes the use of "he or she" makes the text convoluted)
Plaintiff:	The term used for a claimant before 26 April 1999
Recoverability:	The ability to recover CFA success fees and ATE premiums from an opposing party
Rule Committee:	Civil Procedure Rule Committee
Woolf reforms:	The reforms recommended by Lord Woolf in 1996 and implemented in 1999

TABLE OF CASES

TABLE OF STATUTES

TABLE OF STATUTORY INSTRUMENTS

Part One

THE PROCESS OF REFORM AND THE PRINCIPLE OF PROPORTIONALITY

CHAPTER 1

INTRODUCTION

1. THE ROLE OF CIVIL JUSTICE

Starting point. Our starting point must be that the effective administration of justice, including civil justice, is vital to the well-being of every community. This proposition can be demonstrated both at the theoretical level and as a matter of practical reality.　　**1–001**

From Aristotle to Rawls in one paragraph. Legal philosophers from Aristotle[1] to Rawls have recognised the critical importance of civil justice to society.　　**1–002**

- In Aristotle's view,[2] justice embraces moral excellence and, more specifically, both corrective justice and distributive justice. Justice, like all virtues in Aristotle's scheme of things, is a mean. Corrective justice seeks the mean between the loss suffered by the victim and the gain made by the wrongdoer. Distributive justice requires a proportionate sharing of benefits and burdens.[3]

- Rawls, writing over 2,000 years later, maintains that justice "is the first virtue of social institutions, as truth is of systems of thought".[4] From this starting point, Rawls proceeds to develop his theory of justice as fairness and the role of justice in a well-ordered society.

A survey of jurisprudence during the two millennia which separate Aristotle and Rawls is beyond the scope of this book. The important point is that most serious thinkers have recognised the critical importance of civil justice (as well as criminal justice). It is implicit in all such writings that the administration of justice should be accessible to those involved in conflict.

---

[1] Aristotle looked at legal philosophy from a broad perspective, since he was an authority on everything else as well.

[2] Aristotle, *Nicomachean Ethics*, book 5; *Eudemian Ethics*, book 6.

[3] See also Hart's analysis of justice and morality in Ch. 8 of *The Concept of Law*, which seems to be a development of Aristotle's thinking.

[4] John Rawls, *A Theory of Justice*, chapter 1.

1–003   **Bentham strikes a discordant note.** Jeremy Bentham, the famous expounder of utilitarianism, was strongly critical of the courts for their single minded pursuit of justice, without regard to the costs and delay involved.[5] He argued that in their quest to arrive at the right answer courts should not admit every possible piece of evidence, but only as much evidence as could be justified by his felicific calculus.[6] As Sorabji demonstrates,[7] Bentham's theories did not provide a satisfactory foundation on which to build any procedural code. Bentham's contribution was to highlight that the proper administration of justice was not the same as achieving a legally perfect outcome in every case. That approach did not find favour at the time, but it is now gaining traction in modern theories of case management.

1–004   **Practical importance of civil justice.** At the practical level, the importance of civil justice is self-evident. Sir Jack Jacob QC stated in his 1987 Hamlyn lectures:

> "[T]he system of civil justice is of transcendent importance for the people of this country, just as it is for the people of every country."[8]

More recently, Professor Dame Hazel Genn returned to this theme in her 2008 Hamlyn Lectures.[9] In her first lecture, she took the following propositions as her starting point:

> "[T]he machinery of civil justice sustains social stability and economic growth by providing public processes for peacefully resolving civil disputes, for enforcing legal rights and for protecting private and personal rights. The civil justice system provides the legal architecture for the economy to operate effectively, for agreements to be honoured, and for the power of government to be scrutinised and limited. The civil law maps out the boundaries of social and economic behaviour, while the civil courts resolve disputes when they arise. In this way, the civil courts publicly re-affirm norms and behavioural standards for private citizens, businesses and public bodies."

1–005   **Economic importance of civil justice.** The civil courts play a crucial role in sustaining and attracting economic activity. Commercial contracts must be capable of effective enforcement. For all major enterprises, occasional litigation is an incident of carrying on business. Therefore an efficient civil litigation process is vital for their operations. Furthermore, parties to international contracts choose English law, because they have confidence in the English courts. This in turn attracts both transactional work and dispute resolution to this country.

1–006   **The availability of civil litigation provides an essential backdrop.** Most transactions between government and governed and most dealings between individuals or companies proceed smoothly. This is because people voluntarily

---

[5] See the excellent review of Bentham's works in Sorabji, *English civil justice after the Woolf and Jackson reforms*, Pt 1, "Theories of justice".

[6] See Jeremy Bentham, *Introductory view of the rationale of judicial evidence*. In *Principles of judicial procedure*, Bentham incorporated utilitarianism into his theory of substantive justice.

[7] John Sorabji, *English civil justice after the Woolf and Jackson reforms*, Ch. 3, "Substantive justice is no end in itself".

[8] Sir Jack Jacob, *The reform of civil procedural law*.

[9] Professor Dame Hazel Genn, *Judging civil justice* (Hamlyn Lectures 2008).

comply with their legal obligations. When disputes arise, such disputes are usually resolved before the issue of legal proceedings or, failing that, before trial. This is because the participants can predict what the courts will (or at least might well) decide. Thus, the law and the accessibility of the civil courts provide an essential backdrop for the way people do business and live their lives.

Civil litigation develops the law. Those few civil disputes which proceed   1–007
to trial fulfil a valuable public function in reaffirming the framework within which everyone must regulate their affairs. Professor Genn describes this as the "shadow" which judicial decisions cast.[10] Accordingly, she argues that "a flow of adjudicated cases is necessary to provide guidance on the law and, occasionally, to make new leaps". The Lord Chief Justice, Lord Thomas, made similar points in his 2016 lecture entitled "Developing commercial law through the courts: rebalancing the relationship between the courts and arbitration".[11]

2. A Short History of Civil Justice Reform since 1870

The Judicature Acts.[12] The reports of the Judicature Commission, published in   1–008
1868 and 1869, recommended radical restructuring of the civil justice system. The Supreme Court of Judicature Act 1873 as amended by the Judicature Act 1875 (collectively "the Judicature Acts") implemented the Commission's recommendations. The Judicature Acts swept away the previous superior courts[13] and created a single "Supreme Court of Judicature". The Supreme Court of Judicature contained both the Court of Appeal and the High Court. The High Court comprised the Chancery Division, the Queen's Bench Division, and the Probate, Divorce and Admiralty Division. The Judicature Acts also achieved the fusion of common law and equity.

An enduring structure, but adapted to modern circumstances. The struc-   1–009
ture established by the Judicature Acts still remains in place, which is a testament to the breadth of vision of the Victorian law reformers. The "Supreme Court of Judicature" was renamed the "Senior Courts" in 2008, when the newly created Supreme Court replaced the Judicial Committee of the House of Lords as the final appellate court of the UK. The divisions of the High Court are now the Chancery Division, the Queen's Bench Division and the Family Division. Within those divisions are various specialist courts, such as the Patents Court, the Administrative Court, the Technology and Construction Court, and the Admiralty and Commercial Court.

---

[10] See Genn's comment in her first Hamlyn Lecture:
   "Adjudication in civil justice has a critical public function in providing the framework or the "shadow" in which settlement of disputes can be achieved".
[11] Bailii Lecture, 18 March 2016, available on the Judiciary website: *https://www.judiciary.gov.uk/* [Accessed 1 July 2016].
[12] See generally Sir William Holdsworth, *A History of English Law*, Vol. 1, pp. 638-645, and Vol. 15, *passim*.
[13] Court of Queen's Bench, Court of Common Pleas, Court of Exchequer, Courts of Chancery, Court of Probate, Court of Divorce, High Court of Admiralty.

1–010   **Rules of the Supreme Court 1883.**[14] High Court judges have always possessed the common law power to make rules regulating the procedures of their courts. Section 1 of the Civil Procedure Act 1833 put that power on a statutory basis. The Judicature Acts conferred the power to make rules on a newly created Rule Committee. The Rule Committee made the Rules of the Supreme Court ("RSC") 1883, which remained in force subject to amendments for some 80 years.

1–011   **Civil justice reform projects between 1883 and 1950.** During this tumultuous period of British history, numerous committees and commissions examined the workings of the civil courts. These included the Gorrell Committee, the Royal Commission on Delays in the King's Bench Division, the Hanworth Committee, the Peel Commission and many others. These learned bodies were all seeking to expedite civil proceedings and reduce costs. Their reports resulted in a variety of amendments to the RSC 1883, but the problems remained intractable. Finally, in the middle of the twentieth century, came the Evershed Committee.

1–012   **Evershed Committee.** The Committee on Supreme Court Practice and Procedure, over which Sir Raymond Evershed MR presided, deliberated for six years. It delivered two interim reports and a final report, which was dated July 1953. The control of costs was one of the committee's principal concerns. It seriously considered recommending a version of costs management, but drew back from that. In para. 700 of its final report, the committee stated:

> "While some of us at any rate cherish the hope that it may at some future date be possible to evolve some workable scheme for fixing costs in advance, we are not prepared at this date, and with the evidence now before us, to recommend such a radical departure from the present system. Upon any view we think that the introduction of any such far-reaching scheme would have to wait until more experience had been gained as the result of the less ambitious proposals which we are more disposed to recommend."

1–013   **Rules of the Supreme Court 1965.** The Evershed Committee's main recommendation was that there should be a complete rewriting of the RSC. This work was duly put in hand. The result was the Rules of the Supreme Court 1965, which replaced the Rules of the Supreme Court 1883. The new rules made numerous drafting improvements and revisions, but no substantial procedural changes.[15] The RSC 1965 remained in force until the end of the twentieth century.

1–014   **Civil justice reform projects in the late twentieth century.** Unfortunately, both delay and high levels of costs continued to plague the civil justice system. New committees and reformers set to work. The Winn Committee in 1968 and the Cantley Committee in 1979 both focused on delays in personal injury litigation. In 1988, the Report of the Review Body on Civil Justice[16] proposed 91 reforms,

---

[14] Sir Jack Jacob, *The reform of civil procedural law*, pp. 213–214; Sir William Holdsworth, *A History of English Law*, Vol. 1, pp. 645–647.
[15] See the preface to the White Book 1967, p. x.
[16] Cmd 394, 1988.

including a substantial extension to the jurisdiction of the county courts in order to relieve pressure on the High Court. The Courts and Legal Services Act 1990 implemented many of those recommendations. In 1993, a working party set up by the Law Society and the Bar Council, chaired by Hilary Heilbron QC, published a formidable report on civil justice reform. The general theme of reports during this period was that courts should do more to restrain the excesses of civil litigation and that all involved should co-operate to secure the early resolution of issues. These reports and the continuing concern about costs and delay led to the establishment of the Woolf Inquiry.

Woolf Inquiry. Lord Woolf's Inquiry into Access to Justice ran for two years.   **1–015** His assessors[17] tendered their advice, but Lord Woolf alone decided on the contents of his reports. The inquiry involved wide consultation, seminars around the country and contributions from working groups. Lord Woolf delivered an interim report in 1995 and a final report in 1996. He proposed a number of reforms to streamline the litigation process. A key proposal was that the court should take an increased role in the management of cases. Lord Woolf recommended that new Civil Procedure Rules should be drawn up. They would be a unified code, governing proceedings in both the High Court and the county courts. The new rules would be written in clear and simple language.

Introduction of the Civil Procedure Rules in 1999. A new Civil Procedure   **1–016** Rule Committee ("the Rule Committee") was established. It drew up the Civil Procedure Rules 1998 ("CPR"). The CPR came into force on 26 April 1999. They replaced the former RSC and the former County Court Rules.

Unification of the county courts. In January 2008, the Judicial Executive   **1–017** Board invited Sir Henry Brooke, a retired lord justice of appeal, to conduct an inquiry into the question of unifying the civil courts. Sir Henry delivered his report in August 2008. His principal recommendation was that the various county courts around the country should be unified into a single court. This recommendation was adopted. In 2014, the new County Court came into existence. It continued to operate in the same buildings as the former county courts.

Civil justice reform projects in the early twenty-first century. The reforms   **1–018** of Lord Woolf undoubtedly reduced delays and expedited civil litigation. Unfortunately, however, costs continued to escalate. This was largely due to some disastrous reforms in April 2000,[18] which were nothing to do with Lord Woolf. Those events generated a "costs war".[19] In litigation, unaffected by the April 2000 reforms, costs continued to mount. There were concerns about the expense of commercial litigation, especially after the collapse of BCCI's action against the Bank of England with huge costs on both sides. This led to the establishment of the Long Trials Working Party, chaired by Sir Richard Aikens. The working party recommended a number of wise reforms, in particular early identification of

---

[17] I was the barrister assessor and learnt much from Lord Woolf's conduct of the inquiry.
[18] Discussed in Ch. 5, below.
[19] Described in Ch. 3 of the Review of Civil Litigation Costs Preliminary Report ("Preliminary Report", "PR").

issues and focusing case management on the identified issues. The Admiralty and Commercial Court implemented those recommendations.

1–019   **Review of Civil Litigation Costs.** It was against the background described above that, in 2008, Sir Anthony Clarke MR announced the setting up of the Review of Civil Litigation Costs. He appointed the most junior member of the Court of Appeal to carry out that review. Chapter 2, below, summarises the course of that review. Later chapters discuss the resulting reforms and how they have fared.

3. WHY IS IT SO DIFFICULT TO CONTROL LITIGATION COSTS?

1–020   **Lots of very clever people have wrestled with this problem. Surely they've cracked it by now?** Well, yes. Civil justice reformers have done much to tackle the excesses of litigation costs. But England and Wales still remain one of the most expensive jurisdictions in which to litigate.[20] That is why Sir Anthony Clarke MR set up the Costs Review.

1–021   **Professor Zuckerman's analysis.** Professor Zuckerman offers a penetrating analysis of the issue in Ch. 27 of *Zuckerman on Civil Procedure*. He identifies the underlying problem as

> "the combined effect of two features of the English costs system: the costs shifting principle (transferring the burden from the successful party to the unsuccessful one) and the method of remunerating lawyers on an hourly basis".[21]

Professor Zuckerman is right on both counts. Research has demonstrated that costs shifting tends to drive up costs on both sides.[22] Self-evidently, remuneration on a time spent basis incentivises inefficiency—the longer you spend doing a task, the more you get paid for it.

1–022   **So what's the answer then?** Given the starting point (a common law system with costs shifting deeply embedded in the culture), the only way to control costs is to do so in advance. That means (a) introducing fixed recoverable costs, or (b) setting budgets for each case and holding the parties to those budgets, or (c) a combination of the two. The Review of Civil Litigation Costs came down in favour of option (c), as explained in later chapters. If recoverable costs are controlled in advance, this changes the dynamics of litigation. The parties are less inclined to engage in an "arms race". They are more inclined to restrict expenditure on their own side, possibly even holding their own lawyers to a budget.

---

[20] See Hodges, Vogenauer and Tulibacka, *The Costs and Funding of Civil Litigation*, at p. 104, para. 25.
[21] Adrian Zuckerman, *Zuckerman on Civil Procedure*, at p. 1456, para. 27.384.
[22] See PR Ch. 9.

Will that approach make you popular? No, unfortunately it won't. For **1–023**
entirely understandable reasons, lawyers much prefer to have a free hand during
litigation and to leave the quantification of costs until later. Add up the bill at
the end and recover as much of it as you can from the other side (assuming you
have won). When Lord Woolf had the temerity to suggest that costs should be
controlled in advance, he provoked an "outcry" from the legal profession and was
persuaded to drop the idea: see pp. 81–82 of Lord Woolf's Final Report. Sadly, it
has now become clear that anyone who seriously wants to tackle the problem of
litigation costs will have to upset the legal profession—and possibly the judiciary
as well, if they are required to start controlling budgets.

But surely you can't make litigation affordable just by tweaking the costs **1–024**
rules? Good point. Any project to make civil litigation affordable requires a combination of five strategies:

- Amend the rules of procedure, so as to streamline the litigation process and
  cut out unnecessary work.

- Amend the funding rules, so that (a) no method of funding generates
  increased costs and (b) there are as many different funding options as
  possible.

- Facilitate and incentivise early settlement of disputes.

- Simplify and streamline the method of quantifying what the loser pays to
  the winner.

- Control the amount of recoverable costs in advance, as discussed above.

Did the Review of Civil Litigation Costs achieve that? The jury is still out, **1–025**
but see Ch. 22, below. Part of the problem is that most of the "jurors" are lawyers,
who—for reasons explained above—are destined to dislike the reforms. There
is a natural inclination for people to say that any reform which they dislike is
counter-productive. "Costs budgeting drives up costs"; "denying us recoverable
success fees inhibits access to justice"; etc. All these arguments will require
careful scrutiny, not acceptance at face value. When the recent reforms have
bedded in properly, it is hoped that someone (perhaps the economics department
of a university) will carry out an objective assessment. It is essential that those
carrying out such an assessment should start with an open mind and should not
receive funding from any stakeholder groups who have a vested interest in the
outcome.

Chapter 2

THE CIVIL LITIGATION COSTS REVIEW AND PROPOSALS
FOR REFORM

1. The Review of Civil Litigation Costs

Establishment of the Review of Civil Litigation Costs. On 3 November **2–001**
2008, the Master of the Rolls, Sir Anthony Clarke, established the Costs Review
with the support of the Ministry of Justice.

Terms of reference. The terms of reference for the costs review were: **2–002**

"To carry out an independent review of the rules and principles governing the costs of
civil litigation and to make recommendations in order to promote access to justice at
proportionate cost.

Terms of reference:
In conducting the review Lord Justice Jackson will:

- Establish how present costs rules operate and how they impact on the behaviour
of both parties and lawyers.

- Establish the effect case management procedures have on costs and consider
whether changes in process and/or procedure could bring about more proportionate costs.

- Have regard to previous and current research into costs and funding issues; for
example any further Government research into Conditional Fee Agreements –
'No win, No fee', following the scoping study.

- Seek the views of judges, practitioners, Government, court users and other
interested parties through both informal consultation and a series of public
seminars.

- Compare the costs regime for England and Wales with those operating in other
jurisdictions.

- Prepare a report setting out recommendations with supporting evidence by 31
December 2009."

Assessors. The assessors were Mr Justice Cranston, Professor Paul Fenn, **2–003**
Senior Costs Judge Peter Hurst, Jeremy Morgan QC, Michael Napier CBE QC,
Andrew Parker and Colin Stutt. The assessors met regularly throughout the

Review. They gave invaluable advice and assistance. Inevitably, they disagreed with one another on many issues. They are not responsible for the contents of the Preliminary or Final Reports.

2–004   **Judicial assistants and clerk.** The judicial assistants were Pete Given (Allen & Overy LLP) from January to February, Ilona Groark (Herbert Smith Freehills LLP) from March to July, and Hannah Piper (Hogan Lovells International LLP) from September to December 2009. Julian Bailey of CMS Cameron McKenna LLP gave intermittent assistance throughout the year, in particular with analysis of the overseas material. The accountant judicial assistants (both from Deloitte LLP) were Lucy Harrison from 27 July to early October, and Chris Tune from October to December 2009. All the judicial assistants worked long hours and made a real contribution to the project.

2–005   **Phase One of the Costs Review.** Phase One of the review ran from January to April 2009. It involved fact finding, a study of academic research, a tour of overseas jurisdictions, preliminary consultation with stakeholder groups, collection of evidence and available statistics/costs data. The work product of Phase One was the Preliminary Report.

2–006   **Judicial survey.** During the four-week period 19 January to 13 February 2009, every first instance judge was asked to provide details of every case in which they made a summary assessment of costs, a detailed assessment of costs, or an order for interim payment on account of costs. The results of the survey were published in the Preliminary Report. They were the subject of much analysis by the accountant judicial assistant and also by many stakeholders who sent in submissions.

2–007   **Overseas visits.** The overseas jurisdictions visited were France, Germany, Hong Kong, Australia (New South Wales, Victoria and Western Australia), New Zealand, USA and Canada. The Preliminary Report includes an account of those jurisdictions and also other jurisdictions based on desk study and phone calls.

2–008   **Preliminary Report ("PR").** The Preliminary Report comprised 64 chapters and 30 appendices on a CD. The report (excluding appendices) was 663 pages long. It provided details of the costs of different categories of litigation gathered from a variety of sources. It summarised:

- relevant academic research;
- the positions of major stakeholder groups on the principal issues;
- the current means of funding civil litigation and options for reform;
- the issues surrounding fixed costs;
- the rules for summary and detailed assessments;
- case management procedures and options for reform, including costs management;
- the costs and procedural regimes of nine overseas jurisdictions.

The report reviewed 11 specialist areas of litigation. It examined the effects of (a) cost shifting and (b) regimes where there was no costs shifting, such as employment tribunals. The Preliminary Report identified issues for consideration during Phase Two.

Appendices to the Preliminary Report. Appendices 1–8 set out the results   2–009
of the judicial survey. Appendices 9–30 set out in digestible form a vast mass of data provided by stakeholder groups. These included the Association of Personal Injury Lawyers ("APIL"), various insurers, the Commercial Court Users Committee, individual firms of solicitors, the Media Lawyers Association ("MLA"), the National Health Service Litigation Authority ("NHSLA"), the Medical Protection Society and others. The appendices were on a CD, but if printed out would run to about 300 pages.

Data from the Legal Services Commission. PR Ch. 6 sets out data from   2–010
the Legal Services Commission. This gave a clear picture of costs in 14 identified areas. These areas were welfare, public law, consumer claims, debt claims, education, employment, actions against the police, community care, personal injury, mental health, clinical negligence, immigration, housing and "miscellaneous". These costs were broken down by reference to the stages at which cases settled.

Total volume of material in the Preliminary Report. The total volume of   2–011
material in the Preliminary Report and its appendices was vast. Only a brief description is offered here.

Phase Two of the Costs Review. Phase Two was the consultation period,   2–012
running from May to July 2009. Stakeholder groups, practitioners, court users and others sent in several thousand pages of written material. Numerous firms of solicitors and other organisations hosted meetings at which issues of concern to themselves and their clients were debated. Legal commentators pitched into the fray with gusto.

Working groups. During Phase Two, working groups considered the follow-   2–013
ing areas and reported back:

- personal injury damages;
- fixed costs in insolvency proceedings;
- costs management of insolvency proceedings;
- disclosure;
- libel;
- costs management generally.

2–014   **Seminars.** There were:

- four major seminars (organised by the Master of the Rolls' office) at Cardiff, Manchester, Birmingham and London; and

- eight "informal" seminars, each devoted to a specific topic: CFAs, CLAF/ SLAS/DBAs, fixed costs, chancery litigation, judicial review, SMEs' business disputes, case + costs management, assessment of costs.

2–015   **Pilots and working groups during Phase Two.** Two costs management pilots were established during Phase Two. The first was in the Birmingham specialist courts. The second was a pilot of costs management for defamation proceedings in London. Seven working groups were established to consider specified topics and report back.

2–016   **Phase Three of the Costs Review.** Phase Three ran from mid-August to December 2009. The first month was spent reading and analysing the accumulated the material. Thereafter, the Final Report was written at the rate of five chapters per week (i.e. one chapter per day). By late November, the whole of the Final Report was in first draft. That allowed a month for revising and polishing. The Final Report was complete by Christmas 2009.

2–017   **Visits during Phase Three.** The principal task was report writing at this stage, so visits were kept to a minimum. Nevertheless, Phase Three included a trip to Scotland for a conference marking the launch of Lord Gill's report. It also included visits to three solicitors' offices: Irwin Mitchell LLP in Sheffield, Beachcroft LLP in Birmingham and Olswang LLP in London. The purpose of these visits was to study work in progress and gain an insight into preparations for detailed assessment, costs negotiations and budgeting.

2. PROPOSALS FOR REFORM

2–018   **Final Report ("FR").** The Final Report was 558 pages long. It comprised 46 chapters and 10 annexes. It set out additional statistical material which was not available at the time of the Preliminary Report, including details of 1,000 cases closed or settled by the NHSLA in the period 1 April 2008 to 1 March 2009.

2–019   **Structure of chapters of the Final Report.** Each chapter set out a summary of the relevant evidence, a summary of the written submissions received and the competing arguments deployed during Phase two. It then set out conclusions and supporting reasons.

2–020   **Recommendations.** The Final Report made 109 recommendations. Most of the proposals required amendments to the CPR. Some required primary legislation. Some of the proposals related to the state of the common law and were a matter for judicial consideration in future cases. Some of the recommendations were directed to particular bodies, such as providers of professional training or the Judicial College (then known as the Judicial Studies Board).

What reforms did the Final Report propose? Rather a lot, actually. Anyone **2–021** seeking the full answer should read the report or at least have a look at the list of recommendations on pp. 463–471. The following chapters of this book set out and discuss the principal recommendations and some of the others.

Interrelationship between the recommendations. The reforms were designed **2–022** as an interlocking package. The links between them include the following:

- The new rules about proportionality govern case management, costs management, funding reforms, summary assessment and detailed assessment.

- The abolition of recoverable success fees and recoverable after-the-event insurance ("ATE") premiums. This is necessary to prevent (a) recoverable costs being grossly disproportionate and (b) distortion of incentives on both sides, which further drives up litigation costs.

- The introduction of qualified one-way costs shifting ("QOCS") is necessary to compensate for the abolition of recoverable ATE premiums.

- The 10% increase in damages is part of a package of measures to compensate personal injury ("PI") claimants for the loss of their former right to recover against defendants the success fees payable to their own lawyers.

  Other elements of that package are (a) the cap on the amount of the success fee which a lawyer can charge his or her own client in a PI case, and (b) the enhanced reward for effective claimant offers under CPR Pt 36.

- The introduction of damages-based agreements ("DBAs"), the promotion of before-the-event insurance ("BTE") and the proposal for a contingent legal aid fund ("CLAF") are part of a policy to establish new means of funding litigation (which do not drive up costs) in a world where success fees and ATE premiums are no longer recoverable.

- The case management reforms are intended to go hand in hand with costs management. The general idea is that courts will manage cases in accordance with approved (and proportionate) budgets.

- The costs management rules, together with the abolition of recoverable success fees and recoverable ATE premiums, are intended to facilitate alternative dispute resolution ("ADR") (as well as reduce the costs of litigation).

- The proposals concerning court IT are designed to facilitate effective case management and costs management.

- Increased docketing is necessary in order to facilitate more effective case management and costs management.

- The new measures to control the scope of witness statements and expert reports enable the court to limit written evidence to that which is proportionate, having regard to the approved budgets.

- The reforms to the disclosure rules should enable the court to limit disclosure` to that which is proportionate, having regard to the approved budgets.

- Referral fees drive up the costs of personal injury litigation, because competition inures to the benefit of the referrers rather than the claimants; that is a driver of disproportionate costs and must stop.

- Fixed costs across the fast track are the best way to achieve certainty and to ensure that costs are proportionate. Once referral fees are banned, it becomes possible to fix the costs of fast track personal injury cases at a proportionate level.

- The proposals for future fixing of costs in the lower reaches of the multi-track are a logical extension of costs management and fast track fixed costs. Experience gained from those exercises will feed into any future grid of fixed costs.

- The proposal for a new form bill of costs fits with (a) the proposal to make effective use of modern IT and (b) the existence of approved costs budgets.

2–023   **Appendix A.** Appendix A at the end of this book illustrates graphically some of the links between reform proposals in the Final Report.

2–024   **Launch of the Final Report.** The text of the Final Report was delivered to the Lord Chancellor and the Master of the Rolls in late December 2009. The report was printed in early January 2010 and published on 14 January 2010.

CHAPTER 3

THE ORGANISING PRINCIPLE – PROPORTIONALITY

1. WHAT IS PROPORTIONALITY?

Aristotle's long shadow. As noted in Ch. 1, above, Aristotle's twin concep-   **3–001**
tions of justice embody proportionality. Izhak Englard, in his essay on corrective
and distributive justice,[1] has demonstrated how the Scholastic movement picked
up and developed these ideas. Aquinas, in *Summa theologica*, appreciated that
corrective justice was not a simple equal measure, but a proportionate measure
adapted to the particular circumstances.[2] Through the Scholastic movement,
Aristotle's ideas came to infuse modern European jurisprudence.

Professor Zuckerman's analysis. Professor Zuckerman classifies proportion-   **3–002**
ality as a civilian principle. He describes it as a tool of administrative law

"for assessing the use of authority by state organs, such as the police, so as to determine
whether their use of power was excessive or unnecessary in relation to the particular
intended objective".[3]

Whilst accepting that summary, it is right to say that similar principles are embedded in the common law.

Blackstone on the limits of law. In his distillation of English law during the   **3–003**
eighteenth century, Sir William Blackstone described the limits of the law as
follows:

"Political therefore, or civil, liberty, which is that of a member of society, is no other
than natural liberty so far restrained by human laws (and no farther) as is necessary and
expedient for the general advantage of the publick [*sic*]."[4]

---

[1] Izhak Englard, *Corrective and distributive justice: from Aristotle to modern times.*
[2] See Englard's analysis of *Summa Theologica* at p.20 of *Corrective and distributive justice: from Aristotle to modern times.*
[3] Adrian Zuckerman, *Zuckerman on Civil Procedure*, Ch 1, para. 1.35.
[4] Sir William Blackstone, *Commentaries on the Laws of England*, 1st edn (1765), Ch. 1, p.121.

Interestingly, Blackstone cites Justinian's *Institutes* as authority for this proposition, even though the Institutes omit the crucial restriction on the ambit of law.[5]

3–004   **Proportionality as a restraining principle.** It is, therefore, a long established feature of both civil and common law jurisdictions that there are limits upon the extent to which the law can intrude upon private rights. The proportionality principle is one way of expressing those limits.

3–005   **Lord Reed's analysis.** Lord Reed traced the emergence of proportionality as a principle of both common law and civil law in *Bank Mellatt v HM Treasury (No. 2)* [2013] UKSC 39; [2014] AC 700 at [68]–[76]. Although Lord Reed did not specifically cite Englard, *Summa Theologica*, Justinian or Zuckerman, his analysis is along the same lines as set out in the preceding paragraphs.

3–006   **What does proportionality actually mean?** Proportionality means that there is a proper relationship between subject and object. If applied to the action of an administrative body, it means that there is a proper relationship between the administrative action and the objective to be achieved. If applied to a judicial decision, it means that there is a proper relationship between (a) the subject matter of the litigation and (b) any remedy ordered and/or any steps taken to achieve that remedy. Proportionality is the antithesis of "zero tolerance".

3–007   **A European concept.** The principle of proportionality has underpinned the European Community (now the EU) since it was established in 1957. The fourth paragraph of Article 5 of the Treaty on the European Union provides:

> "Under the principle of proportionality, the content and form of Union action shall not exceed what is necessary to achieve the objectives of the Treaties."

This is widely accepted as enshrining the proportionality principle. In *R v Ministry of Agriculture, Fisheries and Food, ex p Fedesa and others* (C–331/88) [1990] ECR I-4023, the European Court of Justice stated at [13]:

> "The Court has consistently held that the principle of proportionality is one of the general principles of Community law. By virtue of that principle, the lawfulness of the prohibition of an economic activity is subject to the condition that the prohibitory measures are appropriate and necessary in order to achieve the objectives legitimately pursued by the legislation in question; when there is a choice between several appropriate measures recourse must be had to the least onerous, and the disadvantages caused must not be disproportionate to the aims pursued."

The most recent analysis of proportionality in EU law is to be found in *R. (Lumsdon) v Legal Services Board* [2015] UKSC 41; [2015] 1 WLR 121.

---

[5] Justinian, *Institutes*, at 1.3.1:
"Et libertas quidem est, ex qua etiam liberi vocantur, naturalis facultas eius, quod cuique facere libet, nisi si quid aut vi aut jure prohibetur."

Proportionality as a principle of English law. In *SS (Nigeria) v SSHD* **3–008**
[2013] EWCA Civ 550; [2014] 1 WLR 998, the Court of Appeal was considering
whether the deportation of a foreign criminal would be disproportionate. Laws
LJ (with whom Black LJ and Mann J agreed) neatly distilled the proportionality
principle at [38] as follows:

> "But the true innovation effected by proportionality is not, in my judgment, to be
> defined in terms of judicial intrusion or activism. Rather it consists in the introduction
> into judicial review and like forms of process of a principle which might be a child of the
> common law itself: it may be (and often has been) called the principle of minimal inter-
> ference. It is that every intrusion by the State upon the freedom of the individual stands
> in need of justification. Accordingly, any interference which is greater than required for
> the State's proper purpose cannot be justified. This is at the core of proportionality; it
> articulates the discipline which proportionality imposes on decision-makers."

A month later, the Supreme Court reviewed the role of proportionality in a very dif- **3–009**
ferent context. In *Bank Mellatt v HM Treasury (No. 2)* [2013] UKSC 39; [2014] AC
700, the Bank of England in the exercise of its powers under s.62 of the Counter-
Terrorism Act 2008 issued a direction which had the effect of shutting the claimant
(an Iranian Bank) out of the UK financial sector. The purpose was to hinder the
pursuit by Iran of its nuclear weapons programme. The claimant applied under
s.63 of the 2008 Act to set aside the direction. The High Court judge dismissed the
application, as did the Court of Appeal. The Supreme Court reversed that decision,
holding that the measure taken by the Bank of England was disproportionate. Lord
Sumption gave the leading judgment for the majority. At [21], he noted that the
principles of rationality and proportionality overlapped. After identifying a line of
authorities on these two principles, he concluded with a pithy summary:

> "Their effect can be sufficiently summarised for present purposes by saying that the
> question depends on an exacting analysis of the factual case advanced in defence of
> the measure, in order to determine (i) whether its objective is sufficiently important to
> justify the limitation of a fundamental right; (ii) whether it is rationally connected to the
> objective; (iii) whether a less intrusive measure could have been used; and (iv) whether,
> having regard to these matters and to the severity of the consequences, a fair balance
> has been struck between the rights of the individual and the interests of the community.
> These four requirements are logically separate, but in practice they inevitably overlap
> because the same facts are likely to be relevant to more than one of them."

2. PROPORTIONALITY IN ADJECTIVAL LAW

Adjectival law. Adjectival law is a collective term for the rules of procedure **3–010**
and practice which enable persons to (a) enforce the rights and remedies conferred
by substantive law, or to (b) resist baseless claims. Some of these rules embody
fundamental principles, for example *audi alteram partem* – listen to both sides
before deciding. Even so, the rules of adjectival law are not ends in themselves.
They are subordinate to the principles of substantive law. You don't listen to
both sides just for the fun of it. You do so in order to decide the relevant issue
in accordance with substantive law. As Sir Jack Jacob observed in the Eighth
Upjohn Lecture, 1979:

"Procedure is not the master but the servant of justice, and its function is ever to study and conform to the needs of the times."[6]

3-011   **The procedural rules must not licence a free-for-all in which every point is pursued without limit.** As Bentham noted two hundred years ago,[7] it is not possible to deliver perfect justice in every case without regard to costs or delay. Such an approach would be a denial of justice because most litigants could not afford to participate in the process. The question therefore arises as to what restrictions should be placed upon the obtaining and presentation of evidence. This question becomes all the more acute in the digital age. In many cases, the potentially relevant electronic documents are unlimited. Parties can produce with ease pleadings, witness statements, expert reports and written submissions of inordinate length. The more the written material expands, the more there is to talk about at oral hearings.

3-012   **How should litigation be regulated in the digital age?** The answer is that the principle of proportionality, which has now emerged in substantive law, should also be the guiding principle of adjectival law. Sorabji describes this approach as "the revolutionary change that the Woolf and Jackson reforms brought about".[8]

3-013   **How should the proportionality principle be formulated for this purpose?** The proportionality principle in the context of adjectival law may be formulated as follows: Procedural requirements should be proportionate to the subject matter of the litigation. This proposition is subject to qualifications, for example in the event of misconduct by parties.

3-014   **Can you give examples to illustrate 'proportionate' and 'disproportionate' in adjectival law?** Here are two illustrations:

Illustration (i). Absent special circumstances (e.g. the litigation is a test case), it would be disproportionate to require the parties to spend £1 million on disclosure, if the sum in dispute is only £200,000. The rules must be sufficiently flexible to enable the court to make proportionate disclosure orders in every case.

Illustration (ii). The purpose of sanctions is to secure that (a) litigation proceeds efficiently and at proportionate cost towards resolution in accordance with the substantive law, and that (b) there is a general culture of compliance with rules, practice directions and orders. (In the absence of such a culture, litigants (a) will be inhibited from enforcing their rights and remedies or from resisting baseless claims, alternatively (b) they will only do so at increased cost and inconvenience.[9]) Therefore any sanctions imposed by the rules or by the court must be proportionate to that purpose. This inevitably involves a balancing exercise. That balancing exercise is neatly illustrated by recent experience.

---

[6] Jacob, *The reform of civil procedural law*, p.2.
[7] See section 1 of Ch. 1, above.
[8] John Sorabji, *English civil justice after the Woolf and Jackson reforms*, pp.2–3.
[9] An award of costs thrown away by an adjournment or an amendment seldom refects the true loss suffered by the opposing party. See e.g. *Denton v TH White Ltd* [2014] EWCA Civ 906; [2014] 1 WLR 3926 at [89].

- Under the pre-2013 CPR, the courts made insufficient use of sanctions. The consequence was that litigation was so lax that parties generally were less likely to achieve resolution at proportionate cost or in accordance with the substantive law. The Law Society's submissions quoted in section 2 of chapter 11 below graphically described that state of affairs.

- As a result of the decision in *Mitchell v News Group Newspapers Ltd* [2013] EWCA Civ 1537; [2014] 1 WLR 795 (or at least that decision as generally interpreted), for several months the courts went to other extreme and imposed or maintained sanctions which were unduly tough, for example disallowing costs because a party had been 45 minutes late in filing its budget.

What is required is a proportionate approach to sanctions, which lies some-   **3–015**
where between those two extremes. Chapter 39 of the Review of Civil Litigation Costs Final Report ("FR"), para. 6.5 advocated such a proportionate approach. The amendments made by the Rule Committee to CPR r.3.9 struck the right balance and thereby achieved a proportionate approach. It appears that—after some initial mishaps—the courts are now applying this rule correctly.

Amendments made to the overriding objective with effect from 1 April   **3–016**
2013. The Rule Committee made two amendments to the overriding objective with effect from 1 April 2013. The purpose of the first amendment was to promote proportionality. The purpose of the second amendment is less clear.

The first amendment to the overriding objective. The first amendment   **3–017**
was the insertion of "and at proportionate cost" into CPR r.1.1(1) and (2). As explained in section 5 of this chapter, I accept some responsibility for this amend-ment, having proposed it to the Rule Committee. It was part of a package of linked amendments, designed to make costs proportionate.

The second amendment to the overriding objective. The second amendment   **3–018**
to the overriding objective was to add at the end of r.1.1(2) a new sub-paragraph as follows: "(f) enforcing compliance with rules, practice directions and orders".

Comment. The second amendment to the overriding objective was not one of   **3–019**
my recommendations. It is, of course, none the worse on that account. The second amendment will be beneficial if it is understood as promoting the purpose stated in illustration (ii) above. That purpose is to secure that (a) litigation proceeds effi-ciently and at proportionate cost towards resolution in accordance with the sub-stantive law, and (b) there is a general culture of compliance with rules, practice directions and orders. On the other hand, the provision will be disproportionate if it is understood as introducing formalism or making strict compliance in every case an end in itself, rather than the means to an end. The correct construction of the provision is, of course, a matter for the courts, not for this book.

Conclusion. A major objective of the Woolf reforms was to introduce a regime   **3–020**
of proportionate case management. The creation of separate rules for different tracks played a significant part in achieving that objective. The purpose of the

various procedural reforms proposed in the Final Report was to achieve that same objective. Chapters 8–14 below discuss reforms to the management of litigation and the facilitation of ADR. All those reforms have the objective of promoting the resolution of disputes not only in accordance with the substantive law, but also proportionately.

3. PROPORTIONATE COSTS – THE GOAL OF THE 2009 COSTS REVIEW

3–021   **Terms of reference for the 2009 Costs Review.** The terms of reference for the Costs Review required the reviewer "to make recommendations in order to promote access to justice at proportionate cost". This required (a) consideration of what "proportionality" meant in the context of litigation costs and (b) the formulation of specific proposals to achieve proportionality (as defined in answer to the first question), so far as that was possible. Neither of those tasks was particularly easy.

3–022   **The case law.** The existing case law offered only limited assistance to anyone tackling those two questions.[10] Indeed this was one of the reasons why the Master of the Rolls set up the Costs Review.

3–023   ***Lownds v Home Office.*** *Lownds v Home Office* [2002] EWCA Civ 365; [2002] 1 WLR 2450 posed a particular problem. The guidance given by the Court of Appeal in that case was that the assessment of costs should proceed in three stages: (a) assessing "reasonable" costs; (b) determining whether the total of those reasonable costs is proportionate; if not, (c) disallowing any items of costs which were unnecessary (a test to be applied without setting too high a standard). The effect of *Lownds* was that the court could, and in many cases did, make awards of costs which were disproportionately high. This decision has come in for some criticism from several quarters. Sorabji describes it as "disastrous".[11]

3–024   **The effect of recoverable success fees and recoverable ATE premiums.** To make matters worse, when the courts were considering whether or not the costs claimed were proportionate, the then current rules required judges to disregard the amount of any recoverable success fee or ATE premium: see s.11 of the Costs Practice Direction as it stood in 2009.

3–025   **An inescapable consequence.** It was an inescapable consequence of the terms of reference that the Costs Review would have to tackle the problems posed by *Lownds* and by the regime of recoverable success fees/recoverable ATE premiums, as well as the problems of definition discussed above.

---

[10] See e.g. *Willis v Nicolson* [2007] EWCA Civ 199 at [18]–[19].
[11] John Sorabji, *English civil justice after the Woolf and Jackson reforms*, p.242.

4. RECOMMENDATIONS CONCERNING PROPORTIONATE COSTS IN THE FINAL REPORT OF JANUARY 2010

The principal recommendation. The principal recommendation in the Final   **3–026**
Report was that successful parties should only recover proportionate costs.[12] In
truth this recommendation was inevitable, given the terms of reference. It was
nonetheless highly controversial.

Defining "proportionate" costs. This turned out to be one of the most chal-   **3–027**
lenging tasks in the whole of the Costs Review. Chapter 3 of the Final Report
(entitled "Proportionate Costs") underwent radical revision more than once as discussions with the assessors proceeded during the autumn of 2009. Paragraphs 5.1
to 5.13 of that chapter set out some important conclusions reached after hearing
the valuable (but differing) views[13] of the experienced assessors:

"5.1 **The two relevant principles.** To what extent should the winning party in litigation
recover the costs which it has incurred against the losing party? Two principles are relevant to
the debate which this question has generated. They are compensation and proportionality.[14]

5.2 **Compensation.** The principle of compensation is embedded both in common law
and in equity. The essence of compensation is that a wrongdoer should restore the innocent
party to the position in which he would have been, if the wrong had not occurred. The
principle of compensation underlies the law of contract, the law of tort, the law of damages
and the remedies of equity.

5.3 **Proportionality.** As explained in section 3 of this chapter, proportionality is a more
recent arrival on the scene. Proportionality is an open-textured concept. It now pervades
many areas of the law, both substantive and adjectival. The essence of proportionality is
that the ends do not necessarily justify the means. The law facilitates the pursuit of lawful
objectives, but only to the extent that those objectives warrant the burdens thereby being
imposed upon others.

5.4 **Interaction of the two principles.** The principle of compensation requires that a
party whose claim or defence is vindicated should be made whole. In other words, that
party's costs should be paid by the other side. However, the principle of proportionality requires that the costs burden cast upon the other party should not be greater than the
subject matter of the litigation warrants. The focus of this chapter is upon the extent to
which the second principle limits the operation of the first principle.

5.5 **Proportionality of costs.** Proportionality of costs is not simply a matter of comparing the sum in issue with the amount of costs incurred, important though that comparison
is. It is also necessary to evaluate any non-monetary remedies sought and any rights which
are in issue, in order to compare the overall value of what is at stake in the action with the
costs of resolution.

---

[12] On an assessment of costs on the standard basis.
[13] The function of the assessors was to advise, not to achieve unanimity. They brought to bear a vast
wealth of experience, but seldom were in agreement with each other.
[14] See e.g. *Erlanger v New Sombrero Phosphate Company* (1878) 3 App Cas 1218 at 1278–1279;
Newbigging v Adam (1886) 34 Ch D 582 at 595; *Livingstone v Rawyards Coal Company* (1880) 5 App
Cas 25 at 39. This principle is sometimes referred to as *restitutio in integrum*.

5.6 The comparison exercise set out in the previous paragraph produces a strong indication of whether the costs of a party are proportionate. Before coming to a final conclusion, however, it is also necessary to look at the complexity of the litigation. There can be complex low value claims where the costs of litigation (if conducted properly) are bound to exceed the sum at stake. Equally, there can be high value, but straightforward, commercial claims where the costs are excessive, despite representing only a small proportion of the damages. It is also relevant to consider conduct and any wider factors, such as reputational issues or public importance.

5.7 It is therefore necessary to consider proportionality of costs by reference to (a) the sums at stake, (b) the value of any non-monetary remedies claimed and any rights in issue, (c) the complexity of the litigation, (d) conduct and (e) any wider factors, such as reputational issues or public importance.

5.8 Professor Zuckerman pithily summarises proportionality as follows: 'The aim of the proportionality test is to maintain a sensible correlation between costs, on the one hand, and the value of the case, its complexity and importance on the other hand.'[15]

5.9 In borderline cases it will be a matter of subjective opinion whether the costs in any particular case are disproportionate. Nevertheless, despite the difficulty of determining in borderline cases whether or not costs are proportionate, there are many cases where it is readily apparent that costs are or are not proportionate, having regard to all the circumstances of the case.

5.10 **Disproportionate costs do not become proportionate because they were necessary.** If the level of costs incurred is out of proportion to the circumstances of the case, they cannot become proportionate simply because they were "necessary" in order to bring or defend the claim. It will be recalled from chapter 12 of the Preliminary Report that the Legal Services Commission applies a cost / benefit test when deciding whether to support a case with public funds. Any self-funding litigant would do the same. The fact that it was necessary to incur certain costs in order to prove or disprove a head of claim is obviously relevant, but it is not decisive of the question whether such costs were proportionate.

5.11 At the time when *Lownds* was decided, it seemed to myself and others that this decision was a neat way of applying the proportionality test, which would bring costs under proper control. Experience, however, has taught otherwise. In my view, the time has now come to say that the guidance given by the Court of Appeal in *Lownds* is not satisfactory, essentially for the reasons given by the President of the QBD at the Cardiff seminar. The effect of *Lownds* was to insert the Victorian test of necessity into the modern concept of proportionality.

5.12 **Disproportionate costs should be disallowed in an assessment of costs on the standard basis.** If a judge assessing costs concludes that the total figure, alternatively some element within that total figure, was disproportionate, the judge should say so. It then follows from the provisions of CPR rule 44.4(3) that the disproportionate element of costs should be disallowed in any assessment on the standard basis. In my view, that disproportionate element of the costs cannot be saved, even if the individual items within it were both reasonable and necessary.

5.13 In other words, I propose that in an assessment of costs on the standard basis, proportionality should prevail over reasonableness and the proportionality test should be applied on a global basis. The court should first make an assessment of reasonable costs, having regard to the individual items in the bill, the time reasonably spent on those items and the other factors listed in CPR rule 44.5(3). The court should then stand back and

---

[15] Adrian Zuckerman, *Zuckerman on Civil Procedure: Principles of Practice*, 2nd edn (2006), para.26.88.

consider whether the total figure is proportionate. If the total figure is not proportionate, the court should make an appropriate reduction. There is already a precedent for this approach in relation to the assessment of legal aid costs in criminal proceedings: see *R v Supreme Court Taxing Office exp John Singh and Co* [1997] 1 Costs LR 49."

And what conclusion did all that lead to? Chapter 3 of the Final Report **3–028** reached two conclusions. The first was that "proportionality" should be redefined to include the matters discussed above. The second conclusion was that on a standard basis assessment the successful party should not recover more than proportionate costs. In other words, proportionality should trump reasonableness.

New definition of proportionate costs. Paragraph 5.15 of FR Ch. 3 proposed **3–029** the following definition of proportionate costs[16]:

"Costs are proportionate if, and only if, the costs incurred bear a reasonable relationship to:
   (a) the sums in issue in the proceedings;
   (b) the value of any non-monetary relief in issue in the proceedings;
   (c) the complexity of the litigation;
   (d) any additional work generated by the conduct of the paying party; and
   (e) any wider factors involved in the proceedings, such as reputation or public importance."

Reversal of *Lownds* by rule change. Paragraph 5.16 of FR Ch. 3 recom- **3–030** mended that the Rule Committee should reverse the effect of *Lownds* by rule change.

Well that's fine, but how could the *actual* costs of litigation be brought **3–031 down to proportionate levels?** Fair question. Merely saying that the winner will only recover proportionate costs is a good first step. It will encourage economy by all parties, but that alone is not enough. You cannot make litigation affordable simply by amending the costs rules. The body of the Final Report, therefore, proposed a series of procedural reforms to make case management more proportionate, as summarised in section 2 above.

5. IMPLEMENTATION

Amendments to CPR Pt 44. The Rule Committee implemented the recommen- **3–032** dations in FR Ch. 3 by amending CPR Pt 44 to include the following provisions:

"44.3 (2) Where the amount of costs is to be assessed on the standard basis, the court will –

---

[16] *Zuckerman on Civil Procedure* in the latter part of Ch.27 expresses reservations about this formulation, because it is multi-dimensional. On the other hand, if proportionality is *only* defined as an arithmetic concept, this leads to all sorts of nonsenses. This became apparent in 2009 when a variety of different formulations were tested against imaginary cases.

(a) only allow costs which are proportionate to the matters in issue. Costs which are disproportionate in amount may be disallowed or reduced even if they were reasonably or necessarily incurred; and

(b) resolve any doubt which it may have as to whether costs were reasonably and proportionately incurred or were reasonable and proportionate in amount in favour of the paying party.

(5) Costs incurred are proportionate if they bear a reasonable relationship to –

(a) the sums in issue in the proceedings;
(b) the value of any non-monetary relief in issue in the proceedings;
(c) the complexity of the litigation;
(d) any additional work generated by the conduct of the paying party; and
(e) any wider factors involved in the proceedings, such as reputation or public importance."

3–033   **Self-evident consequence of the amendments to r.44.3.** At the risk of stating the obvious, any court assessing recoverable costs under the new r.44.3 will sometimes find itself constrained to cut down substantially the costs which the receiving party reasonably incurred in order to "win" the case.[17] The court will have regard to the subject matter of the litigation, as well as the other factors set out in r.44.3(2), and will only award such sum as is proportionate.

3–034   **Amendment to the overriding objective.** The Rule Committee amended the overriding objective by inserting the words "and at proportionate cost" into CPR r.1.1(1) and (2).[18] So CPR r.1.l(1) now reads:

"These Rules are a new procedural code with the overriding objective of enabling the court to deal with cases justly and at proportionate cost."

3–035   **Cumulative effect of the above amendments.** The cumulative effect of the amendments to rr.1.1 and 44.3 is to put the concept of proportionate costs, as now defined, at the heart of civil procedure. Both the court and the parties are under a duty to manage litigation at every stage to ensure, so far as possible, that the *actual* costs are no more than proportionate. The second sentence of r.44.3(2)(a) recognises that this goal cannot be achieved in every case.

3–036   **Proportionate costs rules.** For convenience, the fnal words of r.1.1(1) ["and at proportionate cost"], r.44.3(2) [reversing *Lownds*] and r.44.3(5) [the definition of proportionate costs] will be referred to collectively as "the proportionality rules".

3–037   **Should there be supplementary guidance about the meaning of proportionality in a practice direction?** During 2011 and 2012, there was much debate about whether a practice direction ("PD") should supplement the definition of proportionate costs. Many practitioners argued that there should be supplementary guidance. The third implementation lecture stated the case against that approach, including the following warning:

---

[17] As happened in *BNM v MGN Ltd* [2016] EWHC B13 (Costs).
[18] I proposed this draft amendment to the Rule Committee at its meeting on 9 March 2012.

"If the rule is supplemented by an elaborate practice direction, opportunities for satellite litigation will increase exponentially, as practitioners explore the relationship between the provisions, possible interstices in the language and so forth. One lesson from the Costs War is that lawyers leave no stone unturned when it comes to arguing about costs."

Fifteenth Implementation lecture. In the fifteenth implementation lecture, **3–038** Lord Neuberger MR stated the case against providing supplementary guidance more fully:

"14. While the change in culture should reduce the scope of costs assessments at the conclusion of proceedings, it will not obviate the need for a robust approach to such assessments. Again the decision as to whether an item was proportionately incurred is case-sensitive, and there may be a period of slight uncertainty as the case law is developed.
15. That is why I have not dealt with what precisely constitutes proportionality and how it is to be assessed. It would be positively dangerous for me to seek to give any sort of specific or detailed guidance in a lecture before the new rule has come into force and been applied. Any question relating to proportionality and any question relating to costs is each very case-sensitive, and when the two questions come together, that is all the more true. The law on proportionate costs will have to be developed on a case by case basis. This may mean a degree of satellite litigation while the courts work out the law, but we should be ready for that, and I hope it will involve relatively few cases."

Outcome. In the end, the view that there should be no PD giving supplemen- **3–039** tary guidance prevailed. Some commentators and practitioners are concerned about this.[19] Others accept that this is for the best.

Why are we better off with no supplementary practice direction? Rule **3–040** 44.3(5) states all of the general principles to be applied in determining whether costs are proportionate. The application of those principles in any given case is fact-specific and involves the exercise of discretion. If a PD were to give more detailed guidance, it would inevitably be lengthy. The PD would be helpful in some cases and confusing in others. No legislator can foresee all the vagaries of litigation. Any detailed PD would generate satellite litigation about the relation-ship between the rule and the practice direction. Then we would have r.44.3(5) + a lengthy PD + an encrustation of case law, followed up inevitably by much learned commentary from the academic community. Surely we are better off without all that?

Guidance on the application of r.44.3(5). For a helpful commentary on the **3–041** application of r.44.3(5), readers should consult *Questions & Answers*,[20] Ch. 3 "Proportionality". There is also helpful judicial guidance on the proportionality test to be found in *Hobbs v Guy's and St Thomas' Foundation NHS Trust* [2015] EWHC B20 (Costs).

---

[19] See e.g. *Costs Law: An Expert Guide*, Ch 7 entitled "Proportionality – a brief plotted history from Woolf to Hobbs (via Jackson)".
[20] Hurst, Middleton and Mallalieu, *Questions & Answers*, 2nd edn (2016).

3–042   **There is no halfway house between r.44.3(5) and fixed costs.** Anyone seeking guidance which will convert the provisions of r.44.3(5) into hard figures is really asking for a fixed costs regime. It is certainly possible to draw up a fixed costs regime on the basis of the general provisions of r.44.3(5). Indeed that is quite likely to come in the near future for the lower reaches of the multi-track, as discussed in Ch. 19, below. It is not, however, practicable to draw up any useful practice direction which will hover in the middle region between r.44.3(5) and a fixed costs regime.

6. Implications of the New Proportionality Rules

3–043   **Impact on all areas of litigation.** As discussed above, the new proportionality rules infuse all areas of litigation. The following paragraphs give some illustrations of how they do so.

3–044   **Effect on the retrospective assessment of costs.** The new rules for detailed and summary assessment are set out in Chs 20 and 21, below. The proportionality rules now guide every detailed or summary assessment of costs on the standard basis. It will no longer be possible for successful parties to recover the absurd levels of costs which previously caused disquiet.[21]

3–045   **Effect on costs management.** The new proportionality rules directly impact upon costs management, which is discussed in Ch. 14, below. The costs managing judge will only approve budgets which satisfy the new definition of proportionality. This will not only encourage economy on the part of the parties, but it will also affect the case management directions which the judge will give.

3–046   **Effect on case management.** A series of case management reforms have been implemented, which are intended to bring down the actual costs of litigation towards more proportionate levels. These are discussed in Chs 11 to 13, below. They include provisions to control factual and expert evidence, as well as measures limit the scope of disclosure. The intention is that the case managing judge will use these powers in order to manage the case within the budget that he/she has set. The Chief Chancery Master has given an excellent explanation of how he exercises his case and costs management powers.[22]

3–047   **Implication for developing fixed costs.** The new proportionality rules pave the way for developing a fixed costs regime. It now becomes possible to devise rules for fixed costs, which will translate the general provisions of r.44.3(5) into hard figures. This was not possible so long as *Lownds* prevailed. Chapter 19, below will discuss how to do this.

3–048   **Effect on funding.** The new proportionality rules are inconsistent with any regime which allows a successful party to recover additional costs by reason of

---

[21] See e.g. FR Ch. 2, paras 4.7 and 4.8.
[22] See section (i) of the Annexe to the Harbour Lecture of 15 May 2015, available in the "Reviews" section of the Judiciary website (*https://www.judiciary.gov.uk/* [Accessed 1 July 2016]).

the funding mechanism chosen. Consistently with that approach, the Legal Aid, Sentencing and Punishment of Offenders Act 2012 ("LASPO") has brought to an end the indefensible regime of recoverable success fees and recoverable ATE premiums. This is explained in Ch. 5, below. Other forms of funding which do not lead to disproportionate recoverable costs have been promoted, as explained in Chs 7 and 8, below.

Economic consequence. The reduction of recoverable costs to that which is **3–049** proportionate changes the incentives upon both litigants and lawyers. Market forces will incentivise lawyers to reduce the actual costs of litigation (i.e. the costs paid by the client, which normally exceed those recovered from the other side) so far as possible. The closer actual costs charged by a lawyer are to recoverable costs, the more business that lawyer is likely to attract.

Effect on referral fees. Referral fees added a new layer of costs to per- **3–050** sonal injury litigation. This is inconsistent with the proportionality principle. Accordingly, the Final Report recommended that such referral fees should be banned. Parliament has implemented that recommendation, as discussed in Ch.17, below.

Appendix A. As can be seen from Appendix A, the new proportionality rules **3–051** are linked directly or indirectly to all of the reforms proposed in the Final Report.

IMPLEMENTATION

1. APPROACH TO IMPLEMENTATION

Judicial Steering Group. In January 2010, the Judicial Executive Board set up a Judicial Steering Group ("JSG") to oversee implementation on behalf of the judiciary. The JSG comprised: **4–001**

- Lord Neuberger, Master of the Rolls,

- Lord Justice Maurice Kay, Vice-President of the civil division of the Court of Appeal,

- Lord Justice Moore-Bick, Deputy Head of Civil Justice,

- Lord Justice Jackson ("RJ").

JSG procedure. The JSG met fortnightly. It oversaw steps being taken by RJ to promote implementation of the reforms and it authorised future action.   **4–002**

Government's position. In January 2010, the Labour Government indicated its general acceptance of the recommendations in the Final Report. That Government fell in the general election of May 2010. The incoming Coalition Government considered the proposals afresh and went out to consultation on them in November 2010. In March 2011, the Coalition Government announced its acceptance of the principal recommendations and the Ministry of Justice ("MoJ") set about preparing the necessary legislation.   **4–003**

Legal Aid, Sentencing and Punishment of Offenders Act 2012. The primary legislation required to implement the FR reforms was contained in Pt 2 of LASPO. This provided for: **4–004**

- abolition of recoverable success fees, subject to specified exceptions;

- abolition of recoverable ATE premiums, subject to specified exceptions;

- authorisation of DBAs, subject to regulations;

- authorisation of enhanced rewards for effective claimant Pt 36 offers;

- banning of referral fees.

LASPO came into force on 1 April 2013.

4–005   **Amendments to the CPR—held back until the general implementation date.** The FR reforms required a large number of additions, deletions and amendments to the CPR. RJ and others prepared draft rules to implement the reforms. The Rule Committee considered the drafts and approved them after making appropriate amendments. The Rule Committee decided at an early stage to hold back most of the rule changes until the general implementation date. As a consequence, during 2011 and 2012 there was a growing stockpile of rule amendments which remained in escrow.

4–006   **Implementation lectures.** The existence of the stockpile of rule amendments in escrow provided an opportunity to publicise the rule changes in advance and to explain how they gave effect to the FR reforms. A series of implementation lectures was intended to serve this purpose. The lectures were and still are on the Judiciary website. You can access them by clicking on "Reviews" at the top right-hand corner of the home page. The following are the lectures in the series:

1. *Legal aid and the Costs Review reforms* (5/9/2011) Jackson LJ.

2. *Contingency legal aid fund and supplementary legal aid fund* (11/10/2011) Jackson LJ.

3. *Technical aspects of implementation* (31/10/2011) Jackson LJ.

4. *Focusing expert evidence and controlling costs* (11/11/2011) Jackson LJ.

5. *Achieving a culture change in case management* (22/11/2011) Jackson LJ.

6. *Third party funding or litigation funding* (23/11/2011) Jackson LJ.

7. *Controlling the costs of disclosure* (28/11/2011) Jackson LJ.

8. *Assessment of costs in the brave new world* (26/1/2012) Jackson LJ.

9. *Docketing: completing case management's unfinished revolution* (9/2/2012) Lord Neuberger MR.

10. *Why ten per cent?* (29/2/2012) Jackson LJ.

11. *The role of ADR in furthering the aims of the Costs Review* (8/3/2012) Jackson LJ.

12. *The reform of clinical negligence litigation* (23/3/2012) Jackson LJ.

13. *Reforming the civil justice system – the role of IT* (27/3/2012) Jackson LJ.

14. *Keynote address to Association of Costs Lawyers conference* (11/5/2012) Lord Neuberger MR.

15. *Proportionate costs* (30/5/2012) Lord Neuberger MR.

16. *Costs management: a necessary part of the management of litigation* (30/5/2012) Ramsey J.

17. *IP litigation: implementation of the Jackson Report's recommendations* (14/2/2013) Arnold J.

18. *The application of amendments to the Civil Procedure Rules* (22/3/2013) Lord Dyson MR.

The pilots. Because of the long time lag between publication of the Final   **4–007** Report and the general implementation date, it was possible to pilot a number of the proposed reforms at specific court centres. With the approval of the JSG and the Rule Committee, the following pilots were established:

* costs management of defamation cases in London;

* docketing in Leeds;

* concurrent expert evidence in the Manchester specialist courts;

* provisional assessment of costs in Leeds and York;

* costs management in the specialist courts, initially at Birmingham but subsequently at all court centres.

Monitoring of pilots. Professor Dame Hazel Genn of UCL monitored the   **4–008** concurrent evidence pilot and published her findings.[1] Nicholas Gould of King's College and Fenwick Elliott monitored the principal costs management pilot and put his report online.[2] RJ monitored the provisional assessment pilot (with much help from the judges involved) and summarised the results in the eighth implementation lecture. Nick Taylor of Leeds University and Ben Fitzpatrick of York University monitored the docketing pilot. They provided published their findings in *Civil Justice Quarterly*.[3] One great benefit of the pilots was that they exposed teething troubles and glitches. The final rules were modified to deal with those difficulties.

Working groups. A number of working groups took forward the implemen-   **4–009** tation of specific recommendations. Michael Napier QC chaired a group which developed a code for third party funders. An editorial advisory board (chaired by Lord Neuberger and Lord Clarke) oversaw the publication of an ADR handbook. HH Judge Simon Grenfell chaired a working group, which developed a series of standard directions and model directions for cases of common occurrence. A Civil Justice Council ("CJC") working group embarked upon revising the pre-action protocols. Michael Napier chaired a working group which advised the MoJ on rules for damages-based agreements. Senior Costs Judge Peter Hurst chaired a working group which undertook the necessary re-writing of the costs rules and practice directions (CPR Pts 43–48).

General implementation date. The general implementation date for the   **4–010** reforms was 1 April 2013. This was the date when LASPO and most of the rule amendments came into force. It was not possible to bring literally everything into

---

[1] *Getting to the Truth: experts and judges in the "hot tub"* (2013) 32 CJQ 275–299.
[2] Available on the Judiciary website: *https://www.judiciary.gov.uk/publications/costs-management-pilot/* [Accessed 1 July 2016].
[3] *Docketing lite: an analysis of a process of assigning multi-track cases to individual judges* (2012) 31 CJQ 430–450.

force on the same day. Some of the rule changes happened earlier.[4] Some of the rule changes were postponed. In particular, the introduction of fixed costs for fast track personal injury cases was deferred until 31 July 2013.

4–011   **No-one is indispensable.** On 28 April 2012, RJ underwent an operation followed by medical treatment. RJ played no further part in the implementation process between then and late 2013. Mr Justice Ramsey took over the lead role in implementation during that period and did a first class job.

2. THE INHERENT PROBLEM OF IMPLEMENTATION

4–012   **What was the problem?** The real problem of implementation was that the reforms were a coherent whole, but individual recommendations were directed to different groups. It did not necessarily follow that everyone would agree with the proposals. Civil justice reform is a contentious subject, about which most lawyers have their own ideas. The principal bodies which needed to be persuaded were:

- the MoJ,
- Parliament,
- the Rule Committee,
- the Judiciary (in particular, as to the appropriateness of raising general damages by 10%),
- the Judicial College,
- the profession,
- third party funders (in particular, as to the need for serious self-regulation).

4–013   **The danger.** Since the reforms were interlocking, it would have been very damaging if key pieces of the jigsaw had been rejected. For example, if Parliament had ended recoverable success fees, but the senior judiciary had rejected the recommendation to raise the level of general damages by 10%; or if Parliament had ended recoverable ATE premiums, but the Rule Committee had declined to introduce QOCS. Furthermore, any adverse judicial decisions in key cases such as *Simmons v Castle* [2012] EWCA Civ 1039, 1288; [2013] 1 WLR 1239 or *Wagenaar v Weekend Travel* [2014] EWCA Civ 1105 would have disrupted the reforms and unbalanced the package.

4–014   **Consequence.** If the general package of the reforms was going to remain intact, it was necessary that RJ should (a) take part in the debate which followed publication of the Final Report and (b) provide any necessary explanations. The reforms threatened many vested interests. Not everyone who was attacking the proposals had read the Preliminary Report and the Final Report from cover to

---

[4] e.g. the new r.36.14(1A) to reverse the effect of *Carver v BAA* [2008] EWCA Civ 412; [2009] 1 WLR 113.

cover. Sometimes the responses to concerns raised were to be found within those reports or their appendices.

General proposition. If anyone undertakes a substantial civil justice reform   **4–015** project, it is not enough simply to write a report and then retreat into dignified silence.[5] Given the scale of such a project and the volume of accumulated material (approximately 300 ring files in the present case), no-one other than the individual who has written the report and attended all the seminars, meetings, etc, has all the details at their fingertips and knows where to find relevant evidence. This does not mean that the author must be an obsessive or wedded to every detail of his recommendations. It does mean that the author must stand ready to attend hostile meetings, answer questions and respond to criticisms.

Should the author of a civil justice report take part in any formal public   **4–016** **consultation about his own proposals?** RJ concluded that it was necessary to do so, in order to preserve the integrity of the reform package. With the approval of the Judicial Executive Board and the JSG, RJ responded to three public consultations and put those responses on the Judiciary website for any interested party to read during the consultation period. The consultation responses can be found on the Judiciary website.[6] They are entitled:

- *Lord Justice Jackson's Response to MoJ Consultation Paper CP 13/10* (civil litigation funding and costs),

- *Lord Justice Jackson's Response to MoJ Consultation Paper CP6/2011* (solving disputes in the county courts),

- *Lord Justice Jackson's response to MoJ Consultation Paper CP 16/11* (costs protection for litigants in environmental judicial review cases).

The response to Consultation Paper CP13/10. The first of the three consulta-   **4–017** tion responses was the most important one, as it dealt with the key elements of the reforms. It is reproduced as Appendix B at the end of this book. It was written in more trenchant terms than a judge would normally adopt in public debate. In view of the ferocity of the attacks being made upon the Final Report and the fact that some of those attacks were not hugely well-informed, it was felt necessary to put in a robust response.

3. DEBATE SINCE THE GENERAL IMPLEMENTATION DATE

The ongoing debate. Debate about the reforms has continued with some   **4–018** vigour in legal periodicals over the last three years. There are now signs, however,

---

[5] Lord Woolf not only drafted his two reports, but also took part in the subsequent rule drafting and oversaw implementation of his reforms. He frequently attended meetings at which his views were challenged.
[6] Consultations are available through the Reviews webpage: *https://www.judiciary.gov.uk/reviews/* [Accessed 1 July 2016].

that the debate is dying down as the reforms are bedding in and the profession is becoming more familiar with costs management.

4–019   **Conferences to discuss the FR reforms during 2013 and 2014.** There were three conferences to discuss the reforms in the 18-month period following implementation. They were:

- the UCL conference on 13 November 2013, entitled "Justice after Jackson";
- the CJC conference on 21 March 2014, entitled "Impact of Jackson reforms";
- the Law Society conference on 20 October 2014, entitled "Commercial litigation: the post-Jackson world".

The papers prepared for those conferences are available online. RJ's paper for the Law Society Conference on 20 October 2014 set out the case for amending the Damages-Based Agreements Regulations 2013 in order to permit hybrid DBAs.

4–020   **Post-implementation lectures in 2015–2016.** During the period 2015–2016, RJ has given lectures for two purposes. The first purpose is to assist practitioners and judges who are applying the new rules in practice. The second purpose is to draw attention to areas where implementation is incomplete and to suggest further steps which might be taken. The principal lectures in this series are:

- the Harbour Lecture on 13 May 2015, entitled "Confronting costs management";
- the Mustill Lecture on 16 October 2015, entitled "The civil justice reforms and whether insolvency litigation should be exempt";
- the Insolvency Practitioners Association ("IPA") annual lecture on 28 January 2016, entitled "Fixed costs – the time has come";
- the Keynote speech at the Solicitors' Costs conference on 2 February 2016, entitled "The case for a CLAF";
- the Keynote speech at the Law Society's Civil Litigation conference on 21 April 2016, entitled "The new form bill of costs".

4–021   **Impact of post-implementation lectures.** RJ does not have any official role apart from being one of 39 judges in the Court of Appeal and therefore is not (and never has been) able to dictate what people do about the reforms proposed in the Final Report. The only avenue is to seek to persuade others by rational argument. The effect of the post-implementation lectures so far has been as follows:

- The Harbour Lecture contained numerous recommendations in order to promote the smooth running of costs management. Some of those recommendations have been taken up, for example the proposal for a time-limited moratorium on costs management in clinical negligence cases at the RCJ.

- The Mustill Lecture proposed ending the exemption of insolvency litigation from the LASPO reforms. The Government has ended that exemption with effect from 1 April 2016.

- The IPA annual lecture proposed introducing fixed recoverable costs in the remainder of the fast track and the lower reaches of the multi-track. The Government has said that it supports the principle of fixed recoverable costs and is considering those proposals.

- The speech at the Solicitors' Costs Conference invited the profession to establish a Contingent Legal Aid Fund. The Law Society, the Bar Council and the Chartered Institute of Legal Executives have set up a joint working group to take forward that proposal. It is very much hoped that this will lead to action. Following the retraction of legal aid, there is great need for a CLAF. Such bodies operate successfully overseas.

- The speech at the Solicitors' Costs Conference on 21 April 2016 proposed steps which the Rule Committee should take in order to develop a new form bill of costs. The Rule Committee has set up a sub-committee to consider those proposals.

4. OVERALL POSITION

Most but not all of the FR proposals have now been implemented. Many of the **4–022** reforms are working smoothly and people have forgotten that they are part of the FR reforms. Some remain controversial, although that controversy is diminishing. One or two major proposals are still work in progress. This applies in particular to fixed recoverable costs and the new form bill of costs.

Part Two
FUNDING

CHAPTER 5

CONDITIONAL FEE AGREEMENTS, AFTER-THE-EVENT INSURANCE AND INCREASED DAMAGES

1. CONDITIONAL FEE AGREEMENTS: BACKGROUND

Should litigation lawyers be paid by results? Until 1995, the law did not **5–001** allow solicitors or barristers conducting litigation to be paid by results. The reason for this prohibition was the fear that if lawyers had a personal stake in the outcome, it would compromise their objectivity. They may be tempted to behave improperly. There is undoubtedly some force in those concerns. On the other hand, if lawyers are allowed to be paid by results, this opens up a new means of funding for those who could not otherwise afford to litigate. Lawyers can take on a portfolio of cases on a no-win-no-fee basis. They receive nothing in cases which fail, but they make up their losses by receiving extra payment in cases which succeed. Clients who cannot otherwise afford to litigate thereby gain access to justice. After much anguished debate, policy makers decided that the "access to justice" argument should prevail.

The birth of CFAs. Hence the idea of conditional fee agreements ("CFAs") **5–002** was born. In essence, a CFA provides that (a) the lawyers charge no fee if they lose, but (b) they charge the normal fee (called "base costs") plus a success fee if they win. Section 58 of the Courts and Legal Services Act 1990, which came into force in 1995, permitted CFAs in three types of cases, namely personal injury, insolvency litigation and ECHR applications. The benefit to claimants from these arrangements was obvious. The downside, however, was that if they won, they had to pay part of the damages to their own lawyers as success fees. Claimants could not recover that element of their costs from the other side.

Extended use of CFAs. Section 27 of the Access to Justice Act 1999 permitted **5–003** the use of CFAs in all types of civil litigation as from April 2000. Numerous variants of CFAs came into use. The agreement could provide for a "low fee" instead of "no fee", if the case was lost. In some cases, both solicitors and counsel worked on CFAs. In other cases, the solicitors had CFAs, but counsel worked on the normal basis of being paid in any event. Although CFAs were designed to assist claimants, sometimes defendants used them. In that situation, "success" was defined as defeating the claim, or perhaps reducing quantum below a certain level.

5–004   **Reforms in 2000 to make success fees recoverable.** In April 2000, there was a substantial retraction of legal aid. In particular, personal injury claims (excluding clinical negligence claims) fell outside the scope of legal aid. The Government decided that in order to assist personal injury claimants and others who were ceasing to benefit from legal aid, the rules for CFAs should be changed. Parties with the benefit of CFAs should be entitled to recover the success fees (due to their own lawyers under the CFAs) from the other side. Section 27 of the Access to Justice Act 1999 and rules made pursuant to that section gave effect to this reform. These provisions came into force in April 2000.

5–005   **First decade of the twenty-first century: the "costs war".** The new regime brought in its wake all manner of unforeseen problems, as discussed in section 3, below. Because the costs burden on defendants was substantially increased, liability insurers looked for ways to avoid liability. They began raising ingenious objections to their opponents' CFAs, arguing that because of technical breaches the claimants were not entitled to recover any costs at all. Claimant lawyers for their part fought to recover substantial, some would say excessive, success fees. These skirmishes, which filled many pages of the law reports, became known as "the costs war".[1] That episode reflected little credit on the legal profession or the civil justice system.

2. AFTER-THE-EVENT INSURANCE: BACKGROUND

5–006   **Nature of after-the-event insurance.** After-the-event insurance ("ATE") was developed during the 1990s. The insured takes out insurance against the risk of losing his case. The insurance is called "after-the-event", because the accident or incident about which the client is litigating has already happened. The client, who is usually a claimant but could be a defendant, is taking out insurance against the risk of losing his case. If sadly the client does lose, then the insurer pays out (a) the costs due to the other side and (b), under most ATE policies, the insured's disbursements, such as expert fees.

5–007   **The premium itself is insured.** A special feature of most ATE policies is that the premium itself is usually insured. In other words, insurers receive enhanced premiums in cases which are successful, but no premium at all in cases which are unsuccessful.

5–008   **Combination of CFAs and ATE.** During the 1990s, claimants started to make use of CFAs in conjunction with ATE. The benefit of this arrangement was that if they lost, they had no costs liability either to their own solicitors or to the other side. In other words, they had a completely free ride. On the other hand, if the

---

[1] See PR, Ch. 3, section 5 (pp. 27–38).

claimants won, they paid success fees to their lawyers and ATE premiums to their insurers. They had to make those payments out of the damages recovered. The Law Society recommended that the total of those payments should always be limited to 25% of damages recovered. The Law Society model CFA agreement included a provision to that effect. According to the Association of Personal Injury Lawyers, this regime worked well.[2]

Reforms in 2000 to make ATE premiums recoverable. In 1999, the   5–009
Government decided that in order to assist personal injury claimants and others who were ceasing to benefit from legal aid, the rules for ATE should be changed. Parties with the benefit of ATE should be entitled to recover the ATE premiums from the other side as part of their recoverable costs if they won. Section 29 of the Access to Justice Act 1999 and rules made pursuant to that section gave effect to this reform. These provisions came into force in April 2000.

3. What was the Overall Effect of the Reforms of April 2000?

A disaster. The reforms of April 2000 ("recoverability") were, with the utmost   5–010
respect to all concerned, a disaster, essentially for five reasons.

First reason: recoverability drives up the costs of litigation. Take a cohort   5–011
of 100 cases in which the claimants have CFAs and ATE. Assume that the claimants win 80 cases and lose 20. In theory, if the success fees and ATE premiums are set at the right level, then:

(i) The solicitors bear their own costs in the 20 unsuccessful cases, but recover those costs by means of success fees on the 80 successful cases.

(ii) The ATE insurers receive no premiums in the 20 unsuccessful cases, but instead they pay out the defendants' costs and the claimants' disbursements in those cases. The ATE insurers make up for all those losses by means of the premiums which they receive in the 80 successful cases.

(iii) Thus, at the end of the day, if everything goes perfectly to plan, the defendants end up paying all the claimants' costs in all 100 cases. The claimants, on the other hand, have a completely free ride. They never pay their own costs and never pay any adverse costs, regardless of the outcome of any individual case.

(iv) In fact, lawyers are human and also business people. By and large, they will only back winning cases on CFAs. Likewise, ATE insurers will generally only back winning cases. The result is that lawyers will recover more on success fees in successful cases than they lose on unsuccessful cases. Likewise, ATE insurers will recover more in premiums on successful cases than they pay out on the "lost" cases. On top of that, the ATE insurers have to recover from premiums received their own overheads and profits. **The**

---

[2] See Lord Woolf, *Final Report on Access to Justice*, pp. 26–27.

practical consequence is that in our imaginary cohort of 100 cases, the defendants will end up paying substantially more than all of the costs of both sides in all 100 cases, regardless of the outcome of any individual case.

(v) Thus, the recoverability regime drives up the total costs of litigation. The main beneficiaries are the lawyers and the ATE insurers.

5–012 **Professor Andrews' analysis.** Professor Andrews illustrates the effect of the recoverability regime in Vol. 1 of *Andrews on Civil Processes*.[3] The regime led to a raft of cases in which courts felt compelled to award exorbitant sums by way of costs.

5–013 **Second reason: distortion of incentives.** If one side is litigating at no risk as to costs and the other side is at risk of paying out something approaching four times the costs of the action (own costs + other side's costs + other side's success fee + other side's ATE premium), that distorts incentives.[4] The party at no risk as to costs takes no interest in the costs which its lawyers are running up. The normal disciplines which control costs are lacking. This is illustrated by the data in FR Appendix 1.

Table 1 summarises a batch of "successful" cases tried by district judges. Where claimants did not have CFAs, their costs were on average 51% of the damages. Where claimants did have CFAs, their costs were on average 158% of damages.

Table 5 summarises a batch of "successful" cases tried by circuit judges. Where claimants did not have CFAs, their costs were on average 55% of the damages. Where claimants did have CFAs, their costs were on average 203% of damages.

5–014 **Third reason: unfairness.** Fair litigation requires a level playing field. It is grossly unfair if one side is at massive risk as to costs and the other side is at no risk whatsoever. During the Costs Review, there were stories of many cases where one side was driven to cave in not because its claim or defence was weak, but simply because of the crushing costs risk which it faced.

5–015 **Fourth reason: the recoverability regime was not targeted on those who needed support.** The legal aid regime (which the new scheme of recoverability was in large measure intended to replace) was targeted upon those who needed support, because they had meritorious cases but lacked means. The new recoverability regime was not directed to those who merited support. Anyone could use it. For example, in an ordinary commercial action, one party used the regime in order to shift much of the costs risk onto the other party: *Sandvik Intellectual Property AB v Kennametal UK Ltd* [2012] EWHC 245 (Pat). On occasions, defendants could and did use the regime against claimants. Sometimes businesses used it against consumers.

5–016 **Other bizarre examples.** Household insurers, who pay out on claims for tree-root damage to houses, frequently sue local authorities to recover their

---

[3] See Vol. 1, "Court Proceedings", Ch. 20, pp. 576–580.
[4] See *Zuckerman on Civil Procedure*, Ch. 27, p. 1387.

losses. After 2000, household insurers started using CFAs and ATE in such cases, thereby imposing substantial additional burdens upon council tax payers. International finance companies suing the Civil Aviation Authority used CFAs and ATE. So did large contractors who were suing public authorities in procurement disputes. The recoverability regime was never intended to support large commercial enterprises. It was quite wrong that they should be able to shift their own costs burden onto the public purse in every case (regardless of the outcome).

Fifth reason: a very expensive form of one-way costs shifting. As explained   **5–017** in Ch. 16, below, the system of recoverable ATE premiums introduced a hugely expensive form of one-way costs shifting.

4. RECOMMENDATIONS IN THE FINAL REPORT OF JANUARY 2010

Abolition of recoverability regime. The Final Report recommended that   **5–018** Parliament should abolish the recoverability regime. Parties with CFAs should no longer be able to recover the success fees if they won. Parties with ATE should no longer be able to recover the ATE premiums if they won. In place of the recoverability regime, Parliament should put in place a series of measures to assist those claimants who needed support, principally PI claimants.

Measures to assist claimants. The Final Report proposed the following   **5–019** package of measures to assist claimants in the new era:

(i) The level of general damages for personal injuries, nuisance and similar wrongs should increase by 10%.

(ii) In PI cases, the success fees which the lawyers may charge should not exceed 25% of damages, excluding any damages referable to future care or future losses.

(iii) The rewards for "effective" claimant offers under CPR Pt 36 should be enhanced.

(iv) In PI cases and in other litigation where parties are in an asymmetric relationship, claimants should have the protection of "qualified one-way costs shifting", generally known as "QOCS". If the claimants won, they should recover their costs. If they lost, they should have no costs liability—except to the extent that it was reasonable having regard to (a) the financial resources of each of the parties or (b) their conduct in the litigation. In other words, there would be one-way costs shifting, except in rare cases: e.g. where the claimant is wealthy and the defendant is uninsured, or where the claimant has persisted in bringing a frivolous claim.

(v) Other means of funding litigation should be developed. In particular, contingency fees or DBAs should be permitted; before-the-event insurance and third party funding should be promoted.

5–020   **Was this package of measures sufficient to support personal injury claimants?** Yes, it was. Professor Paul Fenn analysed the data on 63,998 PI cases. He found that under the proposed package of reforms, 61% of claimants would be better off and 39% of claimants would be worse off. The last section of the Appendix B of this book sets out the details, including separate tables for road traffic accident cases, employers' liability cases and public liability cases.

5. IMPLEMENTATION IN APRIL 2013

5–021   **Abolition of recoverability.** Sections 44 and 46 of the Legal Aid, Sentencing and Punishment of Offenders Act 2012 ("LASPO") ended the recoverability of success fees and ATE premiums. They achieved this by amending s.58 of the Courts and Legal Services Act 1990 ("the 1990 Act") and inserting a new s.58C into the 1990 Act. These provisions came into effect on 1 April 2013.

5–022   **Exceptions.** Parliament made four exceptions. They were:

(i) In clinical negligence cases, that part of an ATE premium which related to the cost of expert reports on liability or causation would still be recoverable: see s.58C(2)–(5) of the 1990 Act and the Recovery of Costs Insurance Premiums in Clinical Negligence Proceedings (No. 2) Regulations 2013 (SI 739/2013).

(ii) Sections 44 and 46 of LASPO would not be brought into effect in relation to diffuse mesothelioma proceedings until the Lord Chancellor had carried out a further review: see s.48 of LASPO.

(iii) In relation to defamation and privacy claims, the implementation of ss.44 and 46 of LASPO was deferred until costs protection was introduced for such proceedings: see the written ministerial statement of 12 December 2012 by the Parliamentary Under-Secretary of State for Justice[5] and art.4(b) of the Legal Aid, Sentencing and Punishment of Offenders Act 2012 (Commencement No. 5 and Saving Provision) Order 2013 (SI 77/2013).

(iv) In relation to proceedings brought by liquidators, trustees in bankruptcy and companies in administration, the implementation of ss.44 and 46 of LASPO was deferred for two years: see the written ministerial statement of 24 May 2012 by the Parliamentary Under-Secretary of State for Justice[6] and art.4(b)–(f) of the Legal Aid, Sentencing and Punishment of Offenders Act 2012 (Commencement No. 5 and Saving Provision) Order 2013 (SI 77/2013).

5–023   **Increase in the level of general damages.** It is the courts which set the level of general damages. The Final Report therefore did not recommend legislation to raise the level of damages. Instead, the Final Report recommended that judges

---

[5] *Hansard*, HC Vol.555, col.38WS (12 December 2012).
[6] *Hansard*, HC Vol.545, col.94WS (24 May 2012).

should achieve this reform by means of judicial decision. The senior judiciary heard argument on this issue in *Simmons v Castle* [2012] EWCA Civ 1039 and 1288; [2013] 1 WLR 1239 and accepted the recommendation. The Lord Chief Justice, sitting with the Master of the Rolls and the Vice-President of the Civil Division of the Court of Appeal, held that the level of general damages would increase by 10% with effect from 1 April 2013 (except in cases which were proceeding on pre-LASPO CFAs). The Court of Appeal confirmed the universal application of this increase in the level of general damages in *Summers v Bundy* [2016] EWCA Civ 126.

Restriction on deductions from claimants' damages in personal injury 5–024 **cases.** In PI cases, claimant solicitors cannot charge a success fee exceeding 25% of the damages recovered, ignoring for the purpose of this calculation any damages referable to future pecuniary losses. Future pecuniary losses are, in this context, essentially future care costs and future loss of earnings. Parliament implemented this restriction on the recoverable success fee through s.44(2) of LASPO and art.5(1) (a) of the Conditional Fee Agreements Order 2013.

The other recommended measures to assist claimants. These were also put 5–025 into effect on 1 April 2013. They are dealt with in Chs 6, 7, 10 and 16, below.

6. DISCUSSION OF THE FOUR EXCEPTIONS

(i) *First exception*

The underlying policy. The policy underlying s.46 of LASPO is clear. The 5–026 Government has decided that clinical negligence claimants should have a mechanism for recovering from the public purse the costs of their medical reports on liability and causation. No-one could criticise that policy decision and it is certainly not the intention of this chapter to do so.

The current method of achieving that policy objective. It is nevertheless 5–027 submitted that an unduly expensive method has been chosen for achieving that policy objective. This is for two reasons:

- Recoverable ATE premiums are not targeted on those who merit support. There is no means test.
- This mechanism adds an unnecessary layer of cost to the process, namely the overheads and profits of the ATE insurers.

The taxpayer (through the NHSLA) bears these additional costs.

A better method. There is a much more economical way for the taxpayer to 5–028 meet the costs of medical reports, namely by means of legal aid. Legal aid is means tested and is only made available to those claimants who need financial support. The Legal Aid Agency exists and it can administer payments of this character most efficiently. Indeed, the legal aid authorities did so for over half a century up until 31 March 2013.

5–029   **First implementation lecture. Time for reconsideration?** These arguments were deployed in the first implementation lecture, delivered at Cambridge on 5 September 2011.[7] The arguments did not find favour with the Government. At the present time, however, when there is concern about the costs of clinical negligence litigation, it might be thought appropriate to look again at the issue. This is a clear example of a cutback in legal aid which was counterproductive.

(ii) *Second exception*

5–030   **Lord Chancellor's decision.** In December 2013, the Lord Chancellor decided to bring ss.44 and 46 of LASPO into force in respect of mesothelioma claims. This would have brought mesothelioma claims into line with all other PI litigation.

5–031   **Judicial review challenge.** Mr Tony Whitston, a member of the Asbestos Victims Support Groups Forum UK, challenged the Lord Chancellor's decision in judicial review proceedings. That challenge succeeded on the basis that s.48 of LASPO required the Lord Chancellor to carry out a review of the effects of ss.44 and 46 in relation to claims for diffuse mesothelioma claims; the Lord Chancellor had not carried out such a review. See *Whitston v Secretary of State for Justice* [2014] EWHC 3044 (Admin).

5–032   **The future.** The continuation of recoverable success fees and recoverable ATE premiums for mesothelioma claims is only intended to be a temporary measure. It is the most expensive method imaginable for funding such claims. In the long term, the possibilities would appear to be:

- bringing ss.44 and 46 into force in respect of mesothelioma claims, after carrying out a satisfactory review; or

- providing legal aid for such claims; or

- setting up a tribunal scheme to deal with such claims, possibly with the tribunal having investigative powers and its own medical panel.

(iii) *Third exception*

5–033   **Defamation and privacy claims.** The problems with maintaining a recoverability regime for defamation and privacy claims is the burden which this places on defendants, of whom some are well resourced but others are not. The problem is illustrated by the decision of the European Court of Human Rights in *MGN Ltd v UK* [2011] ECHR 66.

5–034   **Final Report proposals.** The Final Report has proposed that:

- There should be QOCS for defamation and privacy claims.

- Recoverable success fees and recoverable ATE premiums for such claims should come to an end.

---

[7] Available on the Judiciary website: *https://www.judiciary.gov.uk* [Accessed 1 July 2016].

As discussed in Ch. 18, below, the Government has gone out to consultation on that proposal, but has not yet reached a decision.

Implications of QOCS. If a QOCS regime is introduced for defamation and   **5–035**
privacy claims, it should follow the form suggested in the Final Report, rather than that adopted in CPR rr.44.14 to 44.16. The means of the claimant should be taken into account in determining whether he or she should benefit from QOCS. It would not be satisfactory if a wealthy claimant had the benefit of QOCS in litigation against a poorly resourced local newspaper.

(iv) *Fourth exception*

The two-year exemption for insolvency litigation. In relation to insol-   **5–036**
vency litigation, the stated purpose of deferring implementation was to allow practitioners time to adjust to the changes. Quite why insolvency practitioners needed this special indulgence was not obvious, since more than three years had elapsed between the publication of the Final Report and the implementation of its recommendations.

Extension of the exemption. In February 2015, the Government announced   **5–037**
that it would further delay the implementation of ss.44 and 46 of LASPO in relation to insolvency litigation "for the time being". Some commentators thought that this extension was unwise.[8]

Ending of the fourth exception. Following an announcement in December   **5–038**
2015, the insolvency exemption was brought to an end on 6 April 2016. CFAs for insolvency proceedings made after that date are not exempt from ss.44 and 46 of LASPO.

---

[8] See the Mustill Lecture 2015, which is on the Judiciary website.

DAMAGES-BASED AGREEMENTS

1. BACKGROUND

Terminology. "Damages-based agreements" and "contingency fees" are both 6–001 terms used to describe arrangements whereby a lawyer is paid a percentage of the winnings in the event of success, but no fee[1] in the event of failure. In this book, the term "DBA" will be used to describe such an arrangement.

The position overseas.[2] In Estonia, Finland, Hungary, Italy, Japan, Lithuania, 6–002 Slovakia, Slovenia, South Africa, Spain, Taiwan and the USA, DBAs have been permitted for many years. In Ontario, DBAs are permitted in the context of a costs shifting regime.

The position in England and Wales in 2009. Litigants and lawyers were not 6–003 allowed to use DBAs in contentious business. That meant all forms of litigation in court. On the other hand, DBAs were permitted in employment tribunals, subject to certain statutory restrictions, because employment claims were classified as "non-contentious" business. Such a classification was bizarre, to say the least, as anyone who has fought out cases in employment tribunals will confirm.

The principal arguments for disallowing DBAs. The principal arguments 6–004 which were advanced for disallowing DBAs in England and Wales were the following:

- DBAs are liable to give rise to greater conflicts of interest between lawyer and client than in the case of CFAs.

- It is wrong in principle for the lawyer to have an interest in the level of damages.

- If CFAs and contingent fees co-exist, lawyers would conduct lower value claims on CFAs and higher value claims on DBAs. This dual system

---

[1] Whether a DBA should allow a low fee in the event of failure is a matter of controversy.
[2] See Hodges, Vogenauer and Tulibacka, *The Costs and Funding of Civil Litigation*, Table 2 on pp. 132–133.

would maximise recovery for lawyers and give rise to a conflict of interest between lawyer and client.

- If part of the DBA fee is not recoverable from the other side (as is the case in all jurisdictions where DBAs are currently permitted), then clients will lose part of their damages. This is unacceptable in PI cases, especially insofar as damages represent the cost of future care.

- DBAs create an incentive to settle a case early.

- DBAs will only be viable if the level of general damages for personal injuries increases. That is not going to happen, as is apparent from the non-implementation of the Law Commission's 1998 report.

- DBAs are only acceptable in the USA because damages are extremely high and include non-compensatory elements. This is not the case here.

- The introduction of DBAs would be damaging to the solicitors' profession.

- The introduction of DBAs would be contrary to the existing professional culture, which makes the Commercial Court attractive to overseas litigants.

6–005   **The principal arguments for ending the ban and permitting DBAs.** The principal arguments which were advanced for ending the ban and permitting DBAs were the following:

- The principle of no win-no fee has been established by CFAs, so there can be no principled objection to DBAs.

- DBAs are simpler than CFAs. They are easier to understand and would avoid some of the problems of CFAs.

- DBAs offer less scope for conflicts of interest than CFAs.

- Many clients would prefer DBAs to CFAs.

- If DBAs are permitted as well as the existing funding mechanisms, this can only increase access to justice.

- Under a DBA, the fees payable to the lawyer are always, and by definition, proportionate.

- DBAs give the lawyer a direct incentive to maximise recovery for his client.

- There is no danger of DBAs creating a US-type situation here. In England and Wales, (a) juries do not assess damages and (b) judges are not elected.

- DBAs work well in employment tribunals. They also work well in appeals to the VAT and Duties Tribunal.

- There can be no possible objection to sophisticated clients (e.g. large public limited companies with in-house counsel) entering into contingency fee agreements, if that is what both they and their solicitors want to do.

Growing doubts about the ban. Many commentators, in particular Professor   6–006
Michael Zander, were critical of the current position and maintained that DBAs
should be permitted as a means of promoting access to justice. This was clearly
a live issue for consideration in the 2009 Costs Review and was flagged up for
consideration in PR Ch. 20.

2. DEBATE DURING THE COSTS REVIEW

Consensus impossible. It became clear at an early stage in the consultation   6–007
period that no form of consensus was possible on this issue. The views on both
sides of this issue were strongly held.

Votes at meetings. Votes were taken at many of the meetings during the   6–008
consultation period. The majority usually voted in favour of allowing DBAs in
principle. It was not practicable to take votes on the question of what safeguards
were appropriate. At the seminar on 10 July 2009, Professor Kritzer, a prominent
US authority on the subject, gave an account of how contingency fee regimes
operated in the USA.

Stakeholder views. The Law Society broadly favoured DBAs. Personal   6–009
injury lawyers opposed DBAs. Commercial lawyers were divided in their views.
Third party funders were supportive of DBAs on the grounds of freedom of
choice. That was interesting because the ban on DBAs presumably got them
more business.

3. RECOMMENDATIONS IN THE FINAL REPORT OF JANUARY 2010

Chapter 12 of the Final Report. FR Ch. 12 summarised the conflicting views   6–010
expressed during the consultation period, but came down in favour of allowing
DBAs subject to appropriate safeguards.

Reasoning. The arguments in favour of allowing DBAs, as set out in section   6–011
1 above, clearly outweighed the arguments in favour of maintaining the ban. The
following were particularly important considerations:

- DBAs would provide an additional means of funding litigation. The existence of as many funding options as possible was very much in the public
  interest.

- Unlike the then current CFAs, DBAs would not prejudice opposing parties.
  If an opposing party lost, it would not have to pay any additional costs by
  reason of the DBA.

- Once the principle of payment by results was accepted, DBAs were preferable to CFAs. DBAs tended to incentivise efficiency, whereas CFAs
  tended to incentivise inefficiency. It was illogical to ban DBAs while permitting CFAs.

- In the commercial context, where both parties are experienced business people, why on earth shouldn't they run litigation on a DBA basis if that is what they both want? There must be some good reason for banning people from doing things. In this instance there is no good reason.

6–012 **Review of overseas regimes.** After reviewing overseas regimes, FR Ch. 12 concluded that the Ontario model was best suited to the needs of this jurisdiction.

6–013 **Conclusion.** Chapter 12 of the Final Report concluded with two recommendations:

> "(i) Both solicitors and counsel should be permitted to enter into contingency fee agreements with their clients. However, costs should be recoverable against opposing parties on the conventional basis and not by reference to the contingency fee.
> (ii) Contingency fee agreements should be properly regulated and they should not be valid unless the client has received independent advice."

6–014 **Links to costs management.** If litigation is subject to costs management, the party with a DBA will know as from the first case management conference ("CMC") how much costs they are likely to recover if they win and how much costs they are likely to pay out if they lose. It will then be straightforward to compare the anticipated costs recovery from the other side with their contractual liability for costs to their own lawyers under the DBA.

6–015 **Link to recommendation for fixed recoverable costs.** The proposal to allow DBAs fits neatly with the recommendation for fixed costs. Once both of these reforms are properly in place, a party entering into a DBA with their lawyers will know from the outset and with precision (a) what costs they will pay to the lawyers if they win and what costs they will recover from the other side, and (b) what costs they will have to pay out if they lose. Such an arrangement creates clarity as to the financial position before any proceedings are issued. This is of considerable assistance in decision-making.

6–016 **Link to proposed new form bill of costs.** Once the new form bill of costs and accompanying software are in place, as discussed in Ch. 20, below, solicitors will have a convenient tool for comparing their actual costs being incurred against anticipated recovery under the DBA.

4. IMPLEMENTATION

6–017 **The Government's position.** After consultation, the MoJ resolved to accept the FR recommendations in favour of DBAs, but without imposing any requirement for independent advice. It announced this decision in March 2015.

6–018 **Legislation.** Section 45 of LASPO permitted the use of DBAs with effect from 1 April 2013. This was subject to the provisions of the Damages-Based Agreements Regulations 2013 ("the DBA Regulations").

The scheme. The general scheme follows that in Ontario. As between solici- 6–019
tor and client the DBA governs what the client pays, subject to the restrictions
imposed by the DBA Regulations. As between the parties, costs recovery is on
the conventional basis: see CPR r.44.18. That means that the receiving party must
prepare a bill of costs in the standard form.

The problems. Unfortunately, the drafting of the DBA Regulations is 6–020
unsatisfactory. This has thrown up a large number of problems, as identified in
Questions & Answers.[3] Professor Rachael Mulheron discussed those problems
in her article "The Damages-Based Agreements Regulations 2013: some conun-
drums in the 'Brave New World' of funding".[4] The fact that the Government has
not (or at least not yet) abrogated the indemnity principle, as recommended in
FR Ch. 5, makes those problems more acute. As a result and most unfortunately,
solicitors and clients seldom make use of DBAs.

Civil Justice Council Report. In 2014, the CJC, at the request of the MoJ, 6–021
set up a working group to consider the problems and propose appropriate revisions to the DBA Regulations. Professor Rachael Mulheron was the chair.
In August 2015, the working group delivered an excellent report, making 56
detailed recommendations. At the time of writing, that report is still under
consideration.

Fixing the problem. It is not surprising that the MoJ is still considering the 6–022
CJC report. The drafting issues are complex and it is vital that the MoJ gets it right
next time. When the amended DBA Regulations are published, it is very much
hoped (and expected) that these will create a workable regime. There is a very
substantial need for such a regime.[5]

One particular issue. This book is not the place to debate the minutiae of the 6–023
problems with the DBA Regulations. But one particular issue does merit discussion, namely the question of hybrid DBAs. This will be addressed in the next
section.

5. HYBRID DBAs

What is a "hybrid" DBA? A "hybrid" DBA is a no win-low fee DBA. In other 6–024
words, if the case is lost, the lawyers are still allowed to charge a fee, albeit significantly less than their normal fees. The risk of receiving only a low fee entitles
the lawyers to receive the agreed share of the winnings if the case is successful.
In the commercial context, lawyers and clients quite often wish to enter into a
hybrid DBA.

---

[3] Hurst, Middleton and Mallalieu, 2016 at pp. 21–24.
[4] (2013) 32 CJQ 241–255.
[5] Professor Mulheron made a powerful speech urging the implementation of her recommendations at
the Westminster Legal Policy Forum seminar on 23 May 2016. The seminar was well attended both
by the legal profession and by Government officials.

6–025   **The present position.** The DBA Regulations appear not to permit hybrid agreements. There seems to be no willingness on the part of the Government to amend the regulations in order to allow hybrid DBAs.

6–026   **Proposal.** It is suggested that this issue should be looked at again. There are eight reasons why hybrid DBAs should be permitted.

6–027   **First reason.** DBAs are particularly suited to commercial litigation. It may not be practical for lawyers to undertake a long commercial action on the basis that they will recover no payment for their labours if the case is lost. On the other hand, they may well be willing to work for (a) reduced fees in the event of defeat, and (b) a share of the winnings if the case is won. If that is what both lawyers and clients want, why should they not be allowed to proceed on that basis?

The answer is that there is no reason of either principle or practicality why that should not be allowed. The old argument that lawyers should not be allowed to act on a speculative basis fell away twenty years ago when CFAs were permitted.

6–028   **Second reason.** Between April 2000 and April 2013, the CFA regime was an instrument of injustice and, on occasions, oppression. It meant that one party litigated at massive costs risk, while other party proceeded at no or minimal costs risk. None of those objectionable features are present in hybrid DBAs. The presence or absence of a hybrid DBA makes no difference to the position of the other party. The amount of costs which a successful party recovers from his adversary will be precisely the same, regardless of whether the successful party has an ordinary DBA, a hybrid DBA or no DBA. The means by which a litigant chooses to fund his legal costs is his own business. It should not concern his opponent.

6–029   **Third reason.** Hybrid DBAs are allowed in Canada. Section 28.1(2) of the Solicitors Act in Ontario provides:

> "A solicitor may enter into a contingency fee agreement that provides that the remuneration paid to the solicitor for the legal services provided to or on behalf of the client is contingent, in whole *or in part*, on the successful disposition or completion of the matter in respect of which services are provided." (emphasis added.)

The phrase "or in part" expressly contemplates that some DBAs will be on a "no win-low fee" basis. According to practitioners, such hybrid DBAs are not regarded as problematic. They work perfectly satisfactorily. No-one suggests that this particular form of DBA is encouraging speculative litigation or unmeritorious claims.[6] On the contrary, the effect of the regime has been substantially to extend access to justice.

6–030   **Fourth reason.** In the Netherlands, hybrid DBAs are the only ones which are permitted. In that jurisdiction, CFAs must include a provision that the client pays some portion of the legal costs in the event of losing.

---

[6] One Canadian judge who was consulted in 2014 suspects that contingency fees generally may encourage questionable claims, although he says that there is no evidential basis for this. More importantly, there is no suggestion that hybrid agreements are relevant to this issue.

Fifth reason. CFAs may be either in the form "no win-no fee" or in the form   **6–031**
"no win-low fee". It is illogical that DBAs do not have similar flexibility.

Sixth reason. Third party funding ("TPF") proceeds on the basis that the   **6–032**
funder meets **some or all** of the litigation costs if the action fails and receives a
share of the winnings if the action succeeds. In other words, TPF is allowed on
a hybrid basis. It is illogical that DBAs (in which the lawyers act as funders) are
not allowed on a hybrid basis. Indeed, it is worse than illogical. DBAs are a more
efficient form of funding than TPF, because only two entities (rather than three)
have a stake in the litigation. Therefore, the law should not be sidelining DBAs
in favour of TPF.

Seventh reason. Some suggest that hybrid DBAs will encourage weak and   **6–033**
speculative claims. Quite the opposite is the case. If both the client and the lawyer
are "investing" in the case, they will not do so unless the chances of success
are considerably more than even. No lawyer will "take a punt" on a weak case.
Professor Kritzer emphasised this point (on the basis of his considerable experience) at the London seminar on 10 July 2009. In practice, the lawyer will do due
diligence on the case, usually taking counsel's opinion, before entering into a
DBA.

Eighth reason. The eighth reason is a simple one. Permitting hybrid DBAs   **6–034**
would promote access to justice. Following the abolition of recoverable success
fees, it is important to open up as many other options for funding as possible.

Conclusion. For a range of policy reasons which Parliament has accepted,   **6–035**
DBAs are a desirable means of funding litigation and thereby promoting access
to justice. There are technical problems with the current DBA Regulations, which
(it is expected) will be overcome following the CJC report. There is also a strong
case for permitting hybrid DBAs. That case has not yet won acceptance, but hopefully it will do so in the future.

OTHER FORMS OF FUNDING

1. RECOMMENDATIONS IN THE FINAL REPORT OF JANUARY 2010

Underlying principles. There are two principles which underlie the funding recommendations in the Final Report. The first principle is that as many different funding options as possible should be made available to litigants. The second principle is that no funding mechanism should be permitted which increases the adverse costs risk imposed upon other parties. In other words, if a winning party's normal entitlement to recoverable costs is £x, he should not be entitled to recover £x + £y because he has chosen to adopt one method of funding rather than another.   **7–001**

Rationale for those two principles. The rationale for the first principle is simple. A spread of funding options is necessary to promote access to justice. The rationale for the second principle is that liability for adverse costs is a necessary evil. It is necessary, so that the successful party is at least partially reimbursed the costs of vindicating his rights. It is an evil because the risk of adverse costs deters some meritorious parties from bringing or defending claims. It is unacceptable for the adverse costs risk to be ramped up in order to generate a new method of funding.   **7–002**

Funding methods discussed in the Final Report. The Final Report discussed the following principal funding methods: **7–003**

- Legal aid in FR Ch. 7,

- Before-the-event insurance ("BTE") in FR Ch. 8,

- After-the-event insurance ("ATE") in FR Ch.9,

- Conditional fee agreements ("CFAs") in FR Ch.10,

- Third party funding ("TPF") in FR Ch.11,

- Damages-based-agreements ("DBAs") in FR Ch.12,

- Contingent Legal Aid Fund ("CLAF") or Supplementary Legal Aid Scheme ("SLAS") in FR Ch.13.

7–004   **The focus of this chapter.** The two preceding chapters have discussed ATE, CFAs and DBAs. The present chapter will address the other forms of funding mentioned above.

2. Legal Aid

7–005   **Chapter 7 of the Final Report.** FR Ch. 7 discussed the legal aid regime as it stood in 2009. Realistically, the chapter accepted that the legal cuts made in 2000 could not, or at least would not, be reversed. Chapter 7 concluded with the following paragraph:

> "4.2 I do not make any recommendation in this chapter for the expansion or restoration of legal aid. I do, however, stress the vital necessity of making no further cutbacks in legal aid availability or eligibility. The legal aid system plays a crucial role in promoting access to justice at proportionate costs in key areas. The statistics set out elsewhere in this report demonstrate that the overall costs of litigation on legal aid are substantially lower than the overall costs of litigation on conditional fee agreements. Since, in respect of a vast swathe of litigation, the costs of both sides are ultimately borne by the public, the maintenance of legal aid at no less than the present levels makes sound economic sense and is in the public interest."

7–006   **The Government's position.** Sadly, that paragraph did not find favour with the Government. In September 2010, the Government put forward proposals for making substantial cutbacks in legal aid.[1] After going out to consultation, the Government announced its decision in June 2011. The decision was to go ahead with the proposed cutbacks to civil legal aid subject to some modest adjustments.

7–007   **LASPO.** Part I of LASPO, namely ss.1 to 43, gave effect to the Government's decisions on legal aid. Those provisions do not in any sense give effect to recommendations in the Final Report. Therefore, they do not call for discussion in this chapter.

7–008   **Have the cutbacks in legal aid saved any public money?** This is not an easy question. The cutbacks have obviously produced some top line savings in public expenditure. On the other hand, they have generated additional costs elsewhere in the system, in particular as a consequence of the increased number of litigants in person.[2] It must be for economists to assess the overall financial impact of these developments. It is neither possible nor appropriate for a judge to venture any opinion on this question.

7–009   **Medical reports in clinical negligence litigation.** There is one cutback in legal aid which can be demonstrated to have driven up costs. That is the with-

---

[1] MoJ Consultation Paper CP 12/10, November 2010.
[2] King LJ described some of the consequences in *Minkin v Landsberg* [2015] EWCA Civ 1152; [2016] 1 WLR 1489.

drawal of legal aid for medical reports on liability and causation issues in clinical negligence cases. Taxpayers are now paying more for those reports than they did under legal aid: see the discussion in section 6 of Ch. 5 above.

3. Before-the-event Insurance

Advantages of before-the-event insurance. Before-the-event insurance is 7–010
by definition cheaper than after-the-event insurance. That is because the "event" has not happened and probably will not happen. The premium is reduced accordingly. In many ways, BTE is the ideal way to fund litigation. The legal costs are spread across a large number of insured individuals, most of whom will not sue or be sued in any given year. For example, the majority of those who have legal expenses cover as an add-on to their household insurance never ask their household insurers to fund litigation. The real problem is that the take-up of BTE cover is very low (except in respect of road traffic accidents, where different considerations apply).

Role of BTE in small business disputes. There is scope for making greater use 7–011
of BTE in the disputes which, from time to time, inevitably arise in the running of small businesses. The Federation of Small Businesses made the following pertinent comments in its submissions to the Costs Review:

> "The FSB agrees with the suggestion in the [Preliminary Report] that overall SMEs will be better protected if BTE insurance cover was extended across the SME community. The FSB insurance package does cover BTE legal expenses insurance chiefly for the defence of employment claims against business but also in respect of limited other areas. All members have the defence package of BTE insurance as it is embedded within the subscription. The FSB legal team confirm that the reach of BTE insurance is increasing, either through the growth of the FSB and similar organisations, or purchased as a 'stand alone' offering through commercial brokers. The FSB package is one of the most cost effective ways of purchasing BTE insurance. However, there are barriers to the increased take up of BTE insurance by FSB and SMEs, namely the combination of cost and product or benefit awareness, particularly in the current, difficult, economic climate. Cost alone may exclude many smaller FSB members from extending their BTE cover and such cover may always be limited in scope because of the enormous variety of business derived disputes making standardised cover difficult for insurers to package."

Comparison with Germany. In Germany, where admittedly litigation costs 7–012
are lower, there has been a high take up of BTE ever since the 1950s: see generally PR Ch. 55. A study carried out in 2007 revealed that in Germany, 35% of litigants were funded by BTE.[3] In England, the equivalent figure was 4%. Even that 4% figure may be misleading, because most of it probably related to road traffic accident claims. In 2007 (because of the distorted costs regime prevailing), most road traffic accident claims made on BTE generated *profit* rather than cost for the insurers. Such BTE did not serve any useful purpose, since most of the "insureds"

---

[3] PR Ch. 55, para. 4.6 and Table 55.2.

could perfectly well have litigated at no cost to themselves without any help from BTE insurers.

7–013   **Final Report.** The Final Report proposed measures (discussed elsewhere in this book) to put road traffic insurance on a more rational basis. These included ending recoverable success fees and recoverable ATE premiums, banning referral fees, etc. More relevantly for present purposes, FR Ch. 8 recommended that steps be taken encourage a higher take up of "proper" BTE cover. In the period following publication of the Final Report, this recommendation attracted some interest. Subsequently, however, it has received less attention.

7–014   **Government support for the recommendation.** Both in its consultation paper of November 2010 and in its response paper of March 2011, the Government stated:

> "The Government therefore supports Sir Rupert's view on BTE insurance and would welcome a change in culture so that there is a greater use of existing BTE policies and the development of the market to expand BTE insurance coverage."

7–015   **Effect of the FR recommendation.** It has not been possible to obtain any reliable figures for the take up of BTE since the Final Report made that recommendation and the Government expressed its support. A working group has recently been set up by the CJC to look at a number of matters. These include how to promote the use of BTE as an effective means of funding civil litigation. Professor Rachael Mulheron chairs the working group. It is hoped that this will give renewed impetus to a FR recommendation which has been somewhat neglected.

4. THIRD PARTY FUNDING

7–016   **The traditional view.** The traditional view was that third party funding ("TPF") was a bad thing. It involved "stirring up litigation" and "officious intermeddling" in other people's disputes. The law of maintenance and champerty developed in order to stamp out such unseemly practices. Modern case law has moved in the opposite direction: see PR Ch. 15 and FR Ch. 11. It is now accepted in a number of jurisdictions[4] that responsible TPF of litigation does not fall foul of the doctrines of maintenance and champerty.

7–017   **Chapter 11 of the Final Report.** FR Ch. 11 identified the following five benefits of TPF:

(i) TPF provides an additional means of funding litigation and, for some parties, the only means of funding litigation. Thus, TPF promotes access to justice.

---

[4] Australia, Austria, Germany, Ireland, the Netherlands and the UK: see Hodges, Vogenauer and Tulibacka, *The Costs and Funding of Civil Litigation*, p. 27.

(ii) Although a successful claimant with TPF foregoes a percentage of his damages, it is better for him to recover a substantial part of his damages than to recover nothing at all.

(iii) The use of TPF (unlike the use of CFAs) does not impose additional financial burdens upon opposing parties.

(iv) TPF would become even more important as a means of financing litigation if success fees under CFAs became irrecoverable (as in fact happened).

(v) TPF tends to filter out unmeritorious cases, because funders will not take on the risk of such cases. This benefits opposing parties.

Should third party funding be regulated? Chapter 11 of the Final Report   **7–018** proceeded on the basis that responsible TPF was a good thing and should be encouraged. The chapter focused principally on how TPF should be controlled. It concluded that for the time being the case for formal regulation had not been made out, but this issue needed to be kept under review. The chapter also noted that at that stage, the Financial Services Authority (which was then the only relevant regulator) was reluctant to undertake the regulation of TPF.

Development of a voluntary code for the third party funders. In 2009, the   **7–019** Civil Justice Council was working with litigation funders to develop a voluntary code, which would regulate TPF. Chapter 11 of the Final Report drew attention to shortcomings in the then current draft of the code. In particular, the provisions about capital adequacy needed to be tightened up. There also needed to be closer restrictions upon when funders could withdraw from ongoing litigation.

Liability for adverse costs. Chapter 11 of the Final Report was critical of the   **7–020** Court of Appeal's decision in *Arkin v Borchard Lines Ltd* [2005] EWCA Civ 655. That decision limited the funder's liability for adverse costs to the extent of funding provided. After reviewing the rival arguments, the chapter concluded that the funder (which stood to make a healthy profit if the case was won) should be liable for all adverse costs if the case was lost.

Recommendations. Chapter 11 of the Final Report concluded with three   **7–021** recommendations:

"(i) A satisfactory voluntary code, to which all litigation funders subscribe, should be drawn up. This code should contain effective capital adequacy requirements and should place appropriate restrictions upon funders' ability to withdraw support for ongoing litigation.
(ii) The question whether there should be statutory regulation of third party funders by the FSA ought to be re-visited if and when the third party funding market expands.
(iii) Third party funders should potentially be liable for the full amount of adverse costs, subject to the discretion of the judge."

Link with other recommendations. The recommendations in respect of TPF   **7–022** mesh in with other FR reforms. TPF works well in conjunction with costs management, as discussed in Ch. 14, below. It will also work well in conjunction with fixed recoverable costs, when the proposals in FR Ch. 16 are implemented. More generally, the expansion of TPF is an expression of the principle that there should be as many different forms of funding litigation as possible, provided that those methods of funding do not drive up costs.

7–023　　**Implementation.** The Association of Litigation Funders ("ALF") was formed. That body worked with the CJC to develop a satisfactory Code of Conduct, which was published in November 2011. The Code addressed the concerns identified in FR Ch. 12.[5] It included a "QC clause", as proposed in the FR. This provided that any dispute between the client and the funder concerning settlement or termination of the funding agreement should be referred to a Queen's Counsel nominated by the chairman of the Bar Council. All third party funders who belonged to the ALF were required to subscribe to the Code.

7–024　　**Revisions of the Code.**[6] Following advice from the CJC, the ALF revised and strengthened the Code in 2014. The provisions concerning capital adequacy now require ALF members to maintain access to a minimum of £2 million, to accept "a continuous disclosure obligation in respect of its capital adequacy" and to submit annual audit reports to the ALF. The Code also requires members to disclose the corporate structures under which they operate.

7–025　　**Expansion of TPF.** Since the publication of the Final Report in 2010, there has been a very substantial expansion of third party funding. This has been the subject of numerous articles in the legal press over the last year.[7] As the funding industry grows, the question whether statutory regulation is required will inevitably arise. The Australian Government is now seriously considering regulating third party funders.[8] Such regulation is not currently on the agenda in the UK, but that may change. It is a matter of concern that some third party funders may be operating, who do not belong to the ALF or subscribe to the Code.[9]

7–026　　**The one recommendation which had been ignored.** The Court of Appeal's decision in *Arkin* still holds sway. It is hoped that in due course either Parliament or the Supreme Court might reconsider this issue in the light of FR Ch. 12.

7–027　　**US report.** In April 2016, the US Chamber Institute for Legal Reform published a report expressing concern about the growth of TPF in England and Wales, without there being any formal oversight of the funding sector. The report pro-

---

[5] See the sixth implementation lecture, which was delivered at the launch of the voluntary code on 23 November 2011.

[6] See R. Mulheron, "England's unique approach to the self-regulation of third party funding: critical analysis of recent developments" [2014] 73 CLJ 570-597.

[7] See, for example, "Third Sector", *Law Society Gazette*, 16 November 2015, and the accompanying leading article headed "The third degree – litigation funders must ward off powerful critics".

[8] Professor Michael Legg of UNSW has expressed concern that some TPF in Australia may be abusive: *"Was Peter Thiel's Funding of the Gawker case an abuse of legal process?"* The *Conversation*, 31 May 2016, available at *https://theconversation.com/was-peter-thiels-funding-of-the-gawker-case-an-abuse-of-legal-process-60167* [Accessed 1 July 2016].

[9] See R. Mulheron, "England's unique approach to the self-regulation of third party funding: critical analysis of recent developments" [2014] 73 CLJ 570 at 576–580.

poses a comprehensive oversight structure with adequate means of enforcement. Those proposals will be for others to consider. There is one proposal urged by the US Chamber which makes obvious good sense, namely that the *Arkin* cap should be removed.[10]

5. CONTINGENT LEGAL AID FUND OR SUPPLEMENTARY LEGAL AID SCHEME

(i) *The position at the time of the Costs Review*

What is a CLAF or a SLAS? Both a CLAF and a SLAS are self-funding **7–028** schemes, which have been proposed as methods of funding litigation. The scheme pays the claimant's costs, win or lose. If the claimant succeeds, the CLAF recovers its costs from the other party and also a share of the proceeds of the action. The normal beneficiaries of such a scheme are claimants, although the scheme could also support counterclaiming defendants. The essential feature of a CLAF is that once it is established, it is expected to stand on its own feet and be fully self-financing. A SLAS, on the other hand, is a self-funding mechanism which is built into or added onto an existing publicly funded legal aid scheme, and administered by the relevant legal aid authority.

History. In 1978, JUSTICE published its original proposals for a CLAF. **7–029** Nineteen years later in 1997, in the run-up to the 1999 Act and removal of PI cases from the scope of legal aid, a range of proposals for CLAFs were made by the Bar Council, the Law Society and the Consumers Association.[11] None of these proposals were implemented, as the Government chose instead to promote and enhance CFAs under the 1999 Act reforms. However, provisions were included within the 1999 Act to provide for a CLAF or SLAS scheme: see s.58B of the Courts and Legal Services Act 1990, which was inserted by s.28 of the 1999 Act. These provisions have not yet been implemented, but they could be. Proposals for a SLAS emerged again in reports by the CJC in 2005 and 2007.

Analysis during the Costs Review. There were numerous conflicting submis- **7–030** sions on this issue during the consultation phase of the Costs Review. Even with the assistance of an able young accountant, it proved impossible to devise a workable financial model for a CLAF. This was in part because there were many other issues to address in a short timescale and the resources of the Costs Review were limited. The fact remains, however, that a number of CLAFs and one SLAS have been successfully established in overseas jurisdictions, albeit on a relatively small scale. Chapter 13 of the Final Report concluded with the following recommendation:

"Financial modelling should be undertaken to ascertain the viability of one or more CLAFs or a SLAS after, and subject to, any decisions announced by Government in respect of the other recommendations of this report."

---

[10] See p. 16 of the report.
[11] See "CLAF – An idea whose time has come", Bar Council 1997; "Proposals to link legal aid and conditional fees", Law Society 1997; CA Policy Paper on CLAF, 1997.

(ii) *The position now and a suggested way forward*

7–031   **Why should a CLAF work now?** The success of third party funding illustrates just how well a CLAF might do. If the Law Society, the Chartered Institute of Legal Executives ("CILEx") and the Bar Council are willing jointly to promote the establishment of a CLAF, it would in effect operate as a not-for-profit third party funder. It could support:

> (i) Some "ordinary" commercial or other cases, assessed in much the same way as litigation funders assess new claims.

> (ii) Some "deserving" cases, i.e. claims for individuals or firms of modest means, where the likely level of damages is not such as to attract one of the established litigation funders.

7–032   **The difference between a CLAF and other third party funders.** Unlike other funders, the CLAF would not have owners or shareholders creaming off the profits. Instead, it would plough all profits back into (a) building up reserves and (b) future litigation funding. The CLAF would be an independent body established by the legal profession in the public interest. Its function would be to promote access to justice.

7–033   **Who should administer the CLAF?** The Bar, the Law Society and CILEx would need to appoint experienced managers. There is no shortage of such people in the City.

7–034   **Who should select the cases to be supported?** In the past, many barristers and solicitors gave up a modest amount of time to sit on committees which considered applications for legal aid. It would be possible to revive that system. An alternative and perhaps preferable approach would be for the CLAF to employ experienced lawyers, who would evaluate and grade the claims. Ideally, the CLAF's costs of evaluation should be recoverable. The evaluation costs could be a fixed sum, determined by reference to the amount finally recovered. It is essential that the cohort of cases supported by the CLAF should be within the discretion of the managers. There should be not be an entitlement to support as of right (subject only to means and merits). This will enable a cautious start up approach to be taken and will avoid flooding the scheme with applications.

7–035   **Where would seed-corn funding come from?** If the governments and the professions in other jurisdictions have managed to find seed-corn funding, surely England and Wales can do the same? There are a number of possibilities:

> (i) Possibly the UK National Lottery might be as generous as the Jockey Club was in Hong Kong. Possibly some charitable foundations would see the merit of the present proposal. Some individual lawyers might be willing to make gift aid donations.

> (ii) The UK Government, which has reduced legal aid, might be willing to put up some initial capital for a CLAF.

(iii) The CLAF might raise capital by means of fixed interest coupons or quasi-debentures. Quasi-debentures would offer a more than average return on a bond but would expose the bond-holder to the risks of the CLAF being unprofitable, thereby sharing both risk and reward on the seed capital. Hopefully, such an arrangement would not prejudice the not-for-profit status of the fund.

But who would invest in the CLAF? Here are two possibilities: 7–036

(i) Individual barristers, solicitors or other professionals may be willing to buy bonds of say £10,000 if they have confidence in the management of the scheme. They would note that (a) investors in certain third party funders have done well and (b) the CLAF does not have any shareholders clamouring for dividends. In this way, the lawyers would be contributing to a much needed scheme, while receiving a reasonable return for only a modest risk.

(ii) A bank or similar institution might assemble a "partnership" of institutional type investors, such as pension funds. Each would put in money, buying a bond with a fixed lifetime and decent percentage annual return, in the expectation that after say 10 years the original capital would be returned because the fund would then be in a position to do so. Thus, £50 million could be raised by persuading ten investors each to put up £5 million.

What happens if there is liability for adverse costs? It is not satisfactory to   7–037
leave litigants of modest means with meritorious cases at the risk of adverse costs. In PI cases (because of QOCS), adverse costs orders are rare and are only made in exceptional circumstances.[12] The claimant should bear the residual risk of adverse costs in those cases. In other cases, there would have to be an agreement between the CLAF and the claimant as to what costs risk each is accepting. If the CLAF takes on the adverse costs risk, then the percentage of damages to which it is entitled (if the case is won) should be higher.

How should the CLAF protect itself against the adverse costs risk? The   7–038
CLAF might take out block or case-by-case ATE cover. Alternatively, the CLAF could self-insure up to a certain point. The CLAF would need a combination of (a) reinsurance above specific levels, and (b) catastrophe insurance in the event that adverse costs in any year exceed the specified catastrophe level.

Effect of costs management. The discipline of costs management will make   7–039
it much easier for the CLAF to assess the adverse costs risk and to keep that risk under review as the action proceeds. Third party funders have always been supporters of costs management and it is anticipated that the managers of the CLAF will take the same approach.

Suppose fixed costs are introduced? The question of introducing fixed   7–040
costs across the whole of the fast track and in the lower reaches of the multi-track is now under active consideration, as discussed in Ch. 19, below. This

---

[12] See Ch. 16.

reform would be beneficial to the CLAF in many respects. There would be certainty as to the adverse costs risk. Additionally, the CLAF would avoid all the expense associated with managing and assessing costs in lower value cases.

7–041   **Well, that all sounds lovely, but is any of it going to happen?** With luck, yes. The above proposal for establishing a CLAF was set out at greater length in a lecture on 2 February 2016.[13] The Law Society, the Bar and CILEx all have copies of the lecture. They have set up a joint working group in order to take the CLAF proposal forward.

7–042   **The goal.** Hopefully, in due course we shall have a properly functioning CLAF in in England and Wales. If and when that happens, we shall have caught up with our colleagues in Hong Kong and Australia, where such schemes are operating successfully.

---

[13] "The case for a CLAF", keynote speech by Jackson LJ at the Solicitors' Costs Conference on 2 February 2016; available on the Judiciary website.

Part Three
CONSENSUAL SETTLEMENT

PRE-ACTION PROTOCOLS

1. BACKGROUND

Woolf reforms. The introduction of pre-action protocols ("protocols") was **8–001** part of Lord Woolf's package of reforms.[1] They are intended to serve two principal purposes:

- Facilitation of settlement without the issue of proceedings where such settlements are possible.
- In cases where the issue of proceedings is unavoidable, promoting a fuller understanding by each party at the outset of the opposing parties' cases.

The protocols in 2009. In 2009, there were ten protocols dealing with specific **8–002** areas of civil litigation ("specific protocols"), namely:

(i) Pre-Action Protocol for Personal Injury Claims.

(ii) Pre-Action Protocol for the Resolution of Clinical Disputes.

(iii) Pre-Action Protocol for Construction and Engineering Disputes.

(iv) Pre-Action Protocol for Defamation.

(v) Professional Negligence Pre-Action Protocol.

(vi) Pre-Action Protocol for Judicial Review.

(vii) Pre-Action Protocol for Disease and Illness Claims.

(viii) Pre-Action Protocol for Housing Disrepair Cases.

(ix) Pre-Action Protocol for Possession Claims based on Rent Arrears.

(x) Pre-Action Protocol for Possession Claims based on Mortgage or Home Purchase Plan Arrears in respect of Residential Property.

---

[1] See *Andrews on Civil Processes*, Vol. 1, "Court Proceedings", pp. 66–67.

8–003   **The practice direction.** There was also the "Practice Direction – Pre-Action Conduct" (the "PDPAC"), which came into effect on 6 April 2009 (towards the end of Phase One of the Costs Review): see PR Ch. 43 para. 3.4. This lengthy practice direction had several different functions. Section II of the PDPAC set out how the courts would secure compliance with the specific protocols. Section III of the PDPAC operated as a general protocol for all civil litigation which was not the subject of specific protocols. Section IV of the PDPAC imposed additional pre-action obligations in respect of all civil litigation, whether or not subject to a specific protocol. Finally, for good measure, three annexes bulked out the PDPAC with five pages of additional verbiage.

8–004   **Controversy concerning protocols.** By 2009, there was a lively debate between the supporters and the opponents of protocols. The supporters saw protocols as an essential tool for (a) encouraging early settlement, and (b) narrowing issues between the parties before the start of litigation. The opponents saw protocols as forcing parties to plead their cases twice—first in correspondence and then for real—thereby adding to the delays and expense of litigation. Chancery and commercial practitioners were generally hostile to protocols. In the construction field, the majority of solicitors were in the supporters' camp, whereas the majority of barristers were in the opponents' camp. Some commentators said that this was because solicitors made money out of the protocol process, whereas barristers made their money out of contested litigation. Those comments were unfair and unduly cynical. The explanation was simply that people were looking at the issue from different standpoints.

8–005   **Preliminary Report.** Chapter 43 of the Preliminary Report summarised the conflicting arguments as follows:

"3.9 The submissions contained very mixed views on the pre-action protocol.
Those championing the pre-action protocols put forward the following reasons:

- They greatly assist in the early exchange of information, which in turn helps to effect early settlement.
- The costs incurred are preferable to trial by ambush.
- One user expressed 'no experience of it working adversely'.
- In environmental and public law cases it is a process to 'be commended'. Similar sentiments have been expressed in relation to personal injury cases.

3.10 Others praise the intentions of the pre-action protocols, but query the continued need for them given the change in attitude effected by the protocols. It is also acknowledged that the protocol can be useful in helping parties to avoid damaging existing relationships (commercial or otherwise), as is often the case once formal litigation has commenced.
3.11 The criticisms in the Phase 1 submissions include the comments that:

- They lead to heavy 'front-loading' of costs.
- They are a 'distraction'.
- There is nothing that a defendant can do to prevent cost accumulation or to commence proceedings if a claimant is unduly prolonging the pre-action process.
- The court has no power to intervene in case management until a claim is issued, by which stage substantial and disproportionate costs may already have been incurred.

- Steps taken pre-issue may be duplicated post-issue (e.g. the statement of case is often the letter of claim re-formulated).
- Once claims are brought within the jurisdiction of the court, the sanctions for non-compliance are not imposed as often as they should be. There is little benefit to be gained from wrapping up any non-compliance in a detailed assessment at the end of the case. One submission referred to Ramsey J's view in *Charles Church Developments Ltd v Stent Foundations Ltd* [2007] EWHC 855 (TCC) 'the courts should generally deal with the cost consequences of failure to comply with a pre-action protocol at an early stage'.
- When effecting this reform, Lord Woolf envisaged the exercise of much more control.
- Overseas litigants find it difficult to understand why so much has to be done pre-issue.
- Many clients (domestic and foreign) find the process frustrating. They see that substantial costs are being incurred but perceive that 'nothing is being done'."

The Preliminary Report described the issues surrounding pre-action protocols as "some of the most intractable questions in the Costs Review": PR Ch. 43, para. 3.23.

2. RECOMMENDATIONS IN THE FINAL REPORT OF JANUARY 2010

The fog lifts. The topic of pre-action protocols was one of the very few areas   **8–006**
where the amount of controversy diminished during Phase Two of the Costs Review. In the course of the seminars and meetings, a consensus started to emerge. There was general agreement that sections III and IV of the PDPAC were unsatisfactory. Disagreements remained about the utility of the protocol for construction and engineering disputes. Most practitioners and court users agreed that the other specific protocols served a useful purpose, although some pruning and amendments were required.

Conclusions in respect of the PDPAC. Chapter 35 of the Final Report con-   **8–007**
cluded that sections III and IV of the PDPAC were flawed, because one size did not fit all. You could not have a universal protocol applying to all the multifarious cases which were not the subject of specific protocols. Compliance with the pre-scriptive provisions of the PDPAC drove up costs to no useful purpose. Therefore sections III and IV of the PDPAC should be repealed.

Conclusions in respect of individual protocols. The Final Report concluded   **8–008**
that the existing specific protocols did serve a useful purpose, but they required a number of adjustments. The FR recommendations in respect of those protocols were scattered across the Final Report in chapters dealing with specific subject areas. The Final Report concluded that no protocols should be created for chancery or commercial cases. These areas of litigation would become protocol-free zones following the repeal of PDPAC, sections III and IV.

Personal injuries protocol. Paragraph 7.2 in FR Ch. 22 stated: **8–009**

"It is clear from all the submissions which I have received that the personal injury protocol has been a success. The front loading of costs which it has generated is more than offset by the number of early settlements (and better informed settlements) which it promotes. Indeed the drop off in contested personal injuries litigation since April 1999, when the protocol came into force, bears witness to this fact. Nevertheless, there are concerns about compliance with the protocol."

Chapter 22 of the Final Report also recommended that the protocol provisions concerning expert evidence, quantum and ADR might be tightened up.

8–010   **Clinical negligence.** The Costs Review identified that late settlement was a particular problem in the field of clinical negligence. The statistics analysed in PR Chs 6 and 11 revealed that only a minority of meritorious clinical negligence claims settled before the issue of proceedings. Chapter 23 of the Final Report identified numerous causes of this problem. These included delays in the provision of health records and the lack of effective communication between the parties. One major cause was the fact that the NHSLA failed to properly investigate claims at the outset. Paragraph 4.11 therefore made the following recommendation:

> "I recommend that the NHSLA should change its practice in relation to independent expert evidence. In respect of any claim (other than a frivolous claim) where the NHSLA is proposing to deny liability, the NHSLA should obtain independent expert evidence on liability and causation during the four month period allowed for the response letter."

8–011   **Consequential amendments to the clinical negligence protocol.** One consequence of the above proposal was that the NHSLA would need more time to consider and respond to the protocol letter of claim. A related problem was that NHS trusts were not always passing on letters of claim promptly to the NHSLA. Chapter 23 of the Final Report therefore recommended amendments to the clinical negligence protocol so that (a) the time for responding to letters of claim should be increased from three to four months and (b) all letters of claim sent to NHS trusts should be copied to the NHSLA.

8–012   **Twelfth implementation lecture.** The twelfth implementation lecture dealt solely with clinical negligence claims. Paragraph 4.1 of the lecture criticised the length of the pre-action protocol. It concluded that "[i]f all the guff is cut out, the protocol will be simpler, clearer and more helpful to practitioners."

8–013   **Housing.** Chapter 26 of the Final Report reviewed three protocols in the field of housing, namely:

- Pre-Action Protocol for Housing Disrepair Cases,
- Pre-Action Protocol for Possession Claims based on Rent Arrears,
- Pre-Action Protocol for Possession Claims based on Mortgage or Home Purchase Plan Arrears in respect of Residential Property.

The chapter was supportive of all three protocols. It proposed amendments for consideration, including provisions for cases where ECHR art. 8 applied.

Construction and engineering protocol. Chapter 35 of the Final Report sum- 8–014
marised the conflicting views of practitioners on the construction and engineering
protocol. It reached the following conclusion:

> "4.16 I am conscious that the decision whether to retain a pre-action protocol for con-
> struction and engineering disputes is finely balanced. There is a strong body of opinion
> to the effect that the protocol serves to increase, rather than reduce, costs. When the
> TCC moves into the Rolls Building in 2011 the anomalous situation will arise that the
> TCC has a pre-action protocol applicable to most of its cases, but the other two jurisdic-
> tions within that building (Commercial Court and Chancery Division) have not.
> 4.17 I recommend that after the TCC has moved into the Rolls Building in 2011, the
> whole question of the protocol should be reviewed. The three jurisdictions in that build-
> ing will all deal with business disputes. There will be benefit in the TCC taking account
> of the position in the Commercial Court and Chancery Division, when the different
> specialist jurisdictions have come together under one roof. The users of the TCC, both
> litigants and lawyers, may possibly conclude at that stage that their pre-action proce-
> dures should be aligned with those prevailing in those other jurisdictions. However, the
> outcome of that review must be a matter for the TCC judges and practitioners after 2011."

Proposed amendments to the construction and engineering protocol. 8–015
Chapter 35 of the Final Report proposed that, if the protocol was to be retained,
there should be a number of amendments to its provisions. These amendments
were all directed to cutting down the costs of compliance. The most important
proposal was that para. 1.5 concerning proportionality should be strengthened.

Other FR recommendations. As indicated above, the Final Report contained 8–016
further detailed recommendations concerning specific protocols, as it lumbered
through the individual areas of civil litigation. An anthology of all those detailed
points would not enhance the readability of this book or serve any other useful
purpose.

3. IMPLEMENTATION

The Burn Committee. The Rule Committee set up a sub-committee, chaired 8–017
by District Judge Suzanne Burn ("the Burn Committee"), to update and revise the
PDPAC and most of the protocols in the light of the FR recommendations and
rule changes. The Burn Committee undertook this substantial task. After approval
by the Rule Committee, the revised protocols came into force between 2013 and
2015.

The PDPAC. Very sensibly, the Burn Committee accepted the recommenda- 8–018
tion to repeal sections III and IV of the PDPAC together with their annexes. The
new slimmed down PDPAC gives concise guidance about sensible pre-action
correspondence, proportionality, expert evidence, the need to consider ADR and
to narrow issues in dispute.

Personal injuries protocol. The Burn Committee made substantial improve- 8–019
ments to the personal injuries protocol. These included strengthening the section

on non-compliance, amplifying the information about quantum to be provided by claimants, revising the provisions on expert evidence, and strengthening the section on ADR. The protocol also takes into account the fixed costs schemes for fast track RTA, employers' liability and public liability cases introduced on 31 July 2013 (discussed in Ch. 19, below), and provides for cases which exit from those new protocols.[2]

8–020   **Clinical negligence protocol.** The Chief Executive of the NHSLA announced in early 2010 that it would accept the FR recommendation concerning its own practice. In future, it would obtain independent expert evidence before sending out response letters denying liability. The Rule Committee reciprocated in 2010 by amending the clinical negligence protocol, so as to (a) allow four months (instead of three) for the response letter, and to (b) require that letters of claim sent to NHS trusts should be copied to the NHSLA.

8–021   Subsequently, the Burn Committee made numerous further improvements to the clinical negligence protocol, all of which were consistent with the FR recommendations. These included removing the paragraphs concerning clinical risk and governance; removing other unnecessary verbiage; adding references to the duty of candour under s.20 of the Health and Social Care Act 2008 and the need for apologies; introducing a letter of notification stage; and also updating the flowchart, the form for obtaining health records and the model letters of claim and response.

The package of amendments to the clinical negligence protocol was particularly important because (as discussed in PR Chs 6 and 11, and in FR Ch. 23) only a minority of meritorious clinical negligence claims were settling before the issue of proceedings.

8–022   **Housing protocols.** These were significantly updated as follows:

- Disrepair: removing the early notification letter and glossary, merging the repetitive guidance notes with the protocol, and updating the section on experts.

- Rent Arrears: adding a new Pt 3 providing guidance on exceptional cases where there might be a valid defence under art.8 of ECHR.

- Mortgage Arrears: adding an encouragement to lenders to check the status of any tenants in occupation, take appropriate steps, and inform the court of the situation on issue of proceedings.

8–023   **Construction and engineering protocol retained.** The London TCC, the Commercial Court and the Chancery Division moved into the Rolls Building in 2011. As expected, the three jurisdictions have come together more closely, with a greater exchange of business between them. There has been some harmonisation of practices. It is common for judges to sit in more than one of the Rolls Building jurisdictions. Despite that coalescence, the TCC and its users decided, no doubt sensibly, to retain their own protocol.

---

[2] Protocol for Low Value Personal Injury Claims in Road Traffic Accidents and Protocol for Low Value Personal Injury (Employers' Liability and Public Liability) Claims.

Amendments to construction and engineering protocol. A number of 8–024 amendments have been made to the construction and engineering protocol along the lines recommended in the Final Report. In particular, para. 1.5 has been redrafted to emphasise that pre-action correspondence, disclosure and exchanges should be kept to proportionate levels and that the costs of compliance should also be proportionate.

Other protocols. The Burn Committee and the Rule Committee worked their 8–025 way through the other protocols during the period 2013 to 2015. They undertook much re-writing and in the process gave effect to many of the FR recommendations. Anyone who is eager to follow up the details should read pp. 2369–2510 of the White Book 2016.

ALTERNATIVE DISPUTE RESOLUTION

1. BACKGROUND

Meaning of Alternative Dispute Resolution. ADR means the resolution of **9–001** disputes by any method other than judicial decision. In its widest sense, therefore, ADR includes arbitration, expert determination, early neutral evaluation, dispute resolution boards, ombudsman schemes, mediation and other means of achieving binding decisions.[1] More importantly (although many would disagree with this definition), ADR also includes negotiated settlements.

A truth universally acknowledged. It has always been the case that the vast **9–002** majority of all civil disputes are resolved by ADR, if one includes negotiated settlements within the definition. Only a small proportion of proceedings issued in the High Court or the County Court actually come to a contested trial.

What's new then? During the 1980s and 1990s, there was a growing realisa- **9–003** tion that the intervention of a third party could lead to more frequent consensual settlement of disputes in cases where bilateral negotiation (a) had broken down or (b) was slow to show results. Such intervention by third parties usually takes the form of mediation but other possibilities exist, such as non-binding early neutral evaluation by an expert or a judge. In 1990 the Centre for Effective Dispute Resolution ("CEDR") was founded with the support of the Confederation of British Industry, a number of law firms and others. Since then, CEDR has done much to promote ADR, in particular mediation. Lord Woolf's Access to Justice Inquiry gave a further boost to ADR.

Lord Woolf's Interim Report. Chapter 18 of Lord Woolf's Interim Report was **9–004** entitled "Alternative Approaches to Dispensing Justice" and contained a review of all the available forms of ADR. At para. 11, he described mediation as follows:

"Mediation is offered by a number of private and voluntary organisations. Unlike other forms of ADR it does not result in a determinative adjudication, but is perhaps best described as a form of facilitated negotiation, where a neutral third party guides the

---

[1] See generally Betancourt and Crook, *ADR, Arbitration and Mediation.* This is a collection of essays on all forms of ADR published by the Chartered Institute of Arbitrators.

parties to their own solution. Mediation can be used in a wide range of disputes, and in many cases produces an outcome which would not have been possible through the strict application of the law."

9–005   **Subsequent growth of ADR.** Following those magisterial comments from Lord Woolf, there was a steady growth in the number of cases resolved by mediation and in the number of bodies offering mediation services. Pre-action protocols first appeared in 1999. These encouraged the use of ADR in order to promote settlement before the issue of proceedings. The newly enacted CPR also encouraged the use of ADR. For example, r.26.4 enabled the court to stay proceedings "while the parties try to settle the case by alternative dispute resolution or other means". The expansion of ADR in the twenty-first century is not unique to England and Wales. It is part of a pan-European, indeed global trend.[2]

9–006   **The Government pledge.** In 2001, the Government set out its pledge on the *"Settlement of government disputes through ADR"*. Government departments undertook, amongst other measures, to consider and use ADR in all suitable cases where the other party accepts it and, where appropriate, to use an independent assessment to reach a possible settlement figure. The Government identified certain types of case which were unsuitable for ADR, such as claims for abuse of power, vexatious litigation or where a legal precedent was required to clarify the law.

9–007   **Judicial encouragement of ADR.** In *Halsey v Milton Keynes General NHS Trust* [2004] EWCA Civ 576, the Court of Appeal gave guidance on the circumstances in which a successful party would be penalised in costs for unreasonable refusal to mediate. The court identified a number of factors which were relevant to determining whether a refusal to mediate was unreasonable. There have been many judgments since then elaborating on the *Halsey* principles.

9–008   **King's College/TCC research project.** The Centre of Construction Law and Dispute Resolution at King's College, London ("King's College") carried out a survey of TCC cases which came to a conclusion in the period 1 June 2006 to 31 May 2008. The survey was set up by agreement between King's College and the TCC judges, following an indication by the judge in charge that empirical data as to the effectiveness of mediation would be helpful.[3] Two large TCC courts participated, namely the London TCC and the Birmingham TCC.

9–009   **Conclusions from the research.** Chapter 34 of the Preliminary Report sets out a detailed account of the survey method. It also sets out King's College's findings. These included the following:

- 60% of the settlements were achieved through conventional negotiation.

- 35% of the settlements were achieved through mediation.

- Within the 35%, the majority of cases would probably have settled anyway

---

[2] See *Andrews on Civil Processes*, Vol 1, 'Court Proceedings', p. 52.
[3] See (2005) 21 Construction Law Journal 265 at 267.

but at a later stage; the financial savings from bringing forward those settlements substantially exceeded the costs of the mediations.

- Within the 35%, a small number of cases on the cusp probably would not have settled absent the mediation; the costs saving achieved by mediation in those cases was enormous.

- A small number of cases in the survey went to trial after unsuccessful mediations; in some of these case the mediation costs were wasted, but in others they achieved valuable benefits such as narrowing the issues.

Chapter 43 of the Preliminary Report. PR Ch. 43 described a number of   **9–010** the mediation schemes which were on offer in 2009. These included the recently established Court of Appeal Mediation Scheme and a number of mediation schemes set up by individual county courts in their own areas. At that time, the county courts in each locality were separate courts, not part of a single County Court as now.

2. CONCLUSIONS AND RECOMMENDATIONS IN THE FINAL REPORT OF JANUARY 2010

Submissions received during the Costs Review. In this area, unlike most   **9–011** others, there was a high degree of consensus amongst the submissions. Most people agreed that ADR in general and mediation in particular were good things and should be encouraged. CEDR stated that in each year there were (on the basis of CEDR's figures) about 2,000 small claims mediations and about 4,000 other mediations. CEDR and other bodies put in powerful submissions advocating mediation on a wider scale. Some enthusiasts proposed compulsory mediation.

Civil Mediation Council. The Civil Mediation Council ("CM Council") is   **9–012** an organisation which promotes mediation in all areas of dispute resolution. In its submission dated 21 July 2009, the CM Council stated that returns from 52 of its provider members reported 6,473 mediations so far that year, which was an increase of 181% over the 2007 baseline. There were 8,204 mediations conducted in 2008 by members. In its submission the CM Council outlined the benefits of mediation in a number of discrete areas, such as Mercantile Court cases, neighbour disputes, chancery litigation etc. The CM Council stated that it was currently holding discussions with the MoJ about the future organisation of the National Mediation Helpline ("NMH") scheme. The CM Council commended the excellent work done by the Small Claims Mediation Service of the county courts, which in 2008 won a CEDR award and an EU award for excellence. It stated that personal injury and clinical negligence practitioners had been particularly resistant to mediation, but even they were now becoming less resistant. The CM Council referred to a number of specific mediation schemes. It stated that public awareness of mediation needed to be increased, especially among small and medium sized businesses, insurers, central and local government bodies. The courts should have in place effective procedures to refer to Law Works litigants who qualify for *pro bono* assistance.

9–013   **Law Society.** The Law Society supported mediation, but sounded a more cautious note. It said:

> "The Law Society continues to support the use of all forms of ADR in circumstances where it may be assist the parties to come to terms and they are willing to do so. We also support the principle of 'legal proceedings as a last resort only'. However, mediation is not the panacea which some consider it to be and is not appropriate in all cases. Neither should it be made mandatory.
>
> Indeed, there are views among practitioners that there is no consistency about which cases are suitable for mediation – some may well be mediated which are more suitable for trial, and vice versa. We consider that firmer guidelines are needed on what is and is not suitable for mediation."

9–014   **Chapter 36 of the Final Report.** FR Ch. 36 reached the following principal conclusions:

> "3.1 *Benefits of ADR not fully appreciated.* Having considered the feedback and evidence received during Phase 2, I accept the following propositions:
>
> (i) Both mediation and joint settlement meetings are highly efficacious means of achieving a satisfactory resolution of many disputes, including personal injury claims.
>
> (ii) The benefits of mediation are not appreciated by many smaller businesses. Nor are they appreciated by the general public.
>
> (iii) There is a widespread belief that mediation is not suitable for personal injury cases. This belief is incorrect. Mediation is capable of arriving at a reasonable outcome in many personal injury cases, and bringing satisfaction to the parties in the process. However, it is essential that such mediations are carried out by mediators with specialist experience of personal injuries litigation.
>
> (iv) Although many judges, solicitors and counsel are well aware of the benefits of mediation, some are not.
>
> 3.2 *Not a universal panacea.* Mediation is not, of course, a universal panacea. The process can be expensive and can on occasions result in failure. I adhere to the general views expressed in the Preliminary Report at paragraphs 4.2.1 to 4.2.6. The thesis of this chapter is not that mediation should be undertaken in every case, but that mediation has a significantly greater role to play in the civil justice system than is currently recognised.
>
> . . .
>
> 3.5 *Need for culture change, not rule change.* I agree with the view expressed by FOIL and others that what is needed is not rule change, but culture change. I do not agree with the proposals made by CEDR for sanctions, including sanctions against all parties. Nor do I agree with the CEDR's proposal for 'compulsion' to be exercised over judges. Judges must have discretion to give such case management directions as they deem appropriate in the circumstances of the individual case.
>
> 3.6 *The pre-action protocols draw attention appropriately to ADR.* The rules enable judges to build mediation windows into case management timetables and some court guides draw attention to this facility. Many practitioners and judges make full use of these provisions. What is now needed is a serious campaign (a) to ensure that all litigation lawyers and judges (not just some litigation lawyers and judges) are properly informed about the benefits which ADR can bring and (b) to alert the public and small businesses to the benefits of ADR.

3.7   *Fragmentation of information.* One of the problems at the moment is that information about ADR is fragmented. In the course of the Costs Review I have received details about a number of providers of mediation from different sources. By way of example, Law Works Mediation Service sent me details of the excellent *pro bono* mediation service which it runs. TML provided similar details to me of its own services. Details of the NMH are available on the HMCS website. CEDR has sent to me a brochure about the excellent mediation services which CEDR offers. Wandsworth Mediation Service has sent to me details of the valuable mediation services which it provides to the community in Wandsworth, either *pro bono* or on a heavily discounted basis. And so forth.

3.8   *Need for a single authoritative handbook.* There already exist MoJ leaflets and material about ADR. There is also a helpful HMCS mediation 'toolkit' in the form of the Civil Court Mediation Service Manual on the Judicial Studies Board ('JSB') website. In my view there now needs to be a single authoritative handbook, explaining clearly and concisely what ADR is (without either 'hype' or jargon) and giving details of all reputable providers of mediation. Because of the competing commercial interests in play, it would be helpful if such a handbook were published by a neutral body. Ideally, this should be done under the aegis of the CJC, if it felt able to accept that role. If possible, the handbook should be an annual publication. The obvious utility of such a work means that it would be self-financing. It needs to have a highly respected editor, perhaps a recently retired senior judge. It needs to become the *vade mecum* of every judge or lawyer dealing with mediation issues. It should be the textbook used in every JSB seminar or Continuing Professional Development ("CPD") training session. I am not proposing any formal system of accreditation, although that would be an option. However, inclusion of any mediation scheme or organisation in this handbook will be a mark of respectability. The sort of handbook which I have in mind will be a work of equivalent status to the annual publications about civil procedure. Most judges and litigators would have the current edition of the proposed handbook on their bookshelves."

Subsequent clarification by CEDR. CEDR has subsequently stated that its   **9–015**
aim is to create a more robust mediation referral culture and practice, rather than compulsion as such.

Recommendations. After discussing the importance of judicial training and   **9–016**
public education in this field, FR Ch. 36 concluded with two recommendations. These were:

  (i)   There should be a serious campaign to (a) ensure that all litigation lawyers and judges are properly informed about the benefits which ADR can bring, and (b) alert the public and small businesses to the benefits of ADR.

 (ii)   An authoritative handbook should be prepared, explaining clearly and concisely what ADR is and giving details of all reputable providers of mediation. This should be the standard handbook for use at all JSB seminars and CPD training sessions concerning mediation.

3. IMPLEMENTATION AND SUBSEQUENT DEVELOPMENTS

Preparation of authoritative handbook on ADR. Following the publication   **9–017**
of the Final Report, Susan Blake, Julie Brown and Stuart Sime set about preparing

an authoritative handbook on ADR to comply with the recommendation in FR Ch. 36. An editorial board, chaired by Lord Neuberger (President of the Supreme Court) and Lord Clarke (a Supreme Court judge, who had set up the Costs Review when Master of the Rolls), provided support and advice. The Judicial College, the CJC and the Civil CM Council endorsed the book. Oxford University Press was the publisher. The book was published in April 2013, in order to coincide with the general implementation date for the FR reforms. It was entitled the *"Jackson ADR Handbook"*. The Judicial College issued copies to all judges dealing with civil work.

9–018   **Growth of ADR since April 2013.**[4] In the three years since April 2013, there has been a substantial increase in the use of ADR, in particular mediation. Courts have more readily granted orders in support of ADR. They have more frequently made costs orders against parties who unreasonably refused to mediate. This cultural change has gone hand in hand with the more intensive focus on case management and costs management discussed elsewhere in this book.

9–019   **A landmark decision.** Many see *PGF II SA v OMFS Co 1 Ltd* [2013] EWCA Civ 1288; [2014] 1 WLR 1386 as a landmark decision. In that case the Court of Appeal held that the defendant's silence in the face of two offers to mediate amounted to an unreasonable refusal to mediate meriting a costs sanction. Briggs LJ gave the leading judgment, with which Maurice Kay and McFarlane LJJ agreed. He began by endorsing the *Jackson ADR Handbook*:

> "4. Although Mr. Seitler [the claimant's counsel] could rely upon on no direct authority for his submission he derived considerable support (as will appear) from the contents and general thrust of the recently published *Jackson ADR Handbook* by Messrs Blake, Brown and Sime, supported by a distinguished editorial advisory board, and endorsed by the Judicial College, the Civil Justice Council and the Civil Mediation Council. The ADR handbook was prepared and published in response to an invitation in Jackson LJ's review of Civil Litigation Costs, see paragraph 3.8 in Chapter 36 of the Final Report. His invitation arose from a conclusion that a culture change was needed among the civil litigation community, so that the widespread benefits of participating in ADR were better recognised."

Briggs LJ went on to discuss the culture change which was taking place and the increased awareness of the benefits of ADR. Turning to the issue of principle in the case he said:

> "34. In my judgment, the time has now come for this court firmly to endorse the advice given in Chapter 11.56 of the ADR Handbook, that silence in the face of an invitation to participate in ADR is, as a general rule, of itself unreasonable, regardless whether an outright refusal, or a refusal to engage in the type of ADR requested, or to do so at the time requested, might have been justified by the identification of reasonable grounds."

Briggs LJ then speculated about particular circumstances in which that general rule may not apply.

---

[4] See the *Jackson ADR Handbook*, 2nd edn, Ch. 1.

What form do costs sanctions take? If the winning party has unreasonably 9–020 refused to mediate, then the court can make an appropriate reduction in its award of costs. If the losing party has unreasonably failed to mediate, that approach is not possible. In *Reid v Buckinghamshire Healthcare NHS Trust* (unreported, 20 October 2015), the court dealt with the matter by ordering the losing party to pay indemnity costs as from the date when it had unreasonably refused to mediate.

EU legislation. Although unrelated to the FR reforms, two important EU 9–021 enactments on ADR were adopted in May 2013 and came into force during 2015 and 2016, namely:

- EU Directive on Consumer ADR (2013/11/EU),
- EU Regulation on consumer ODR (524/2013).

These measures apply to consumer disputes. The ADR Directive requires traders to provide effective, transparent and independent means of alternative dispute resolution and to advertise it to their consumers in a clear and easily accessible way. The ODR Regulation, meanwhile, is concerned with setting up an EU-wide ODR Platform which enables complaints against traders to be filed online. The platform takes the details of the complaint and refers them to providers of ADR in the Member State for resolution. For the UK, this might be CEDR, a professional body such as the Federation of Master Builders or one of the statute-based ombudsman services like the Financial Ombudsman Service.

There is a continuing problem of non-compliance with the EU enactments, as highlighted at a recent conference.[5] Nevertheless, the EU legislation fits well with the continuing efforts to promote ADR in the UK.

Second edition of the Jackson ADR Handbook. A second edition of the 9–022 *Jackson ADR Handbook* is being published by Oxford University Press this year. The second edition describes a number of new ADR initiatives which have emerged since April 2013.

Interaction between ADR and other FR reforms. There are numerous inter- 9–023 connections between the FR reforms. Two are particularly relevant to the present chapter:

(i) During the Costs Review, there was strong evidence that the regime of recoverable success fees and recoverable ATE premiums was hindering the work of mediators. There were reports of mediations which failed because the huge recoverable success fees and/or recoverable ATE premiums proved a stumbling block. The abolition of recoverable success fees and recoverable ATE premiums (discussed in Ch. 5, above) removed this stumbling block. Admittedly, this observation is based on anecdotal evidence, but it gains some support from the Mediation Audits discussed in the next paragraph.

---

[5] Westminster Legal Policy Forum seminar on 23 May 2016.

(ii) Because of costs management, parties now come to mediations knowing (a) what adverse costs they will pay out if they lose; (b) what costs they will recover if they win; and (c) what irrecoverable costs they will have to bear in any event if the case goes to trial. Many mediators say that this is helpful.

9–024   **Seventh Mediation Audit.** CEDR publishes a "Mediation Audit" every two years. The Seventh Mediation Audit published on 11 May 2016 states:

"We asked both mediators and lawyers about the Jackson reforms and whether they had had any impact on either the number of cases coming to mediation or the ease/difficulty of settling cases at mediation.

    (a) What impact have the Jackson reforms had on the number of cases coming to mediation?

	Mediators		Lawyers	
	2016	2014	2016	2014
Decrease	6%	12%	7%	5%
No difference/too early to tell	54%	70%	50%	70%
Increase	41%	18%	43%	25%

    (b) What impact have the Jackson reforms had on the ease/difficulty of settling cases at mediation?

	Mediators		Lawyers	
	2016	2014	2016	2014
Harder	13%	9%	3%	3%
No difference/too early to tell	58%	73%	73%	79%
Easier	29%	18%	24%	17%

So whereas respondents were largely sitting on the fence two years ago – and most still are – those who are prepared to express a view are tending to give the Jackson reforms a positive assessment, although it is clear that there are still mixed views about the double-edged sword of the costs provisions."

9–025   **Online dispute resolution.** It is quite possible for software to carry out much of the ADR process without the need for human intervention, particularly for smaller claims or less complex civil cases. The Portal for fast track PI claims uses such software.[6] New and more ambitious forms of online dispute resolution ("ODR") are now emerging. The Civil Justice Council's Online Dispute Resolution

---

[6] For a description of the process, see *Phillips v Willis* [2016] EWCA Civ 401.

Advisory Group published an excellent report in February 2015, entitled "Online Dispute Resolution for Low Value Civil Claims". It recommended the establishment of a new internet-based court service to assist in resolving such disputes. Briggs LJ is taking these matters forward in the course of his current review.[7]

---

[7] See Briggs LJ's Interim and Final Reports.

PART 36 OFFERS

1. BACKGROUND

Woolf reforms. Before April 1999, there was a procedure for defendants to make payments into court, with costs sanctions for claimants who pressed on and failed to do better at trial. However, there was no procedure in the rules for claimants' offers and there were no incentives for defendants to accept such offers. One of Lord Woolf's reforms was to introduce Pt 36 of the CPR, whereby either party could make a settlement offer to the other party or parties. This procedure is backed up by a scheme of penalties and rewards, in order to encourage the making of reasonable settlement offers and the acceptance of such offers. Part 36 was amended from time to time by the Civil Procedure Rule Committee in the light of experience. In particular, substantial revisions were made to Pt 36 with effect from 6 April 2007.

10–001

General success of Pt 36. Part 36 has generally been regarded as a success, even by those who are otherwise critical of the Woolf reforms. In April 2000, a survey of the FTSE 100 companies revealed that 90% of respondents believed that the Woolf reforms would encourage earlier settlement of disputes. This was seen as the key benefit of those reforms. A survey of lawyers conducted by Mori for the CEDR in April 2000 showed a high level of overall satisfaction with the Woolf reforms, in particular with Pt 36. Evaluations by the Lord Chancellor's Department in 2001 and 2002 came to similar conclusions.

10–002

Views expressed during the 2009 Costs Review. Similar views about the general success of Pt 36 were expressed during the Costs Review. For example, one substantial firm of solicitors in Sheffield, on behalf of one of its clients, wrote:

10–003

"The introduction of Part 36 offers has been a widely successful change introduced by the CPR. Part 36 offers encourage settlement. In practice it has become standard for claimants and defendants to make Part 36 offers."

Two particular issues for consideration in 2009. Despite the positive effects of Pt 36, there were two problematic issues for consideration during the Costs Review. These were:

10–004

(i) the interpretation of "advantageous" in r.36.14(1); and

(ii) the rewards for a claimant whose offer is not beaten.

10–005 **The problem with r.36.1(1) as it was in 2009.** The problem concerning r.36.14(1) in its then form arose from the Court of Appeal's decision in *Carver v BAA plc* [2008] EWCA Civ 412; [2009] 1 WLR 113. The claimant in a personal injuries case, Ms Carver, beat the defendant's Pt 36 offer by £51. The trial judge held that, having regard to all the consequences of going to trial, it could not be said that the final outcome (although £51 higher) was "more advantageous" than accepting the defendant's offer made a year previously. The Court of Appeal upheld that decision. Ward LJ, with whom Rix and Keene LJJ agreed, observed that "more advantageous" was an open-textured phrase. This decision caused much consternation within the profession, as it introduced an unwelcome element of uncertainty into the Pt 36 regime.

10–006 **Inadequate rewards for effective claimant offers.** A number of practitioners were concerned about the unequal playing field. If the claimant failed to beat a defendant's offer, he forfeited recovery of his own costs and became liable for the defendant's costs thereafter. This could amount to a very substantial financial loss. On the other hand, if the defendant failed to beat a claimant's offer, the only consequence was enhanced liability for costs (indemnity not standard basis) and enhanced liability for interest thereafter.

10–007 **Qualified one-way costs shifting.** Finally, a separate issue for consideration was how Pt 36 should operate in those areas where QOCS was introduced.

2. RECOMMENDATIONS IN THE FINAL REPORT OF JANUARY 2010

10–008 **The problem concerning r.36.14(1).** Chapter 41 of the Final Report noted almost unanimity amongst consultees in criticising the decision in *Carver*. Both court users and practitioners wanted certainty and clarity, insofar as that was possible. On this particular issue, both certainty and clarity were achievable. Chapter 41 recommended that the effect of *Carver* should be reversed by rule change.

10–009 **Enhanced rewards for effective claimant offers.** There was quite a wide range of views about what, if anything, should be done to level the playing field. Unison, the trade union, put in a forthright submission:

> "In fact, if further settlement incentives are proposed these should in our view relate to making sure defendants act reasonably in accepting Part 36 claimant offers. This could be readily achieved by attaching greater claimant benefits like greater enhanced damages and higher costs sanctions should that offer be exceeded in court. This would be most beneficial, giving claimants Part 36 offers more teeth – something considered by Woolf many years ago but not implemented."

Others on the claimant side echoed that view. The Association of HM District Judges (looking at matters from the point of view of both parties) proposed that there should be a 10% uplift on damages in cases where the defendant failed to beat the claimant's offer.

Recommendation in respect of effective claimant offers. Chapter 41 of the   **10–010**
Final Report recommended as follows in para. 3.10:

> "In my view, the claimant's reward for making an adequate offer should be increased. The proposal of the Association of Her Majesty's District Judges is the best way forward, namely that there should be an uplift of 10% on damages awarded. Nevertheless, in respect of higher value claims, say over £500,000, there may be a case for scaling down the uplift. If my proposal is accepted in principle, this could be the subject of further consultation."

The chapter also discussed ways of enhancing the claimant's reward for effective offers in the context of non-monetary claims. On p. 472, the Final Report advised that legislation, rather than mere rule change, would be necessary to enable the court to increase any damages awarded by 10%.

Inter-relationship with the CFA reforms. As explained in FR Ch. 41, para.   **10–011**
3.16, this proposal was also relevant to the CFA reforms. The small minority of cases which go to trial generate the highest costs. Claimants on CFAs would no longer recover their success fees from the other side. The enhanced reward for effective claimant offers would form part of a package (which also included the 10% uplift in the level of general damages, QOCS, etc) designed to ameliorate the position of claimants in the new world.

Development of that recommendation. In November 2010, the Government   **10–012**
put some of the FR proposals out to consultation, including the recommenda-
tion for a 10% increase in damages as reward for effective claimant offers. My response (which was put on the Judiciary website during the consultation period) stated:

> " 5.1 *Increasing the rewards for successful claimant offers.* Paras 111 to 114 of the Consultation Paper provide a helpful summary of my proposal to increase the reward for claimants, when defendants reject claimant offers but subsequently fail to beat such offers at trial.
> 5.2 Para 115 of the Consultation Paper raises a concern that this measure may not be effective because only a low percentage of multi-track claims are resolved at trial. I do not share this concern, because once a claimant offer has been rejected, any subsequent settle-ment negotiations will be conducted under the shadow of that unaccepted offer. In other words, if the claimant's offer was well judged his/her subsequent negotiating position will be strengthened.
> 5.3 Having listened to debate about Part 36 at numerous seminars and meetings over the last year, I support both the modifications discussed in para 116 of the Consultation Paper. I would suggest the following scale:

Total damages + value of non-monetary award	Percentage increase
Up to £500,000	10%
£500,001 to £1 million	£50,000 + 5% of excess over £500,000
Above £1 million	£75,000 (with no further increase)

The court must retain a discretion to award less than this sum, if it would be unjust to award the full amount (i.e. the same test as governs the existing rewards for successful claimant offers)."

10–013   **Inter-relationship with QOCS.** Section 4 of FR Ch. 41 recommended as follows:

> "If a claimant fails to accept a defendant's adequate offer under CPR Part 36, the claimant will forfeit or (depending upon the circumstances) substantially forfeit the benefits of one-way costs shifting. The proposed regime of one way costs shifting is 'qualified' because in appropriate circumstances the protection falls away. In the event that qualified one-way costs shifting is introduced as proposed in earlier chapters, no amendment will be required to CPR Part 36 in order to provide incentives for claimants to accept adequate Part 36 offers. The present wording of rule 36.14(2) is sufficient."

3. IMPLEMENTATION

10–014   **Legislation.** Section 55 of LASPO provided the necessary statutory basis for the reforms of CPR Pt 36. The principal provisions of s.55 are:

> "(1) Rules of court may make provision for a court to order a defendant in civil proceedings to pay an additional amount to a claimant in those proceedings where—
>
> (a) the claim is a claim for (and only for) an amount of money,
> (b) judgment is given in favour of the claimant,
> (c) the judgment in respect of the claim is at least as advantageous as an offer to settle the claim which the claimant made in accordance with rules of court and has not withdrawn in accordance with those rules, and
> (d) any prescribed conditions are satisfied.
>
> (2) Rules made under subsection (1) may include provision as to the assessment of whether a judgment is at least as advantageous as an offer to settle.
> (3) In subsection (1) 'additional amount' means an amount not exceeding a prescribed percentage of the amount awarded to the claimant by the court (excluding any amount awarded in respect of the claimant's costs)."

10–015   **Amendments to CPR Pt 36.** With effect from 1 April 2013, the Rule Committee amended CPR r.36.14(1)–(3) to read as follows:

> (1) Subject to rule 36.14A, this rule applies where upon judgment being entered—
>
> (a) a claimant fails to obtain a judgment more advantageous than a defendant's Part 36 offer; or
> (b) judgment against the defendant is at least as advantageous to the claimant as the proposals contained in a claimant's Part 36 offer.
>
> (1A) For the purposes of paragraph (1), in relation to any money claim or money element of the claim, 'more advantageous' means better in money terms by any amount, however small, and 'at least as advantageous' shall be construed accordingly.
> (2) Subject to paragraph (6), where rule 36.14(1)(a) applies, the court will, unless it considers it unjust to do so, order that the defendant is entitled to—

(a) costs from the date on which the relevant period expired; and

(b) interest on those costs.

(3) Subject to paragraph (6), where rule 36.14(1)(b) applies, the court will, unless it considers it unjust to do so, order that the claimant is entitled to—

(a) interest on the whole or part of any sum of money (excluding interest) awarded at a rate not exceeding 10% above base rate for some or all of the period starting with the date on which the relevant period expired;

(b) costs on the indemnity basis from the date on which the relevant period expired;

(c) interest on those costs at a rate not exceeding 10% above base rate; and

(d) an additional amount, which shall not exceed £75,000, calculated by applying the prescribed percentage set out below to an amount which is—

(i) where the claim is or includes a money claim, the sum awarded to the claimant by the court; or

(ii) where the claim is only a non-monetary claim, the sum awarded to the claimant by the court in respect of costs—

Amount awarded by the court	Prescribed percentage
Up to £500,000	10%
above £500,001 to £1 million	10% of the first £500,000 + 5% of any amount over that figure"

These amendments gave effect to all of the FR recommendations discussed above.

Current rules. Part 36 underwent substantial revision with effect from 6 April   **10–016** 2015. The substance of the rules quoted above is now to be found in r.36.17. It remains the case that, under r.36.17(2), a claimant's offer is treated as "more advantageous" if it exceeds the judgment sum by any amount, however small. Very sensibly, however, the Rule Committee has added a provision in r.36.17(5) (e) to deal with cases where the claimant makes an offer which is not "a genuine attempt to settle the proceedings".

A self-contained code. In *Gibbon v Manchester City Council* [2010] EWCA   **10–017** Civ 726; [2010] 1 WLR 2081 at [5], the Court of Appeal held that CPR Pt 36 constituted a complete code. That remains the case following the reforms of 2015: see *Webb v Liverpool Women's NHS Foundation Trust* [2016] EWCA Civ 365; *ABC v Barts Health NHS Trust* [2016] EWHC 500 (QB).

4. INTER-RELATIONSHIP BETWEEN PART 36 AND OTHER REFORMS

Interrelationship with fixed costs. Rule 36.17 is assuming increased impor-   **10–018** tance as we move into an era of fixed costs. If the claimant obtains an order for indemnity costs under r.36.17(4)(b), that is a means of escaping (as from the date when the offer expires) from the fixed costs regime for fast track PI cases: *Broadhurst v Tan* [2016] EWCA Civ 94; [2016] 1 WLR 1928. It may also be a way of escaping from future fixed costs regimes, depending of course upon how the rules for those future regimes are drafted.

10–019 **Interrelationship with costs management.** Rule 36.18, which substantially ties a party to its last approved/agreed budget, applies to an assessment of costs on the standard basis. If the claimant obtains an order for indemnity costs under r.36.17(4)(b), he may escape (as from the date when the offer expires) from the operation of r.36.18: *Denton v T H White Ltd* [2014] EWCA Civ 906; [2014] 1 WLR 3926 at [43].[1] It should also be noted that r.36.23 provides a residual incentive in cases where the offeror has fallen foul of r.3.14 by failing to file a costs budget.

10–020 **Interrelationship with detailed assessment.** As discussed in Ch. 3, above, at a detailed assessment on the standard basis, the receiving party cannot recover more than proportionate costs, even if further costs were reasonably or necessarily incurred: see CPR r.44.3(2). If there is an order for indemnity costs under r.36.17(4)(b), the claimant is not caught by this restriction.[2]

10–021 **Maintaining a level playing field.** The problem in 2009 was that the playing field was tilted in favour of defendants. That was part of the rationale for the FR recommending enhanced damages for effective claimant Pt 36 offers, as implemented by s.55 of LASPO and CPR r.36.14 (now r.36.17). The Rule Committee will need to keep a watchful eye on how the provisions of Pt 36 are playing out in practice, in order to ensure that the playing field remains level. In particular, is r.36.17(5) effectively weeding out Pt 36 offers which ought not to attract indemnity costs? The Rule Committee will need to examine cases such as *Jockey Club Racecourse Ltd v Willmott Dixon Construction Ltd* [2016] EWHC 167 TCC, in order to satisfy itself that the rules are working as intended. It is not the intention of this paragraph to express an opinion either way, merely to identify an important issue which must be kept under review as other aspects of civil procedure develop.

---

[1] There may be difficulties of assessment if the relevant date is part way through a Precedent H Phase: see Hurst, Middleton and Mallalieu, *Questions & Answers*, pp. 74–75.
[2] See Hurst, Middleton and Mallalieu, *Questions & Answers*, p. 207.

Part Four

THE MANAGEMENT OF LITIGATION

CHAPTER 11

CASE MANAGEMENT AND EFFECTIVE USE OF INFORMATION TECHNOLOGY

1. BACKGROUND

Summons for directions. The Rules of the Supreme Court regulated civil   **11–001**
procedure from 1883 until 1999, subject to numerous amendments over the years.
RSC Order 25 required every plaintiff to take out a "summons for directions"
within one month after the close of pleadings. At the hearing of the summons,
the court would consider "the preparations for the trial of the action" and give
appropriate directions. In practice, these were somewhat perfunctory affairs in
which there was little, if any, serious debate about the future conduct of the action.

Strike outs. Unfortunately, plaintiffs or their advisers sometimes failed to issue   **11–002**
summonses for directions in time or at all, with the result that the litigation "went
to sleep". In such cases, after an appropriate interval, defendants would apply to
strike out. Provided that the defendants had waited long enough before applying,
the court usually struck such cases out "for want of prosecution". This was hardly
a good advertisement for civil justice.

Transfer of control. During the second half of the twentieth century, there was   **11–003**
a steady transfer of control of litigation from the parties to the court. Successive
amendments made to the RSC sought to encourage the court to make a more
active role at the hearing of the summons for directions. Then came the watershed
during the 1990s, namely Lord Woolf's Access to Justice Inquiry in 1994–1996,
his Final Report of July 1996 and its implementation in April 1999. The Woolf
reforms involved repealing the RSC and replacing them with the CPR 1998.

Academic analysis. Professor Zuckerman has provided a perceptive and com-   **11–004**
prehensive analysis of these developments (of a kind that is beyond the scope of
this short book) in Ch. 11 of *Zuckerman on Civil Procedure*. There is, inevitably,
a vast wealth of literature on the changing character of case management. The

rise of the managerial judge has been a general trend across the common law world.[1]

11–005   **The philosophy of the Woolf reforms.**[2] Lord Woolf summarised the philosophy underlying his reforms in his Interim Report and explained it more fully in his Final Report. In Chapter 1, para. 3 of his Final Report, he summarised that philosophy as follows:

> "**The basic reforms**
> The interim report set out a blueprint for reform based on a system where the courts with the assistance of litigants would be responsible for the management of cases. I recommended that the courts should have the final responsibility for determining what procedures were suitable for each case; setting realistic timetables; and ensuring that the procedures and timetables were complied with."

11–006   **The functions of case management.** Professor Andrews identifies three main functions of case management, namely the promotion of ADR where this is practicable, promoting the swift and efficient progress of the litigation, and ensuring that judicial resources are allocated proportionately.[3] It is accepted that these are important tasks, but each has its own agenda. The parties and the court need to collaborate in order to focus their efforts on the real issues and to cut out unnecessary work. Parties do not always welcome the prospect of working in harmony with their opponents. No-one should pretend that effective case management is an easy task.

11–007   **Case management conferences.** One of Lord Woolf's many wise innovations was the CMC. This was an occasion when the court would, or at least should, actively case manage. That involved identifying the issues and giving directions which would facilitate the efficient progress of the action up to trial. The court itself sets the date for case management conferences. In other words, the parties did not have to issue a summons or application in order to trigger the case management process. At a stroke, this brought to an end the lamentable saga of cases being struck out for want of prosecution.

11–008   **How effective were case management conferences?** In the specialist courts, such as the TCC or the Commercial and Mercantile Courts, by and large CMCs worked well. The judges really did study the issues. They set directions and timetables which were appropriate to the individual cases. Away from the specialist courts, however, CMCs tended to become formulaic occasions, when judges either rubber-stamped the parties' proposals or gave their own "usual" directions. Certainly this was the very strong feedback which came during the consultation phase of the 2009 Costs Review.

---

[1] Michael Legg provides a description of parallel developments in Australia in *Case Management and Complex Litigation.*

[2] For an excellent analysis of the philosophy underpinning the Woolf reforms and of the historical context of those reforms, see Sorabji, *English civil justice after the Woolf and Jackson reforms.*

[3] *Andrews on Civil Processes*, Vol. 1, p. 198, para. 9.05.

Making proper use of information technology. Lord Woolf discussed the   **11-009**
need to make proper use of information technology in Ch. 21 of his Final Report.
He reviewed the IT systems available and explained how they should be developed for use in the civil courts. In para. 13, he described this task as "crucial if
judicial case management is to succeed". Lord Justice Brooke as Judge in Charge
of Modernisation made valiant efforts to secure the implementation of these
proposals.[4]

Lord Woolf's hopes were not fulfilled. A detailed review of Ch. 21 of the   **11-010**
Woolf Report would serve no useful purpose. Suffice it to say that the IT systems
which Lord Woolf recommended were not developed for the civil courts. In
the mid-2000s, there was a plan to introduce a holistic electronic system across
England and Wales, known as the Electronic Filing and Document Management
("EFDM") project. While EFDM was in development, other projects were post-
poned or cancelled. In late 2008 (just before the Costs Review commenced), the
MoJ halted the EFDM project for lack of funding.

2. RECOMMENDATIONS IN THE FINAL REPORT OF JANUARY 2010

Debate during the Costs Review. During Phase Two of the Costs Review,   **11-011**
there was much lively discussion of case management issues. This tended to
dominate many of the seminars. Many consultees considered that the courts were
too lax in enforcing both their own orders and the rules. Claimant representatives
thought that defendants and liability insurers were "getting away with it" too
often. Defendant representatives took a similarly dim view of indulgences granted
to claimants.

Law Society submission. The Law Society neatly captured this mood in its   **11-012**
written submission, which included the following passage:

> "The Law Society considers that the overriding objective is not applied as rigorously or
> as consistently as it should be.
> The most infrequently applied rules are those that are available to control the progress
> of a case. Lord Woolf introduced a number of ways in which this could be achieved
> (most notably CPR Parts 1.1, 1.4 and 3.1), but the experience of practitioners suggests
> that in practice these are not used fully or at all. Therefore we question whether further
> rules would bring any benefit unless they are applied fully. We suggest there needs to
> be a change in the attitudes of the judiciary and court users so that court rules are fully
> complied with and applied in practice. The unhelpful practice of 'local practice direc-
> tions' which has developed in some courts should be abolished and strictly policed."

Discussion of case management issues in the Final Report. The discus-   **11-013**
sion and analysis of case management issues extended across much of the Final

---

[4] See Brooke LJ "2002: My Essay on Technology and the Judicial Process", 25 October 2015,
available at *https://sirhenrybrooke.me/2015/10/25/my-2002-essay-on-technology-and-the-judicial-
process/* [Accessed 1 July 2016].

Report and does not lend itself to pithy summary. In essence, the Final Report was looking for ways to (a) focus litigation on the issues at an early stage, and (b) cut down the costs which would be wasted in following blind alleys or amassing irrelevant evidence.

11–014   **Enforcing compliance.** In relation to enforcing compliance, FR Ch. 39, para. 6.5 stated:

> "*Enforcement of rules and directions generally.* There is a wide spread of views about this issue, amongst both practitioners and distinguished academic commentators. The conclusions to which I have come are as follows. First, the courts should set realistic timetables for cases and not impossibly tough timetables in order to give an impression of firmness. Secondly, courts at all levels have become too tolerant of delays and non-compliance with orders. In so doing they have lost sight of the damage which the culture of delay and non-compliance is inflicting upon the civil justice system. The balance therefore needs to be redressed. However, I do not advocate the extreme course which was canvassed as one possibility in PR paragraph 43.4.21 or any approach of that nature."

11–015   **A curious twist.** At the time when the Final Report was published, the above proposal for more robust compliance did not generate protest. Most of the other major recommendations led to sustained attacks upon the hapless author of the report from one direction or another. This one, however, did not. It passed under the radar. On the other hand, after implementation this particular reform emerged as the prime target for criticism. Some of that criticism took the form of personal attack.

11–016   **Chapter 39 of the Final Report.** FR Ch. 39 made the following recommendations[5] to promote effective case management:

    (i) Measures should be taken to promote the assignment of cases to designated judges with relevant expertise.

    (ii) A menu of standard paragraphs for case management directions for each type of case of common occurrence should be prepared and made available to all district judges both in hard copy and online in amendable form.

    (iii) CMCs and PTRs should either (a) be used as occasions for effective case management or (b) be dispensed with and replaced by directions on paper. Where such interim hearings are held, the judge should have proper time for pre-reading.

    (iv) In multi-track cases, the entire timetable for the action, including trial date or trial window, should be drawn up at as early a stage as is practicable.

    (v) Pre-action applications should be permitted in respect of breaches of pre-action protocols.

    (vi) The courts should be less tolerant than hitherto of unjustified delays and breaches of orders. This change of emphasis should be signalled by

---

[5] Omitting recommendation (viii), which did not find favour.

amendment of CPR r.3.9. If and insofar as it is possible, courts should monitor the progress of the parties in order to secure compliance with orders and pre-empt the need for sanctions.

(vii) The Master of the Rolls should designate two lords justices, at least one of whom will so far as possible be a member of any constitution of the civil division of the Court of Appeal, which is called upon to consider issues concerning the interpretation or application of the CPR.

Implementation of case management reforms. The Rule Committee and the Judiciary implemented most of those recommendations with effect from the general implementation date, 1 April 2013. The one reform which came into effect early was the set of amendments to the Admiralty and Commercial Courts Guide to promote judicial continuity. This followed a series of discussions with the Commercial Court judges about the FR recommendations during 2011.   **11–017**

Chapter 43 of the Final Report. FR Ch. 43 reviewed the IT systems which were then operating in the civil courts and contrasted them unfavourably with those provided in some overseas jurisdictions. The chapter stated that the civil courts needed an IT system which had the following capabilities: **11–018**

"(i) Electronic filing for claim forms, statements of case, witness statements, expert reports and other documents lodged.
(ii) The ability to maintain all documents lodged by the parties to a case or created by the court in a single electronic bundle relating to that case.
(iii) The electronic bundle for each case should be accessible to the parties, court staff and the judge by means of an extranet with unique password.
(iv) Digital signature technology to authenticate documents and correspondence sent by parties to the court or to each other.
(v) A facility for online payment of court fees and all other payments into court.
(vi) Scanning equipment at all courts, so that parties without IT equipment can lodge documents at court.
(vii) A national database on which the electronic bundles for each case are held (so that cases or hearings can be transferred from one court to another, without any need for transport of papers)."

The chapter then discussed how that objective should be achieved. It concluded with six detailed recommendations directed to that end.

3. RECOMMENDATION (I): DOCKETING

Importance of docketing. Paragraphs 4.1–4.2 of FR Ch. 39 explained the importance of (a) judicial continuity and (b) assigning cases to judges of appropriate experience and expertise. Indeed the vast majority of practitioners supported this proposal. Opposition came from listing officers, who wished to retain flexible use of judge time, and also from some judges. For example, certain judges liked going on circuit for part of each year and did not wish to see that changed. The challenge therefore was to find a way of promoting docketing which would be generally acceptable and workable.   **11–019**

11–020   **The Leeds pilot.** One system of docketing was set up at Leeds. This entailed assigning blocks of cases to individual district judges and giving each of them much greater control over their own listing. Two members of the Law Faculty at Leeds University, Nick Taylor and Ben Fitzpatrick, kindly monitored the pilot. In 2012, they wrote up their findings in an article for Civil Justice Quarterly.[6] They reported that the pilot was "viewed as a success to a greater or lesser extent by all those interviewed". They also noted that the achievement of docketing was very much in the hands of the court staff.

11–021   **General implementation.** District Judge Michael Walker, a judicial member of HM Courts and Tribunals Service Board, prepared guidance for issue to all court staff in March 2012. The guidance was designed to promote greater judicial continuity in the management of cases, bearing in mind that the vast majority of all cases will settle at some point between issue and trial.

11–022   **Commercial Court.** The ninth edition of the Admiralty and Commercial Courts Guide, published in late 2011, included substantial revisions to section D4. The purpose was to promote judicial continuity and thereby more effective case management. That section was amended to read as follows:

"D4.1 An application for the assignment of a designated judge to a case may be made in circumstances where any or all of the following factors:

  (i) the size of or complexity of the case,
  (ii) the fact that it has the potential to give rise to numerous pre-trial applications,
  (iii) there is a likelihood that specific assignment will give rise to a substantial saving in costs,
  (iv) the same or similar issues arise in other cases,
  (v) other case management considerations

indicate that assignment to a specific judge at the start of the case, or at some subsequent date, is appropriate.

D4.2 An application for the appointment of a designated judge should be made in writing to the Judge in Charge of the List at the time of fixing the case management conference. In appropriate cases the court may assign a designated judge regardless of whether an application is made.

D4.3 If an order is made for allocation to a designated judge, the designated judge will preside at all subsequent pre-trial case management conferences and other hearings. Normally all applications in the case, other than applications for an interim payment, will be determined by the designated judge and he will be the trial judge.

D4.4 In all cases the Commercial Court Listing office will endeavour to ensure a degree of judicial continuity. To assist in this, where a previous application in the case has been determined by a judge of the Commercial Court whether at a hearing or on paper, the parties should indicate clearly when lodging the papers, the identity of the judge who last considered the matter, so that so far as reasonably practicable, the papers can be placed before that judge."

---

[6] *Docketing lite: An analysis of a process of assigning multi-track cases to individual judges* (2012) 31 CJQ 430–450.

4. RECOMMENDATION (II): STANDARD DIRECTIONS

Need for consultation. There was a need for wide consultation before any drafting exercise could begin. **11–023**

Establishment of working group. A working group was formed to embark upon this exercise. The group included district judges from across the country and one Queen's Bench master. HH Judge Simon Grenfell, the Designated Civil Judge for Leeds, was chairman. The working group consulted widely and examined the various forms of orders which were in use at different court centres. They then produced (a) a set of standard directions orders and (b) a set of standard paragraphs for inclusion, as appropriate, in directions orders. These can now be found on the MoJ website. **11–024**

Rule amendment. With effect from 1 April 2013, the following provision was added to CPR Pt 29: **11–025**

> "29.1 (2) When drafting case management directions both the parties and the court should take as their starting point any relevant model directions and standard directions which can be found online at *www.justice.gov.uk/courts/procedure-rules/civil* and adapt them as appropriate to the circumstances of the particular case."

Keeping the standard directions up to date. It is necessary that someone keeps the standard directions up to date. That person is the "custodian". It is the custodian's function (a) to keep an eye on the standard directions, as litigation patterns change and (b) to make recommendations to the Rule Committee, if at appears that the standard directions require amendment. **11–026**

The custodian must be a senior and experienced civil judge. At the moment, HH Judge Allan Gore QC, the Designated Civil Judge for Greater Manchester, has that role.

5. RECOMMENDATIONS (III) AND (IV): CASE MANAGEMENT CONFERENCES AND SETTING TRIAL TIMETABLE

More effective case management conferences. In relation to recommendation (iii), there has been an interesting spin off from costs management (discussed in Ch. 14, below). The historic problem with both summonses for directions and CMCs has been that they tended to become formulaic events. They should of course be occasions when the judge **11–027**

> "takes a grip on the case, identifies the issues and gives directions which are focused upon the early resolution of those issues".[7]

One consequence of costs management is that this is now happening. With price tags attached to work, everyone takes more interest. There is serious debate

---

[7] FR Ch. 39, para. 5.5.

about what work is really necessary, what disclosure is required, what experts are needed and so forth. Even practitioners who dislike costs management reluctantly concede this.

11–028   **Directions questionnaires replace allocation questionnaires.**[8] In order to facilitate the proactive case management which is now required, there is a new regime for the provision of information to the court at the outset. The parties are no longer required to complete allocation questionnaires (as they were up to 31 March 2013). Instead, a court officer provisionally allocates the case to a track and sends a notice of proposed allocation to the parties. After receiving this notice, the parties must complete and return directions questionnaires: CPR r.26.3. The parties must consult one another before doing so and provide the information specified in section 2 of PD 26. These provisions serve a serious purpose.[9] They came into force on 1 April 2013 and form part of the coherent package of case management reforms.

11–029   **Directions on paper.** Where there is not going to be any serious debate about either the budgets or the issues in the case, the obvious course is to dispense with the CMC altogether. The availability of standard directions in writing, as discussed above, makes it easier to agree draft directions in a form likely to be approved by the court.

11–030   **Early fixing of trial date.** The Rule Committee implemented this recommendation by means of amendments to CPR Pt 29.

6. RECOMMENDATIONS (V) AND (VI): MORE EFFECTIVE COMPLIANCE

11–031   **Breaches of pre-action protocols.** Recommendation (v) is that where a party is in breach of one of the protocols, it should be possible before litigation commences to seek a court order compelling compliance. This would be a procedure analogous to pre-action disclosure. Unfortunately, this reform requires primary legislation, which has not yet been forthcoming.

11–032   **Tougher enforcement of court orders and the rules.** Recommendation (vi) proposes a more robust approach to enforcing compliance with court orders and rules. This did not require any legislation. The Rule Committee implemented recommendation (vi) by repealing the former CPR r.3.9 and substituting the following:

"**Relief from sanctions**
(1) On an application for relief from any sanction imposed for a failure to comply with any rule, practice direction or court order, the court will consider all the circumstances of the case, so as to enable it to deal justly with the application, including the need –

---

[8] See *Blackstone's Guide to the Civil Justice Reforms 2013* at pp. 61–64.
[9] See Hurst, Middleton and Mallalieu, *Questions & Answers*, p. 60.

(a) for litigation to be conducted efficiently and at proportionate cost; and

(b) to enforce compliance with rules, practice directions and orders.

(2) An application for relief must be supported by evidence."

Glosses on the rule. This new rule has generated extensive academic com-   **11–033**
mentary, much of it critical in tone. The criticism came from several different
viewpoints. Some commentators thought that the rule was too tough. Some
thought that it was too soft. Some thought that it was too vague. The most detailed
analyses of the new rule are to be found in a long series of articles in *Civil Justice
Quarterly* between 2013 and 2016.[10]

Judicial application. Initially, the Court of Appeal took a very tough line   **11–034**
in applying the new r.3.9: see *Mitchell v News Group Newspapers Ltd* [2013]
EWCA Civ 1537; [2014] 1 WLR 795.[11] This decision came in for much criticism.
The Court of Appeal took note of that criticism and adopted a softer approach
in *Denton v TH White Ltd* [2014] EWCA Civ 906; [2014] 1 WLR 3926. *Denton*
strikes broadly the right balance.[12] It requires effective enforcement of compliance so that litigation can progress smoothly and efficiently. At the same time, it
eschews rigid adherence to process for its own sake. Since July 2014, the courts
have been following *Denton* without particular problems or undue complaint. The
academic commentators may still be dismayed, but they have performed a valuable service in articulating the issues and exposing the perils between which the
courts have been finding their way.

7. RECOMMENDATION (VII): PROMOTING CONSISTENCY BY THE COURT OF APPEAL

Nomination of designated judges. In 2012, the Master of the Rolls desig-   **11–035**
nated five judges to form part of any constitution of the Court of Appeal, when
hearing appeals concerning the FR reforms and related issues. They were Lord
Dyson MR, Richards LJ, Jackson LJ, Davis LJ and Lewison LJ. Richards LJ
retired in January 2016 and Lord Dyson is due to retire on 1 October 2016. By
now, however, most of the seminal judgments concerning the reforms have been
handed down.

The future. The next Master of the Rolls will need to consider whether to   **11–036**
nominate a small number of lords justices to form part of any constitution of the
Court of Appeal, when hearing appeals about CPR issues generally. There is good
reason to do this.

---

[10] The two most important (if controversial) articles are Zuckerman, "The revised CPR 3.9: a coded
message demanding articulation" (2013) 32 CJQ 123–138 and Higgins, "CPR3.9: the *Mitchell* guidance, the *Denton* revision, and why coded messages don't make for good case management" (2014)
33 CJQ 379–393. The Zuckerman article was cited in *Denton* at [86].

[11] Fully discussed by Sorabji in *English civil justice after the Woolf and Jackson reforms* at pp.
229–241.

[12] One or two heretics have hinted that they might see some force in the partially dissenting judgment:
see e.g. Hurst, Middleton and Mallalieu, *Questions & Answers*, pp. 2–3.

11–037   **Previous criticism of judicial inconsistency.** There has in the past been scathing criticism of the different approaches to case management adopted by different constitutions of the civil division of the Court of Appeal. See, for example, Professor Zuckerman's 2009 lecture quoted at FR Ch. 39, paras 2.2 to 2.3. That passage begins with the ominous words: "Even more corrosive of good management is the Court of Appeal's inability to speak with one voice."

Although that criticism has not been repeated in recent years, it is important to ensure that the measures taken by Lord Dyson MR to promote continuity of approach to procedural issues should continue in the future. A small group of designated lords justices, one of whom is on the panel in every appeal concerning procedural issues, would achieve that objective.

8. RECOMMENDATIONS IN RESPECT OF INFORMATION TECHNOLOGY

11–038   **Non-implementation, but progress being made.** The aspirations for effective court IT set out in the Costs Review Final Report, like those set out in Lord Woolf's Final Report, have not been fulfilled. On the other hand, many positive steps have been taken, especially in the Rolls Building jurisdictions. Lord Justice Briggs sets out an excellent description of recent developments in his Interim Report at pp. 38–39 and 42–43. In Ch. 6 of his Final Report, he supplements that description and sets out proposals for an Online Court to deal with claims up to £25,000.

11–039   **Cross-over from experience in the criminal courts.** The recent introduction of new IT systems into the criminal justice system has been widely welcomed. This gives cause for optimism that the aspirations expressed in the Woolf Final Report and in the Costs Review Final Report will be achieved in the not too distant future. This will owe much to the efforts of the present Lord Chief Justice[13] and Lord Justice Briggs.

---

[13] See e.g. paras 21–32 of Lord Thomas' lecture on 22 June 2015 entitled "Check against delivery". The Lord Chancellor followed up these issues on 23 June 2015 in his speech "What does a one nation justice policy look like?".

CHAPTER 12

DISCLOSURE

1. BACKGROUND

What is disclosure? Disclosure is the process whereby each party reveals any documents pertinent to the litigation which it holds.[1] The process was known as "discovery" prior to the Woolf reforms and it still retains that name in most common law jurisdictions. The obligation to make extensive disclosure of documents which may damage your case, as well as those which support it, is one of the features which differentiates common law systems from civil law systems. **12–001**

The explosion of documentary of material. During the second half of the twentieth century, the sheer volume of documentary material emerged as a major problem. The invention of photocopiers and fax machines multiplied the numbers of relevant documents which parties felt obliged to disclose or which they wished to place before the court. The next stage was the advent of IT. This vastly increased the quantity of material generated by every business project. By around the turn of the century, most of that material was held in electronic form. **12–002**

Different forms of electronic data grow exponentially. New data sources are emerging almost daily. Examples are Linked-In, Facebook, Twitter and Whatsapp. Many do not lend themselves to printing in a traditional A4 format. All this adds to the complexity of data collection, analysis and production. **12–003**

A major driver of costs. In the larger cases, outside the field of personal injury, disclosure emerged as one of the major drivers of costs. In big commercial cases, teams of young lawyers were engaged for weeks on end upon the process. This has been a source of steady income for city firms, but hardly fun for the trainees and associates working at the coal face. Some firms, however, now use advanced technology for the process or outsource document reviews to others who can do the work more cheaply. **12–004**

---

[1] See generally *Zuckerman on Civil Procedure*, Ch. 15 and *Andrews on Civil Court Processes*, Vol. 1, Ch. 11.

12–005   **What documents did a party have to disclose during the twentieth century?** Prior to 26 April 1999, the Rules of the Supreme Court ("RSC") required parties to disclose all documents "relating to any matter in question between them in the action": RSC Order 24, r.2. The courts construed these words broadly. In *Compagnie Financière et Commerciale du Pacifique v Peruvian Guano Co* (1882) 11 QBD 55, the Court of Appeal held that each party must disclose any document containing information which may enable the other party either to advance his own case or to damage that of his adversary. That included any document "which may fairly lead him to a train of inquiry which may have either of these two consequences". This became known as the "*Peruvian Guano* test". It was well-suited to an age in which solicitors had sufficient time to ponder over each document individually before disclosing it. By the late twentieth century, that was becoming hopelessly unrealistic. The practical consequence was that solicitors tended to disclose everything which related to the projects or incidents which were the subject matter of the litigation (other than privileged documents).

12–006   **The new test introduced by Lord Woolf in April 1999.** The CPR came into force on 26 April 1999, replacing the former RSC. Under CPR Pt 31, the normal order was for "standard disclosure". This required parties to disclose documents which (a) adversely affected their own or another party's case, (b) supported another party's case, or (c) were required to be disclosed by a relevant practice direction. Rule 31.7 required parties to conduct a "reasonable search" for such documents. This new rule reduced the total volume of documents that a party was required to disclose. On the other hand, it required more work by solicitors in order to identify which documents satisfied the "standard disclosure" test. In practice, solicitors often found it easier and safer to disclose everything on the basis of providing background or contextual information, rather than undertake a document-by-document examination.

12–007   **No rules for electronic documents.** The CPR as originally formulated did not contain separate provisions relating to the disclosure of electronic documents. When the Rule Committee was drafting the CPR, the IT revolution was still in its infancy.

12–008   **The position in 2009.** By 2009, there were brief amendments to the practice direction supplementing CPR Pt 31 (PD 31), so as to acknowledge that many "documents" existed only in electronic form. Section 2A of PD 31 gave brief guidance on how to conduct electronic disclosure. Despite the brevity of that guidance, by 2009 electronic disclosure was big business. Specialist service providers had moved into the field and were carrying out much of the necessary collection and processing of electronic disclosure, in order to facilitate review and analysis by solicitors. Chapter 40 of the Preliminary Report gives a fairly detailed account of how people were in practice carrying out electronic disclosure during 2009. It also summarises the rules which then governed electronic disclosure in the USA and Australia.

2. DEBATE DURING THE COSTS REVIEW

Disclosure as a driver of high litigation costs. It was abundantly clear from **12–009** the start of the Costs Review that disclosure was one of the major drivers of high litigation costs. Chapter 4 of the Final Report analysed the causes of disproportionate costs and identified disclosure as one of the culprits: see para. 3.1(x). Not only was the process of disclosure hugely expensive in substantial cases, but so also was its aftermath. Once a party has disclosed documents, the other party has to read them. Witnesses feel the need to comment on them and counsel has to consider them. The litigation process feeds on itself and racks up costs in the process.

Debate during the Costs Review. Views on how to tackle this problem were **12–010** sharply divided. The traditionalist/purist camp maintained that full disclosure was fundamental to our civil justice system and should not be sacrificed on the altar of expediency. The opposing camp argued that the current disclosure regime was prohibitively expensive and in many cases amounted to a denial of justice.

The traditionalist view. The Professional Negligence Bar Association neatly **12–011** summarised the traditionalist view:

> "The rule at the heart of the process (and principle) of disclosure – that opposing litigants must reveal documents to their opponents which are adverse to their own case – has a reach which far exceeds the disclosure process itself. It is fundamental to the way in which litigation in our common law jurisdiction is conducted. There can be legitimate debate as to how that principle is best captured (for example whether by the standard disclosure test provided for by the CPR or by the *Peruvian Guano* test of relevance under the old RSC), but the importance of having a generally applicable test should not be under-estimated (a) because of the need to preserve the essential underlying principle and (b) because a generally applicable test provides a tangible and clear reference point against which the duty of disclosure can be measured."

The alternative view. The Commercial Litigation Association neatly summa- **12–012** rised the alternative view:

> "The IBA system offers a clear means to lower cost. By ensuring only core, crucial documents are collected costs are reduced in all areas. The clear caveat that would need to be placed with this is that the possibility of interlocutory relief from the rigours of the new system could be obtained. . . A comparison with other countries only illuminates the fact that our system is failing and the suggestion that there should be a reduction in the amount of disclosure is welcomed. Their systems should be used as a basis to explore how the reduction can be formulated, with alterations that take into account our adversarial system."

Options identified. After much debate, ten possible options emerged as merit- **12–013** ing serious consideration during Phase Two of the Costs Review. They were:

(i) Maintain the current position with standard disclosure remaining the default disclosure order.

(ii) Abolish standard disclosure and limit disclosure to documents relied upon, with the ability to seek specific disclosure.

(iii) Introduce "issues based" disclosure akin to the approach being trialled by the Commercial Court in 2009.

(iv) Revert to the old system of discovery with the "train of enquiry" test.

(v) No default position with the parties and court being required to consider the most appropriate process for disclosure at the first CMC. This approach was generally referred to as the "menu option".

(vi) More rigorous case management by the court, including greater use of sanctions against parties who provide disclosure late or in a haphazard manner, or ordering the parties to agree a constructive process and scope.

(vii) Use of experienced lawyers as disclosure assessors in "heavy" cases to identify which categories of documents merit disclosure.

(viii) Restrict the number of specific disclosure applications and/or raise the standard to be met.

(ix) Reverse the burden of proof in specific disclosure applications, with the costs of the disclosure exercise being met by the requesting party unless documents of real value emerge.

(x) Allocate a single judge at the outset of substantial cases to enable him or her to become more familiar with the facts and procedural history.

12–014   **Consultation.** There was much discussion of these options at seminars and meetings during Phase Two of the Review, especially with commercial practitioners and court users. A majority view emerged in favour of option (v), the menu option. The Commercial Court Users Committee kindly offered to assist with drafting. A working group drawn from that committee produced a first draft rule. That first draft then became the subject of further consultation.

12–015   **Rules for e-disclosure.** There was general agreement within the profession that section 2A of PD 31, for all its admirable qualities, was not a sufficient basis for the vast amount of electronic disclosure which by 2009 was taking place. The Senior Master chaired a working group on electronic disclosure, which reported in July 2009.

3. RECOMMENDATIONS IN THE FINAL REPORT OF JANUARY 2010

12–016   **E-disclosure.** Chapter 37 of the Final Report reviewed the output of the Senior Master's working group and its proposed practice direction governing disclosure of electronically stored information. It commended the practice direction and urged its adoption by the Rule Committee. That chapter also urged the importance of proper training in this field. Paragraph 2.9 stated:

"I recommend that e-disclosure as a topic should form a substantial part of (a) Continuing Professional Development ('CPD') for solicitors and barristers who will have to deal with e-disclosure in practice and (b) the training of judges who will have to deal with e-disclosure on the bench. Service providers will have a part to play in such CPD or training. Indeed they will have a commercial interest in contributing to the process. However, they should do so within the context of a well structured programme, which is provided or approved by the relevant professional bodies."

Extent of disclosure and control of the process. Having weighed up the **12–017** competing arguments canvassed during the consultation period, FR Ch. 37 recommended that the menu option should be adopted. Standard disclosure should no longer be the default position. Instead, courts should make focused orders for disclosure, tailored to the circumstances of each case.

Exclusion of personal injury claims. By and large, PI claims are not docu- **12–018** ment heavy. Disclosure is not usually a driver of disproportionate costs in PI claims. Accordingly, FR Ch. 37 recommended that the new disclosure rules should not apply to PI claims.

4. IMPLEMENTATION

E-disclosure. The new PD 31B governing electronic disclosure came into **12–019** force in 2010. This provides a comprehensive new code for identifying and disclosing electronic documents, including metadata. Annexed to it is the Electronic Documents Questionnaire, which focuses the minds of the parties on which documents and document repositories should be considered for disclosure.

New rule 31.5. The Rule Committee accepted the recommendations in FR **12–020** Ch. 37. A new r.31.5 of the CPR came into force on 1 April 2013. It provides:

"(2) Unless the court otherwise orders, paragraphs (3) to (8) apply to all multi-track claims, other than those which include a claim for personal injuries.
(3 Not less than 14 days before the first case management conference each party must file and serve a report verified by a statement of truth, which –

    (a) describes briefly what documents exist or may exist that are or may be relevant to the matters in issue in the case;
    (b) describes where and with whom those documents are or may be located;
    (c) in the case of electronic documents, describes how those documents are stored;
    (d) estimates the broad range of costs that could be involved in giving standard disclosure in the case, including the costs of searching for and disclosing any electronically stored documents; and
    (e) states which of the directions under paragraphs (7) or (8) are to be sought.

(4) In cases where the Electronic Documents Questionnaire has been exchanged, the Questionnaire should be filed with the report required by paragraph (3).
(5) Not less than seven days before the first case management conference, and on any other occasion as the court may direct, the parties must, at a meeting or by telephone, discuss and seek to agree a proposal in relation to disclosure that meets the overriding objective.

(6) If –

    (a) the parties agree proposals for the scope of disclosure; and

    (b) the court considers that the proposals are appropriate in all the circumstances,

the court may approve them without a hearing and give directions in the terms proposed.
(7) At the first or any subsequent case management conference, the court will decide, having regard to the overriding objective and the need to limit disclosure to that which is necessary to deal with the case justly, which of the following orders to make in relation to disclosure –

    (a) an order dispensing with disclosure;

    (b) an order that a party disclose the documents on which it relies, and at the same time request any specific disclosure it requires from any other party;

    (c) an order that directs, where practicable, the disclosure to be given by each party on an issue by issue basis;

    (d) an order that each party disclose any documents which it is reasonable to suppose may contain information which enables that party to advance its own case or to damage that of any other party, or which leads to an enquiry which has either of those consequences;

    (e) an order that a party give standard disclosure;

    (f) any other order in relation to disclosure that the court considers appropriate."

12–021   **The menu.** Rule 31.5 (7) contains a "menu" of different possible disclosure orders, as proposed in FR Ch. 20. One possible form of order, which is not expressly set out but which is sometimes made under r.31.6(7)(f), runs along the following lines: by consent, each party gives to the other free access to all its documents (other than privileged documents), so that they can pick out whichever ones they want. Although this might reduce the costs of the producing party, it does little to reduce the overall costs of the action.

12–022   **Judicial training in e-disclosure.** While e-disclosure is not dealt with as a specific topic at the Judicial College, disclosure in general—including PD 31B—is brought to the attention of judges in the civil law introduction course. The Judicial College also makes available a 2012 paper by Morgan J which covers the topic, entitled "An Introduction to E-Disclosure".

12–023   **Professional training in e-disclosure.** For practitioners wishing to learn more in this area, both City University and Wilmington Legal offer specific, targeted courses on e-disclosure. BPP covers disclosure as part of a broader civil litigation course. According to their prospectus, this includes both e-disclosure and the disclosure menu approach recommended by the Final Report. No doubt other providers offer similar training. The hope expressed in FR Ch. 37, para. 2.9 seems generally to have been fulfilled.[2]

12–024   **Available guidance on e-disclosure.** There are now many excellent textbooks available giving guidance on how to conduct e-disclosure, for example *The Electronic Evidence and E-disclosure Handbook*.[3] On occasions, a staged approach

---

[2] This paragraph is not to be taken as endorsing any particular provider. It is merely reviewing whether one particular FR recommendation has been implemented.

[3] Peter Hibbert, *The Electronic Evidence and E-disclosure Handbook* (2015, Sweet & Maxwell).

to e-disclosure is the best way forwards, as in *Goodale v MoJ* [2009] EWHC B41 (QB) and *Daniel Alfredo Condori Vilca v Xstrata Ltd* [2016] EWHC 389 (QBD).

Predictive coding. "Predictive coding" means the use of special computer **12–025** software to assess the likely relevance of documents. Lawyers review samples of the documents and pick out what is relevant, thereby training the computer to do the same. Once the software is sufficiently well trained, they let the computer (a) apply the logic to the entire set of documents and (b) suggest the likely relevance of each document, based on its understanding. The first reported[4] case in which this was ordered was *Pyrrho Investments Ltd v MWB Property Ltd* [2016] EWHC 256 (Ch). Master Matthews gave a clear explanation of the process at [17]–[24]. He set out ten cogent reasons for ordering its use in that case at [33]. Mr Registrar Jones made similar order in *Re Tradeouts Ltd, Brown v BCA Trading Ltd*, petition no. 997 of 2016 on 17 May 2016. Although the "training" process is expensive, in cases where the electronically stored information is vast, predictive coding can achieve huge savings. In *Re Tradeouts*, the parties estimated that predictive coding would cost £120,000, whereas the cost would be nearer £250,000 if paralegals made the search using keywords.

Technology Assisted Review. In addition to predictive coding, many other **12–026** technologies fall under the general heading of Technology Assisted Review ("TAR"). Tools are available which assist with tasks such email threading, near de-duplication, concept searching and clustering.

Foreign language. In some commercial cases, there are many documents in **12–027** foreign languages. Unless the legal team has the requisite capabilities, it is likely that the documents will need to be translated before any legal analysis can begin. This, of course, adds a new layer of costs. Where predictive coding or other TAR products (such as language detection software) are used successfully, this should (a) identify the material in foreign languages and (b) reduce the number of documents needing to be translated.

TeCSA/SCL/TECBAR protocol. In relation to TCC litigation, TeCSA, **12–028** TECBAR and the SCL[5] have produced a very helpful e-disclosure protocol. This protocol guides the parties through the process. In particular, it encourages them to consider all the possible forms of order in the menu option, rather than mechanistically agree "standard disclosure".

The role of the judge in relation to disclosure. If the court is going to make **12–029** effective use of r.31.5, he or she must do more than simply adjudicate upon the parties' competing submissions. It is necessary to test the opposing arguments. One judge writes:

"When disclosure is an issue during case management it is not uncommon to find that the parties' counsel cannot describe the documents which they expect to be relevant, why

---

[4] Courts have approved the use of predictive coding on occasions before 2016.
[5] Technology and Construction Solicitors Association; Technology and Construction Bar Association; Society of Construction Law. Version 0.2 of the protocol is dated 9 January 2015.

they might exist or why they will benefit determination of the issues concerned. This is particularly the case for electronic documents when requests for practical descriptions and examples are usually met with bluster. This and the fact that disclosure issues are relatively rare suggests the fault lies with a failure to properly address the issues either internally or with the other side before the hearing. That conclusion is sustained by the fact that I usually find a general discussion of the need for the disclosure sought, about the practicalities of effecting disclosure and inspection and over the resulting cost produces a solution by agreement without the need for a decision."

12–030   **Great, is everyone now using the new rules properly?** Unfortunately, no. In large commercial actions and other substantial cases, too often people are treating standard disclosure as the default option. Parties frequently agree standard disclosure, seemingly without considering whether other options may be preferable, and the courts accept their agreements. It would be to the public benefit if all involved in the disclosure process gave more attention to the full range of options before simply proposing or agreeing to "standard disclosure".

12–031   **Survey by London Solicitors Litigation Association.** In June 2016, the London Solicitors Litigation Association ("LSLA") carried out a survey of their members. This revealed that neither practitioners nor courts were making proper use of the available disclosure orders contained in CPR r.31.5(7). Commenting on the survey findings, the president of the LSLA stated:

> "[T]he onus must surely be not only on the parties and their advisers to explore and agree a proportionate approach to disclosure in advance of the case management conference (CMC), but also on the courts proactively to challenge parties where they have failed to do so. A more robust and challenging case management approach to disclosure by the courts would be welcomed by many."

The LSLA's June 2016 Litigation Trends Survey went on to criticise lawyers for not making proper use of the new disclosure rules, since proper use of those rules could lead to substantial costs savings.

12–032   **The GC100 disclosure seminar on 27 April 2016.** The GC 100 Group,[6] as regular users of the Commercial Court, raised the growing concerns about disclosure with the Commercial Court. The upshot was a seminar on disclosure in which judges (from the Commercial Court, Chancery Division and TCC), practitioners and court users took part. Principal points emerging from the seminar were:

(i) There was a general recognition that the tools for controlling disclosure have been in place since April 2013, but the parties and the courts are not making sufficient use of them.

(ii) In particular, more use ought to be made of option (b), namely disclosure limited to specific issues. In Commercial Court cases, the parties usually succeed in agreeing a list of issues for the first CMC.

---

[6] This comprises the general counsel and company secretaries of the FTSE 100 companies.

(iii) In patent litigation, there is an established practice of making restricted disclosure orders. This is because the Patents Court and the Intellectual Property Enterprise Court are competing against Continental courts, which have very little disclosure. The litigants have a choice of forum. Parties are generally satisfied with the restrictive approach to disclosure in these cases.

(iv) The use of predictive coding in *Pyrrho* was generally welcomed, but it was accepted that predictive coding was not a panacea to be used in every case.

(v) The new procedure for Shorter and Flexible Trials currently being piloted under PD 51N has very restrictive rules for disclosure. These were generally welcomed.

So where are we now? It is hoped that, as a result of the seminar on 27 April 2016, both practitioners and the courts will make fuller and more effective use of the menu option. A working group was set up at the end of the seminar to take these matters further.   12–033

Link with case management reforms. As discussed in the previous chapter, the Final Report recommended a series of reforms to case management, most of which are now in place. The new disclosure rules obviously fit in with those recommendations. Tailoring disclosure to the real issues in the case obviously goes hand in hand with directions governing the scope of expert reports and factual evidence.   12–034

Link with costs management. The new disclosure rules, which are now contained in CPR r.31.5, were carefully designed to mesh in with (a) the new rules on proportionality and (b) costs management. The intention is that the court should make a disclosure order which is proportionate in all the circumstances of the case. Absent an allegation of fraud, it would be inappropriate to order the parties spend £1 million on disclosure, if the sum at issue is only £1million. The court should, so far as possible, make disclosure orders which are consistent with the approved/agreed budgets. Since the court should be doing case management and costs management together, it can (a) adjust the level of disclosure to fit with the budgets and/or (b) set the budgets to take account of the level of disclosure ordered.   12–035

5. SOME OVERSEAS DEVELOPMENTS

The same problems everywhere. All common law jurisdictions are now grappling with the problems of disclosure and how to control that process in the digital age. Chapter 42 of the Preliminary Report outlined recent developments in the USA and Australia. Legislators and rule-makers are constantly catching up with developments in technology.   12–036

Australia. The Australian Law Commission produced an excellent report in 2011, entitled *Managing Discovery – Discovery of Documents in Federal*   12–037

Courts.[7] Australia is moving in the same direction as the UK, with an emphasis on (a) controlling discovery through judicial case management and (b) limiting the costs of the process.

12–038   The Australian Federal Court substantially adopted the recommendations of the Australian Law Commission in 2011. The court promulgated new rules and practice notes to give effect to the recommendations. McKerracher J stated in *Alanco Australia Pty Ltd v Higgins (No. 2)* [2011] FCA 1063 that those rules were

> "designed to ensure that the Court controls the discovery process to ensure that the parties are not crippled with the cost and delay of that process. The objective is to ensure that discovery will be provided only when necessary for the just resolution of the proceedings as quickly, inexpensively and efficiently as possible".

12–039   **New Zealand.** The New Zealand courts have been engaged in similar reform. The New Zealand High Court Rules—also amended in 2011—adopted the "menu" approach that was recommended in the Final Report. A discovery order

> "must be made at the first case management conference that is held for the proceeding, unless there is good reason for making the order later": r.8.5(2).

The Court can consider standard or tailored discovery (or making no discovery order at all). Importantly, the parties are under an obligation to

> "not less than 10 working days before the first case management conference, discuss and endeavour to agree on an appropriate discovery order, and the manner in which inspection will subsequently take place": r. 8.11(1).

---

[7] ALRC Report 115 (2011).

FACTUAL AND EXPERT EVIDENCE

1. BACKGROUND

The traditional rule—oral evidence at trial. Under the RSC 1883, wit- **13–001**
nesses gave all their evidence at trial orally. This remained the position under
the RSC 1965, as set out in Order 38 r.1. Such a procedure was inefficient and
there were calls for reform. In particular, Sir Jack Jacob argued that the parties
should exchange witness statements and that the written statements should stand
as evidence-in-chief at trial.

Rule changes in the 1980s. During the late 1980s, amendments to RSC Order **13–002**
38 required the parties to exchange witness statements. The new provisions also
gave the court a discretion to treat those statements as evidence-in-chief. In practice, it became increasingly common for written witness statements to stand as
evidence-in-chief. The purpose of these reforms was twofold: first, to save the
time and cost of oral evidence-in-chief and, secondly, to enable each party to
know what evidence it would have to meet. Such a "cards on the table" approach
would in some cases promote settlement and in other cases make for a fairer
trial. Even under the amended Order 80, however, the court sometimes required
witnesses to give oral evidence-in-chief about crucial events or conversations.
Judges still retain this useful power.

Shorter and less substantial cases. Written witness statements have gener- **13–003**
ally achieved their objective in shorter and less substantial cases. In such cases,
witness statements usually lead to a saving of time and costs. The submissions
made during the Costs Review did not suggest otherwise. Nevertheless, sometimes, even in the shorter and less substantial cases, witness statements are unduly
prolix. There can also be problems where witness statements are taken over the
telephone or taken by inexperienced staff. Those, however, are matters for staff
training, not rule changes.

Larger and more substantial cases. The real problem concerning witness **13–004**
statements arose in larger and more substantial cases. There was a concern that the
use of written witness statements, instead of saving costs and promoting fairness,
might have the opposite effect. The statements could grow to immense length and

cover details which the witness was hardly likely to remember. The language was often that of the lawyers or paralegals, not that of the witness.

13–005   **Woolf Report.**[1] Lord Woolf recommended that witness statements (a) should, so far as possible, be in the witness' own words; (b) should not discuss legal propositions; (c) should not comment on documents; (d) should conclude with a statement, signed by the witness, that the evidence is a true statement and that it is in his own words; and (e) in relation to hearsay statements, should give an indication, where appropriate, of the sources of knowledge, belief or information on which the witness himself is relying. Further, he said (at Ch. 12, para.58):

> ". . . In the interim report, I recommended that courts should disallow costs where they thought the drafting of witness statements had been disproportionate. Trial judges, and to some extent procedural judges, will need to make a real effort, especially in the early phase of the new system, to scrutinise witness statements rigorously. This is the only way in which they will be able to pinpoint repetitious or inappropriate material, such as purported legal argument or analysis of documents. This is a fault which must in the main be attributed to the legal profession and not to its clients; wasted costs orders may therefore be appropriate in some instance of grossly overdone drafting. Only if the legal profession is convinced by demonstration that it has an active judicial critic over its shoulder will it be persuaded to change its drafting habits."

13–006   **The position in 2009.** Ten years after the implementation of the Woolf reforms, those aspirations in respect of witness statements were not being fulfilled, certainly in the more substantial cases. Some individual courts were making valiant efforts to bring this problem under control. In particular, the Commercial Court set up a Long Trials Working Party to tackle that and other related problems.

13–007   **Expert evidence.** During the Costs Review, concerns were expressed about the length of expert reports. For example, one experienced circuit judge wrote:

> "Certain disciplines show a marked tendency towards prolixity – in particular, accident reconstruction experts, psychiatrists and pain management clinicians. Notwithstanding the comments of the Court of Appeal in *Liddell v Middleton* there continues to be regular use in serious injury RTAs of accident reconstruction experts. Their reports are long, show a distinct tendency to go outside their remit and are often speculative. All these disciplines display an inclination to analyse witness statements (despite, again, the clear statement in *Liddell* that this is impermissible). Another contributor to lengthy reports is over analysis of medical records."

13–008   **Comments from the profession.** The Law Society acknowledged that experts' fees significantly increased the costs of litigation and proposed that the whole topic of expert evidence should be reviewed by the CJC together with relevant stakeholders. The Bar Council commented that experts' fees could be a "sizeable costs centre" and proposed that, in appropriate cases, the court should determine the scope of expert evidence at the first CMC.

---

[1] See FR Ch. 12, paras 58–60.

For more detail, see the Costs Review reports. Chapter 42 of the Preliminary   **13–009**
Report and FR Ch. 38 set out a full account of the concerns expressed by court
users and the profession concerning witness statements and expert reports.

2. RECOMMENDATIONS IN THE FINAL REPORT OF JANUARY 2010

(i) *Factual evidence*

Chapter 38 of the Final Report. FR Ch. 38 reached the following conclusions: **13–010**

"2.1 *The role of witness statements.* As was explained in chapter 42 of the
Preliminary Report, witness statements serve a number of purposes, including (a)
reducing the length of the trial (by largely doing away with the need for anything more
than short examination-in-chief); (b) enabling the parties to know in advance of the
trial what the factual issues are; (c) enabling opposing parties to prepare in advance for
cross-examination; and (d) encouraging the early settlement of actions. To this I would
add the objective of providing useful and relevant information to the court to enable it to
adjudicate upon the case in an efficient manner.
2.2 Having considered the extensive submissions on this issue, I conclude that witness
statements can and do fulfil the important objectives identified in the previous paragraph.
I do not consider that the fact that some witness statements are too long means that they
should be done away with as a tool of civil litigation. The problem is primarily one of
unnecessary length, rather than whether witness statements should be used at all in civil
litigation. One reason for unnecessary length is that many witness statements contain
extensive argument. Such evidence is inadmissible and adds to the costs.

2.3 *Measures to control prolixity.* There are two primary measures that should be
deployed to try to ensure that witness statements are not unnecessarily lengthy. The first is
case management, and the second is imposition of costs sanctions.

2.4 *Case management.* Under our current system, there are few restrictions in practice
on a party's ability to produce and rely upon witness statements in civil proceedings. The
courts do not, in general, inquire as to how many witnesses a party proposes to call, upon
what matters they will give evidence (and whether those matters are relevant to the real
issues in dispute) and how long their witness statements will be. Nevertheless CPR Part
32 gives the court power to do all of this. The Commercial Court is now exercising these
powers, as part of that court's commitment to more active case management: see section
H1 of the Commercial Court Guide, as revised in May 2009. In my view the best way to
avoid wastage of costs occurring as a result of lengthy and irrelevant witness statements is
for the court, in appropriate cases, to hear argument at an early case management conference (a 'CMC') about what matters need to be proved and then to give specific directions
relating to witness statements. The directions may (a) identify the issues to which factual
evidence should be directed, (b) identify the witnesses to be called, (c) limit the length of
witness statements or (d) require that any statement over a specified length do contain a one
page summary at the start with cross-references to relevant pages/paragraphs.

. . .

2.7 *Costs sanctions.* To the extent that case management does not prevent parties from
producing prolix witness statements, costs sanctions should be applied against the party
responsible for adducing the prolix or irrelevant statements."

(ii) *Expert evidence*

13–011   **Control of expert evidence.** Chapter 38 of the Final Report reached the following conclusions:

> "3.14 *The benefits of good case management.* On those occasions when a proper CMC take place (i.e. the judge actually gets to grips with the issues and debates with counsel what needs to be proved, how and why—rather than making formulaic comments about costs, length of trial etc), huge costs savings can be achieved in relation to the future conduct of the case. This is clear to me both from talking to practitioners and court users and from comments made in written submissions. These comments are confirmed by my own experience as counsel and as judge.
>
> 3.15 The only effective way to control expert costs is by good case management. The suggestion made by the Bar Council and by a set of chambers set out in paragraph 3.3 above is a sensible one, but is only appropriate for cases where the sums at stake and the potential costs make the exercise worthwhile. If (a) the parties are prepared to spend money on a CMC, a large part of which will be devoted to determining the scope of expert evidence, (b) trial counsel attend that CMC well prepared and (c) the judge reads into the case properly first, then such an exercise will yield huge dividends. The judge will be able to make a focused order stating what expert evidence each party can call and upon what issues. The judge can also identify with precision any topics which require a single joint expert.
>
> . . .
>
> 3.17 Even in more routine cases, where expert evidence forms one item amongst many on the agenda for a CMC, good case management can focus the expert evidence. A well drawn order for expert evidence will not only identify the expert or the expert discipline, but also identify the issues which the expert will address.
>
> 3.18 *Orders limiting recoverable expert fees and expenses.* . . . . I recommend that Part 35 or its accompanying practice direction be amended in order to require that a party seeking permission to adduce expert evidence do furnish an estimate of the costs of that evidence to the court. This should not involve extra work or expense, since any solicitor instructing an expert is bound to obtain an estimate of the expert's likely fees and expenses. The solicitor would obtain such an estimate (a) as a matter of good sense and (b) so that he would be able to comply with paragraph 7.2 of the Protocol for the Instruction of Experts annexed to practice direction 35."

13–012   **Concurrent expert evidence—an Australian innovation.** As explained in PR Ch. 58, the Australian courts have developed an extremely effective way taking expert evidence concurrently at trial. The practice began in the Competition Tribunal and was subsequently adopted in the Supreme Court of New South Wales. The experts meet pre-trial in order to identify where they agree and where they disagree. At trial, experts in the same discipline are sworn in at the same time and the judge chairs a discussion between the experts. The pre-trial document recording the matters upon which the experts disagree serves as the agenda. Counsel join in the discussion. They can put questions to the experts, as and when permitted by the judge. In addition, the experts can put questions to each other. This procedure has spread from Sydney to other courts and is quite widely used across a range of courts and states in Australia. The New South Wales judges state that the procedure is effective. It saves both time and costs. It gives back to experts their proper role of helping the court to resolve disputes. It also does away with the "one on one" gladiatorial combat between cross-examining counsel and each expert. Practitioners in New South Wales have confirmed that the procedure is effective, saving both time and costs.[2]

A popular nickname. Some practitioners and judges call the procedure "hot tubbing". Others dislike that graphic term intensely. It is probably safer to call it concurrent expert evidence, at least until you know who your judge is.   **13–013**

Proposal to adopt the concurrent evidence procedure in England and Wales. Chapter 38 of the Final Report proposed that the concurrent expert evidence procedure should be piloted in England and Wales. If effective, the procedure should be adopted in the CPR as an optional procedure for use in appropriate cases.   **13–014**

3. IMPLEMENTATION

(i) *Factual evidence*

New rules regarding witness statements. The Rule Committee amended CPR Pt 32, with effect from 1 April 2013, by adding the following provision to r.32.2:   **13–015**

"(3) The court may give directions:

    (a) identifying or limiting the issues to which factual evidence may be directed;
    (b) identifying the witnesses who may be called or whose evidence may be read; or
    (c) limiting the length or format of witness statements."

Are these new rules working satisfactorily? There is no information available as to the frequency with which courts are exercising their powers under r.32.2 (3) in order to focus witness statements on the issues or to control their length. Nevertheless, Green J gave an extremely helpful review of the operation of this rule in *MacLennan v Morgan Sindall (Infrastructure) plc* [2013] EWHC 4044 (QB); [2014] 1 WLR 2462. This was a personal injury case in which the defendant applied very late in the day for an order limiting the number of factual witnesses whom the claimant could call on the issue of loss of future earnings. The judge gave directions limiting the number of witnesses and the issues which those witnesses were to address.   **13–016**

In *MacLennan*, Green J construed r.32.2(3) against the background of FR Ch. 38. He identified the following five issues as relevant to the exercise of the court's power (at [12]):

    "i) CPR 32 must be read as a whole. The Court needs to use all the powers at its disposal to ensure the efficient and fair conduct of the trial. The power to prohibit the calling of witnesses sits towards the more extreme end of the Court's powers and hence is a power a judge will ordinarily consider after less intrusive measures have been considered and rejected.
    ii) As Lord Justice Jackson observed in the citation above a Court which seeks to regulate the nature and extent of witness evidence will generally wish to do so

---

[2] For a fuller account of concurrent expert evidence in Australia see Legg, *Case Management and Complex Civil Litigation*, pp. 115–120.

at an early stage, before the preparation of the witness statements themselves and before costs are incurred needlessly. At this stage it may also be possible for the parties to identify matters which may be made the subject of admissions and which would, thereby, avoid the need for any further evidence to be adduced.

iii) In the light of (ii) above, whilst it is clear that the power to exclude or control witness statement evidence is best exercised *ex ante* i.e. before the preparation of witness statements, the CPR does not preclude the Court exercising its powers *ex post*, i.e. after witness statements have been drafted, with a view to ensuring an efficient and fair trial.

iv) A judge asked by a party to prohibit the adducing of contemplated future or already prepared witness statement evidence will be doing so before trial. Accordingly there is a risk that a decision by a judge may turn out, albeit with the benefit of hindsight, to have been made in error and to have caused unfairness to one or other of the parties in the conduct of the trial. Accordingly a Court, asked to adopt this course, will wish to be satisfied that it has the fullest possible information available to it. Lord Justice Jackson observed that such a Court will need to have adequate preparation time and be given sufficient guidance from the parties as to which parts of which statements are said to be otiose, prolix, or otherwise inadmissible.

v) Based upon my consideration of the issues in the present case, it seems to me that in cases where a Court *does* seek to limit the calling of witnesses it may be necessary to introduce a safety valve pursuant to which the parties would have liberty to apply and/or, by consent, to vary the order of the Court. In this regard, a Court will be entitled to expect from the parties a considerable degree of cooperation and good sense. The imposition of costs sanctions, after the event, is a blunt instrument whereby the Court may express its displeasure. It is far better for the parties to cooperate at the earlier stage with a view to modifying a Court's prior order so that all factual matters that need to be aired at trial can be done so in an efficient manner. With regard to cooperation the duty of legal advisors is to cooperate with the Court. It can be no justification for a failure to agree sensible directions to say that the relationship between the party's advisors is not a good one (as was submitted to me on the facts of the present case). A Court is entitled to expect legal advisors to cooperate in a pragmatic and sensible manner."

13–017   **When should the court exercise its powers under r.32.2(3)?** The most appropriate time for the court to exercise its powers to limit the number, scope or length of factual witness statements is at an early CMC. At that stage it is possible, in appropriate cases, to save the parties from incurring the (possibly huge) costs of preparing superfluous statements. Even at a late stage, however, as illustrated in *MacLennan*, the court may still exercise its powers under r.32.2(3). In the interests of their respective clients, the legal teams on all sides and the judge should at each stage endeavour to ensure that the factual evidence will be focused upon the real issues in the case.

(ii) *Expert evidence*

13–018   **New rules regarding expert reports.** The Rule Committee amended CPR 35.4, with effect from 1 April 2013, to read as follows:[3]

---

[3] The current sub-rules (3B) and (3C) were later additions to establish fixed costs for certain medical reports, as proposed in FR Ch. 15, para. 5.22. See Ch. 19, below.

"(1) No party may call an expert or put in evidence an expert's report without the court's permission.

(2) When parties apply for permission they must provide an estimate of the costs of the proposed expert evidence and identify—

  (a) the field in which expert evidence is required and the issues which the expert evidence will address; and
  (b) where practicable, the name of the proposed expert.

(3) If permission is granted it shall be in relation only to the expert named or the field identified under paragraph (2). The order granting permission may specify the issues which the expert evidence should address.

(3A) Where a claim has been allocated to the small claims track or the fast track, if permission is given for expert evidence, it will normally be given for evidence from only one expert on a particular issue.
. . .
(4) The court may limit the amount of a party's expert's fees and expenses that may be recovered from any other party."

Judicial guidance. There is a wealth of judicial guidance on the need to control expert evidence. This book is not an anthology of case law. Nevertheless, the recent Tobacco Litigation is a good example of a case with voluminous and complex expert evidence: *R (British American Tobacco (UK) Ltd) v Secretary of State for Health* [2016] EWHC 1169 (Admin). Green J discussed the need for effective case management and judicial supervision of the expert evidence (at [633]–[643]). **13–019**

Concurrent evidence pilot. A procedure for concurrent expert evidence was piloted in the Manchester specialist courts between 2010 and 2013. HHJ David Waksman QC, the Manchester Mercantile Judge, oversaw the pilot. The pilot was voluntary, but a number of practitioners and experts were willing to take part. Judge Waksman held meetings with practitioners (some of which I attended) in order to develop the procedures and gain feedback. Professor Dame Hazel Genn of UCL monitored the pilot. She wrote up her findings in the *Civil Justice Quarterly*.[4] **13–020**

Incorporation of concurrent evidence into the CPR. With effect from 1 April 2013, the following provision was added to PD 35: **13–021**

"11.1 At any stage in the proceedings the court may direct that some or all of the experts from like disciplines shall give their evidence concurrently. The following procedure shall then apply.

11.2 The court may direct that the parties agree an agenda for the taking of concurrent evidence, based upon the areas of disagreement identified in the experts' joint statements made pursuant to rule 35.12.

11.3 At the appropriate time the relevant experts will each take the oath or affirm. Unless the court orders otherwise, the experts will then address the items on the agenda in the manner set out in paragraph 11.4.

11.4 In relation to each issue on the agenda, and subject to the judge's discretion to modify the procedure—

---

[4] "Getting to the truth: experts and judges in the 'hot tub'" (2013) 32 CJQ 275–299.

(1) the judge may initiate the discussion by asking the experts, in turn, for their views. Once an expert has expressed a view the judge may ask questions about it. At one or more appropriate stages when questioning a particular expert, the judge may invite the other expert to comment or to ask that expert's own questions of the first expert;

(2) after the process set out in (1) has been completed for all the experts, the parties' representatives may ask questions of them. While such questioning may be designed to test the correctness of an expert's view, or seek clarification of it, it should not cover ground which has been fully explored already. In general a full cross-examination or re-examination is neither necessary nor appropriate; and

(3) after the process set out in (2) has been completed, the judge may summarise the experts' different positions on the issue and ask them to confirm or correct that summary."

13–022   **Well that's splendid, but is anyone actually using the concurrent expert evidence procedure?** In May 2016, my judicial assistant carried out a short and informal survey of practitioners and judges, mainly in the TCC field. Of those who responded, there was a diverse range of responses. Some practitioners and judges had never received training, never had the chance to use the concurrent evidence procedure and did not expect to use it soon. Some found themselves in the middle ground of increasing exposure and were still getting to grips with the process. At the other end of the spectrum, there was positively enthusiastic uptake.

13–023   **Comments of a TCC circuit judge.** One experienced circuit judge who hears TCC cases at a court centre away from the Rolls Building writes:

"I use hot tubbing regularly. Indeed it is the rule rather than the exception in my court. It is only where there are only one or two discrete issues for the experts (which is a rare case) that I adopt the 'standard procedure', and even then I make a point of having the experts back to back (which practitioners prefer and helps keep the costs of the experts' attendance to a minimum.)

My experience is that construction professionals engage very well with each other, and on occasion will debate a point constructively together leaving the lawyers as interested onlookers. . . .

It helps, of course, that both in the fields of Party Wall Appeals and Tree Root damage cases many experts in the field know each other (and the judge). However my good experience with hot tubbing extends to construction cases where the experts have not met before and are previously unknown to me. I am a firm fan."

13–024   **The experience of a Chancery Division judge.** One Chancery Division judge, who was approached in the recent informal survey, has used the procedure twice since it was introduced. The first case involved a dispute about whether some 50 items of heavy equipment were fixtures. The second case involved a dispute between three parties about defects, breaches of the Building Regulations and remedial costs. The judge's experience in both cases was very positive. He believed that the procedure saved time and focused the expert evidence in a constructive manner.

13–025   **Recent use in a recent competition case.** Mr Justice Roth recently made use of concurrent expert evidence in the competition law case, *Streetmap.EU Ltd v.*

Google Inc. [2016] EWHC 253 (Ch). He found that it not only saved time, but also helped highlight the differences between the experts: see [47] and the discussion at [132] onwards. This is the first time that concurrent expert evidence has been used in a competition law matter. Its use in this field may well expand in the future.

Does concurrent expert evidence mean more work for the judge? Yes. The   **13–026** judge needs to read the expert evidence thoroughly and get on top of the issues before the process starts. On the other hand, that is not a bad thing. The judge will have to master the expert evidence sooner or later anyway. If he or she does so before the experts enter the witness box and then hears their evidence concurrently, the process of judgment writing will be much easier.

How much costs does this procedure save? Difficult to say, because the   **13–027** judges and practitioners consulted did not usually descend to this level of detail. One judge in the recent survey did quantify the saving. He wrote:

"I have only hot tubbed in one 15 day TCC trial. The quantum and building surveying experts were hot tubbed (by discipline) and I felt that considerable time was saved — 2 days were spent with each pair, and I thought that at least double that time might have been spent if each had given evidence separately."

A straw poll of chambers. During May 2016, one major set of construction   **13–028** chambers asked its members for their experience of concurrent expert evidence. There were 15 responses. Seven respondents spoke favourably (or very favourably) about the procedure. Three were critical of the procedure. Four talked generally about the procedure without commenting on its utility or drawbacks. One (who gets the prize for candour) said he had forgotten that the procedure exists.

Will concurrent expert evidence ever catch on more widely in England   **13–029** **and Wales?** Yes, it probably will. It is striking that the majority of those who are hostile to the procedure are judges or practitioners who have never used it (or perhaps only used it once). Most, but certainly not all, judges and practitioners who have used the procedure are supportive.

Incidental points. It became clear from recent responses that some judges stick   **13–030** fairly closely to the procedure set out in section 11 of PD 35, whereas other judges develop that procedure in ways that suit their particular cases. As noted above, in any litigation where there is concurrent expert evidence, the judge must prepare more thoroughly than for an adversarial trial. This is because the judge has a more inquisitorial role. If there is a live transcript (as in *Streetmap*), this is of considerable assistance.

Civil Justice Council review. A CJC working group (chaired by Professor   **13–031** Rachael Mulheron) is currently reviewing the use of concurrent expert evidence in the light of experience to date. It is quite likely that following that review the CJC will propose improvements to the procedure.

13–032   **Conclusion.** It is hoped that the use of concurrent evidence will increase as the benefits become more widely appreciated. Perhaps younger practitioners (for whose benefit this book is principally written) may persuade judges to make use of the procedure more often. As legal systems go, England and Wales are not that different from Australia.

13–033   **Linkage with other FR reforms.** The reforms concerning expert and factual evidence link in with the various case management reforms discussed in Chs 11 and 12, above. Additionally, and self-evidently, there is a link between the new r.35.4 (limitation of future expert costs, when granting permission for expert evidence) and costs management.

COSTS MANAGEMENT

1. BACKGROUND

Development of case management. As discussed in Ch. 11, above, Lord **14–001**
Woolf's reforms gave the court a central role in the management of civil litigation. The concept was that the court should get a grip on the case at an early
stage. The court should focus the parties on the real issues and give directions leading up to trial or settlement. This was unquestionably a positive
development.

The logical consequence. One logical consequence of the Woolf reforms **14–002**
(once they had bedded in) was this. If the court, rather than the parties, was managing the litigation, then the court should do so with an eye on the costs involved.
If the court is going to direct three expert witnesses on each side and extensive
disclosure of documents, the court needs to know what those directions will cost
the parties. The court must also be satisfied that it is reasonable and proportionate for the parties to expend that level of costs on procedural steps. In a claim for
£200,000, for example, it would be absurd to direct the parties to take procedural
steps which will cost each side £1 million.

The position in 2009. The position in 2009 was that, save in exceptional **14–003**
cases, the court did not attempt to control costs in advance. The exceptional
cases were those where the courts made "costs capping" orders. That regime
was problematic. It was seldom invoked in practice and even then only in group
actions. In the general run of cases, the solicitors on both sides charged their
clients on an hourly rate basis. They added up the costs at the end. The winning
party then recovered as much as it could on detailed assessment. By the time of
detailed assessment, the money had been spent and it was too late to say: "this or
that piece of work did not need to be done". Of course the costs judge can disal-
low items, but it is unsatisfactory after the event to tell someone what costs they
should not have incurred. It is also unsatisfactory for the losing party to learn—
after the event—what work someone else was doing at his expense.

Horror stories. In the course of the Costs Review, there were many horror **14–004**
stories about cases where costs had mushroomed out of control. One typical

example was the small boundary dispute. In such a case, the losing party could end up selling their home in order to pay both sides' costs.

2. Debate during the Costs Review

14–005   **Chapter 48 of the Preliminary Report.** PR Ch. 48 raised the question of whether the court should manage costs in conjunction with managing the litigation. The chapter explained how this would fit within the general scheme of the CPR. The chapter reviewed earlier proposals for costs budgeting, which had been advanced by Professors Zuckerman and Peysner. Lord Woolf had considered those proposals but not pursued them because of the general outcry from the profession. Since then, however, the courts have gained experience dealing with summary assessments as well as costs capping and costs estimates in accordance with the provisions of the Costs Practice Direction. Chapter 48 concluded with six questions for consultation, the most important being: "(i) Should costs management become a feature of or adjunct to case management?"

14–006   **Consultation period.** The issues surrounding costs management were the subject of much debate during Phase Two of the Costs Review. Two firms of solicitors (Pinsent Masons LLP and Olswang LLP) demonstrated their budgeting software to the Costs Review team. On 26 May 2009, I attended a meeting of the Users' Committee of the Birmingham specialist courts. After a debate about the topic, they voted by a majority to participate in a voluntary pilot of costs management. That pilot duly started on 1 June. A separate pilot of costs management in defamation cases commenced in London on 1 October 2009. This was a mandatory pilot governed by a practice direction.

14–007   **Submissions during Phase Two.** The submissions on this issue (as on much else) were sharply divided. The Association of HM District Judges broadly supported the proposals for costs management. The Council of HM Circuit Judges opposed the proposal. The Bar Council also opposed the notion of the court managing costs. The Law Society, however, supported the idea.

14–008   **Law Society submission.** The Law Society dealt with the issues thoughtfully and in a balanced way. In the course of its paper, the Law Society stated:

> "The Law Society's Civil Justice Committee supports Professor Peysner's approach to the project management of litigation and some of its members have worked with him in developing those ideas. Support was also shown for the concept at the Law Society's Multi Track event in February 2009 which Jackson LJ attended.
> In commercial litigation a database of hours per task is more elusive as the cases vary so much. However, this does not mean an allocation of time cannot be made. The database reposes within the collective experience of practitioners who apply their professional experience.
> The Law Society agrees with the points made about a possible approach in Chapter 48 paragraphs 3.15–3.20 inclusive of the preliminary report. However, such project management will come at a price as budgets/estimates take time to prepare and authorise which will add to the costs of a case. . ."

The Law Society went on to conclude that the costs generated by costs budgeting were "likely to be offset by real savings if the budgeting regime is applied effectively". The Law Society also emphasised the importance of proper judicial training in costs management.

3. RECOMMENDATIONS IN THE FINAL REPORT OF JANUARY 2010

Chapter 40 of the Final Report. FR Ch. 40 described the costs management pilot which had been established at the Birmingham specialist courts, and summarised the initial results of that pilot. The chapter contained an extensive review of the arguments which had been deployed during Phase Two, both at meetings and in written submissions. The chapter also summarised the conclusions of a costs management working group. The group was supportive of the new discipline.   14–009

Overall conclusion. Chapter 40 of the Final Report reached the overall conclusion that costs management should be pursued, but cautiously and after proper training. Paragraph 7.17 of FR Ch. 40 stated: 14–010

"*A gradualist approach.* In my view, the correct way forward is to adopt a gradualist approach. First there needs to be an effective training programme, as discussed above. At the same time rules should be drafted, setting out a standard costs management procedure, which judges would have a discretion to adopt if and when they see fit, either of their own motion or upon application by one of the parties. At least in the early stages, I think it would be wrong to make costs management a compulsory procedure.

What is costs management? The essence of costs management is as follows:
(i)   At the start of the case each party files a costs budget for the action.
(ii) The parties exchange budgets, endeavour to agree them and lodge them with the court.
(iii) The court then decides whether to make a costs management order.
(iv) If the court makes a costs management order:

(a) The court will examine the parties' budgets (in so far as they are not agreed), make any necessary amendments and then approve them.
(b) Thereafter the court will manage the litigation in accordance with the approved budgets, but with a power to amend the budgets if there is good reason to do so.
(c) At the end of the case the successful party will recover costs in accordance with its approved budget, unless there is some good reason to disregard that budget.

(v)   If the court does not make a costs management order, then the 'old rules' governing costs estimates apply. The court does not approve the budgets. Nevertheless, at the end of the case the successful party will have to provide justification for any bill of costs which exceeds their budget by more than 20%."[1]

Recommendations. Chapter 40 of the Final Report ended with four recommendations: 14–011

---

[1] See now PD 44, subsection 3.

"(i) The linked disciplines of costs budgeting and costs management should be included in CPD training for those solicitors and barristers who undertake civil litigation.
(ii) Costs budgeting and costs management should be included in the training offered by the JSB[2] to judges who sit in the civil courts.
(iii) Rules should set out a standard costs management procedure, which judges would have a discretion to adopt if and when they see fit, either of their own motion or upon application by one of the parties.
(iv) Primary legislation should enable the Rule Committee to make rules for pre-issue costs management."

As will be seen from the following pages, recommendation (iv) in that list has never been implemented. It may be implemented in the future. Alternatively, the view may be taken that pre-issue costs management does not require primary legislation.

4. IMPLEMENTATION

14–012   **Pilots.** Following the publication of the Final Report, successive pilots were established to try out the proposed rules. Chapter 4 of this book summarises the pilots. They generated much useful information, which fed into the rule drafting process.

14–013   **Rule drafting.** In late 2011 and early 2012, I put before the Rule Committee successive drafts of costs management rules which accorded with the description of costs management set out above. The Rule Committee approved the proposed rules in March 2012. In particular, the draft rules made costs management a discretionary process and exempted the Commercial Court.

14–014   **Subsequent decision.** Subsequently, a decision was taken to make costs management (in effect) a mandatory process for all cases within certain financial limits. Thereafter, there was debate about what the financial limits should be and whether the Commercial Court should be exempt. Since the Commercial Court, the TCC and the Chancery Division had a substantial overlap in their fields of work, it was not practicable for them to have different rules in respect of costs management. Accordingly, an exemption for the Commercial Court could not be maintained. The upper financial limit for mandatory costs management was in due costs set at £10 million.

14–015   **Comment on the decision to make costs management mandatory.** Although that decision was contrary to my recommendation, it was a decision which the Rule Committee reached with the best of intentions. The thinking was that, if costs management was a good thing, all litigants should have the benefit of it.

---

[2] The Judicial Studies Board ("JSB") has now become the Judicial College.

The costs management rules. These are contained in CPR Pt 3 at rr. 3.12 to **14–016**
3.18, and in PD 3E. These provisions have undergone a number of amendments
as experience accumulated.

Evaluation of costs management. Since costs management is a new discipline **14–017**
which at the time of writing has been in place for three years, it may be appropriate to carry out an evaluation. This is best done by identifying the benefits and
drawbacks of the procedure in practice.

5. Benefits of Costs Management

Conclusion from the first three years of costs management. The first and **14–018**
most important conclusion to be drawn from the experience of the last three years
is the same as that which was drawn from the pilots. Costs management works.
When an experienced judge or master costs manages litigation with competent
practitioners on both sides, the costs of the litigation are controlled from an early
stage. Although some practitioners and judges regard the process as tiresome, it
brings substantial benefits to court users.

First benefit of costs management: knowledge of the financial position. Both **14–019**
sides know where they stand financially. They have clarity as to (a) what they will
recover if they win (difference between own actual and recoverable costs), and (b)
what they will pay if they lose (own actual costs + other parties' recoverable costs).
In many cases, the litigation costs form a substantial part of what the parties are
arguing about. This information is of obvious benefit for those making decisions
about the future conduct of litigation. Practitioners say the information is extremely
helpful in the context of mediation. Insurers (who in practice end up footing many
litigation bills) also find costs budgets valuable for the purpose of setting reserves.

Views of third-party funders about this benefit. Third-party funders, who play **14–020**
an increasing role in facilitating access to justice, attach particular importance to the
first benefit. They require budgets for their own costs in every case and, wherever
possible, seek costs management orders. Their contracts often link funding to the
court-approved budgets. An experienced QC, who does much work in this field,
states that he does not know of a single funder which dislikes costs management.

Comments of others on this benefit. Most solicitors, including many who **14–021**
are otherwise hostile to costs management, accept that the knowledge gained
is helpful for their clients. The Chief Chancery Master has commented that this
knowledge justifies the requirement to exchange budgets, regardless of whether
or not it reduces costs.

Comments of the Senior Costs Judge. Senior Costs Judge Gordon-Saker **14–022**
stated in his lecture to the Commercial Litigation Association on 1 October 2014:

"Litigation is like a train journey. You cannot get off the train, without injury, unless
everybody else agrees that the train can stop before its destination. Yet if you stay on the

train to the end of the journey, you will only know the cost of the journey after you get off. So we need costs budgeting as a matter of fairness to litigants. . . [He then discussed the lack of court resources and the need for more judicial training.] That said, I am told that – although different judges are taking different approaches to costs budgeting – people are generally happy with the overall results."

14–023   **Second benefit of costs management: it encourages early settlement.** One intractable problem of civil litigation has been that cases which are destined to settle often drag on for far too long before the parties come to terms. Chapter 4 of the Final Report identified this as one of the 14 causes of excessive litigation costs. The new costs management regime makes a contribution to tackling this problem, in that it encourages early settlement. Once all parties can see (a) the total costs of the litigation and (b) the extent of their own exposure, they are inclined to "see sense" or bite the bullet early. Numerous practitioners have confirmed this.

14–024   **Third benefit of costs management: controlling costs.** When costs management is done properly, it controls costs from an early stage. This is for two reasons:

    (i) In some cases,[3] the very act of preparing a budget, which will be subject to critical scrutiny, tempers behaviour. Any party who puts forward an over-elaborate case plan or an excessive budget (a) invites criticism and (b) encourages similar extravagance by the other party/parties.

    (ii) Effective costs management by the court generally reduces the costs payable by the losing party. It also brings down the actual costs of the litigation for both parties, despite the additional costs involved in the costs management process.

14–025   **Interface with the new rules on proportionate costs.** Chapter 40, section 7 of the Final Report discusses how the new proportionality rules interrelate with costs management. Rule 44.3(5) contains a new definition of proportionate costs. Rule 44.3(2) provides that when costs are assessed on the standard basis, no more than proportionate costs will be recoverable. Therefore, the judge at the costs management stage applies the proportionality test and limits the budgets accordingly.[4] It is by no means unusual for a judge to say that (regardless of hourly rates or numbers of hours) no more than £x is proportionate for a particular phase, or that no more than £y is proportionate for the case as a whole. Absent an order for indemnity costs, no losing party should be ordered to pay more than proportionate costs to its adversary.

14–026   **Is it a problem that the winner may recover less costs than in the past?** No. There is extensive academic literature and research to demonstrate that the costs shifting rule tends to drive up costs: see PR Ch. 9. If the 2013 civil justice reforms make a modest inroad into that rule, it is no bad thing. Once people know that they

---

[3] Except QOCS cases, where claimants generally feel no such inhibitions.
[4] Professor Zuckerman argues that the success or failure of costs management will turn upon how the courts apply the proportionality test: *Zuckerman on Civil Procedure*, pp. 1458–1462.

will only recover proportionate costs if they win, they have a greater incentive to be economical.

Fourth benefit of costs management: it focuses attention on costs at the outset of litigation. A number of solicitors and judges have drawn attention to this benefit. In the majority of cases, costs are a major factor. A failure by the victor to recover sufficient costs may render the whole litigation futile.[5] The costs burden on the loser may be crushing, quite regardless of the damages which he may have to pay or the property rights which he may forfeit. It is therefore necessary that all concerned should be forced to focus on the costs involved at the outset.   14–027

Fifth benefit of costs management: an old chestnut is conquered. The "summons for directions" under the pre-1999 RSC was intended to be an occasion when the court would get a grip on the issues and give effective directions. The habitual complaint was that in practice this never happened. Summonses for directions were formulaic and ineffectual. The new style "case management conference" introduced by Lord Woolf was intended to overcome all that and be a real occasion for effective case management. The evidence gathered during the 2009 Costs Review suggested that, outside the specialist courts, this still was not happening. CMCs were simply becoming formulaic occasions. Chapters 37–39 of the Final Report put forward a series of proposals to convert CMCs into effective occasions when the judge   14–028

> "takes a grip on the case, identifies the issues and gives directions which are focused upon the early resolution of those issues".[6]

As discussed in Ch. 11, above, one consequence of costs management is that this is now happening. Price tags attached to the work focus attention on the question of whether certain items of work really need to be done at all.

Sixth benefit of costs management: elementary fairness. It is elementary fairness to give the opposition notice of what you are claiming. The rules require litigants to set out with precision the damages which they seek. Why treat costs differently? From the point of view of the client, costs are often just as important as damages.   14–029

Seventh benefit of costs management: it prevents legal catastrophes. A regional costs judge in Bristol makes the following point about costs management: 14–030

> "It protects losing parties (particularly the 'real' people, as opposed to insurance companies in PI claims) from being destroyed by costs when they lose."

Practitioners are now coping with the new regime. The introduction of the new regime came as an unwelcome shock for many in the profession.   14–031

---

[5] This was the effect of the first instance decision in *Begum v Birmingham CC* [2015] EWCA Civ 386.

[6] FR Ch. 39, para. 5.5.

Nevertheless, a number of practitioners say that their initial fears have not been borne out. A clinical negligence practitioner in Leeds stated that the process has been a learning curve, but in general terms she is now getting reasonable budgets approved. A small firm in Newcastle stated that "costs management is now running fairly smoothly". The Treasury Solicitor's office has generally positive experience of costs budgeting, with one representative stating that he "much prefers" the new regime. AB, the head of the costs department of a major national firm doing claimant clinical negligence work, considers costs management "generally OK" and "a good thing", but he raised a number of specific points which require attention.[7]

14–032 **The proof of the pudding.** In a number of cases where costs management does not apply, one or other party asks the court to manage costs.[8] For example, the *Kenya Litigation* began before April 2013 and so is outside the new rules. There are numerous claimants and that litigation is highly complex. Both parties asked the assigned judge, Mr Justice Stewart, to undertake costs management and he agreed to do so. The *Iraqi Civilian Litigation* began long before April 2013. Nevertheless, as recorded in the Senior Master's judgment of 25 February 2016, both parties agreed that there should be some costs management. The parties differed as to the extent of the budgets which should be lodged for approval, given the advanced stage which the litigation had reached.[9]

6. DRAWBACKS OF COSTS MANAGEMENT

14–033 **Causes of complaint.** The following have emerged as causes of complaint:

(i) Differing approaches adopted by individual judges and courts.

(ii) Delays in listing costs and case management conferences ("CCMCs") as a result of the time spent on costs management, leading to a backlog of work.

(iii) No effective mechanism for controlling costs incurred before the first CCMC.

(iv) Difficulties at detailed assessment if costs budgets and bills of costs are in different formats.

(v) The process of costs management is expensive.

It may be helpful to deal with each of these matters separately.

---

[7] See Harbour Lecture on 13 May 2015. Readers are referred to this lecture, which is available on the Judiciary website, for a fuller analysis of all the issues surrounding costs management.

[8] *Sharp v Blank* [2015] EWHC 2685 Ch was a shareholders' claim for over £200 million. The claimants applied to the court to undertake costs management. Nugee J ordered the parties to exchange budgets. He left open whether he would make a costs management order, since this case was far above the £10 million threshold.

[9] Difficulties arose in the *Iraqi Civilian Litigation*, because the process of costs management had become separated from case management.

(i) Judicial inconsistency. One major city firm, while acknowledging the   **14–034**
benefits of costs management, wrote in 2015:

> "The inconsistent approach being taken by the judiciary, in terms of the detail in which
> costs budgets are examined and the processes involved, is also unhelpful. [Examples
> given.] In general it is unclear whether budgets will be addressed in any detail at the
> CMC, and the approach the court will take if there is to be a detailed consideration
> budgets."

Many practitioners in both London and the regions echoed those concerns.

The solution. The solution to this problem lies in effective judicial training. The   **14–035**
costs management training provided to all civil judges in early 2013 was necessarily brief, because there were many other aspects of the 2013 civil justice reforms to
be covered. Now, however, there is a full-day module on costs management available on judicial refresher courses. It is hoped that as many judges as possible are
taking advantage of this. There is also an excellent chapter on costs management
in the Practical Law Handbook, *Costs and Funding following the Civil Justice
Reforms: Questions & Answers*, which is published annually by Sweet & Maxwell.
Training material on costs management (prepared by District Judges Matharu and
Middleton) is made available to judges in the civil e-library. It is hoped that all
these materials will promote uniformity of approach by case managing judges.

(ii) Delays and backlog. As a result of rules making the procedure manda-   **14–036**
tory, courts have been making costs management orders in virtually every case.
At some court centres, that causes no problem. At others, it has caused delays as
backlogs of cases awaiting CCMCs build up. This problem became most acute in
clinical negligence cases in London. Such delays did not promote access to justice
at proportionate cost. On the contrary, they inhibited access to justice and tended
to drive up costs.

The short-term solution. In May 2015, I proposed that there should be mora-   **14–037**
torium for clinical negligence cases in London.[10] In other words, the Queen's
Bench masters should suspend costs management of clinical negligence cases
until they had caught up with the accumulated backlog. The Senior Master
accepted that recommendation and imposed a moratorium during the summer of
2015, which enabled her colleagues to clear the backlog.

The long-term solution. It is suggested that the rules making costs manage-   **14–038**
ment mandatory should be modified. In place of the current provisions, PD 3E
might set out criteria to guide the courts in deciding whether or not to make a
costs management order. The formulation of the criteria must be a matter for the
Rule Committee. But the committee should perhaps bear in mind the following
principles:

   (i) In most contested Pt 7 cases and in most cases of the type identified in PD
      3E para. 2, costs management by a competent judge or master promotes

---

[10] In the Harbour Lecture on 13 May 2015, section 5.

financial certainty and reduces the costs expended on the litigation to proportionate levels.

(ii) However, the court should not manage costs in any case if (a) it lacks the resources to do so, or (b) the costs management process would cause significant delay and disruption to that or other cases.

14–039 **Parties must still file budgets even if there is no costs management order.** If PD 3E is amended as suggested in the previous paragraph, the parties must still prepare budgets in all relevant cases. They will file their budgets before the court decides whether to make a costs management order. This is an important discipline for each party. It provides valuable information for opposing parties and the court. The filed budgets (even if not agreed or approved) will still exert some restraining effect on recoverable costs, as set out in section 3 of PD 44.

14–040 **(iii) No effective mechanism for dealing with costs already incurred.** There is a concern that in some cases substantial costs have already been incurred before the costs management conference. That is true. On the other hand, the court has a power to "comment" on incurred costs and such comment will carry weight at the detailed assessment. A sensible improvement would be to enable the court in appropriate cases (and when time allows) to make provisional or binding rulings about specific items of past costs. In the longer term, consideration must be given to some form of pre-action costs budgeting, as proposed in FR Ch. 40.

14–041 **General comment about incurred costs.** Even if the costs budgeting regime is ineffective for regulating past costs, it is still a highly worthwhile exercise. The mere fact that money has been wasted in the past is no reason to abandon cost control in the future. At the time of the first case management conference, there is still much to play for, including the future costs of disclosure, witness statements, expert reports, ADR and trial.

14–042 **(iv) Difficulties at detailed assessment.** Except in personal injury/clinical negligence litigation, it is relatively rare for cases which have been subject to costs management to proceed to detailed assessment. This is because the parties are usually able to reach agreement on the basis of the approved budgets. In respect of those cases which do go to detailed assessment, a number of practitioners and judges expressed concern that it was difficult to marry up the approved budget with the final bill of costs. The Rule Committee introduced a temporary solution to the problem in October 2015 in the form of Precedent Q. This enables the costs claimed in the bill to be represented in a form which matches up with the earlier budget.

14–043 **Long-term solution.** The long-term solution to this problem is to adopt the new form bill of costs, as described in Ch. 20, below. At the time of writing, this new form is currently being piloted and is therefore optional. It is hoped that in the future it will become mandatory. The new form bill of costs marries up precisely with Precedent H. It should be possible to complete the new form bill of costs, either using "J codes" or any other software which the solicitors find convenient.

(v) The expense of costs management. Undoubtedly, the costs management 14–044
process does itself have a cost. In precisely the same way, quantity surveyors and others who control the costs of building projects are themselves a costs centre. Nevertheless, if people carry out costs control procedures properly, there is an overall financial benefit. This is what the Law Society predicted during Phase Two of the Costs Review, when it was responding to the Preliminary Report.

Views of legal practitioners. Many legal practitioners, for perfectly under- 14–045
standable reasons, dislike the new discipline of costs management. They are inclined to say that the process should be scrapped because it drives up costs. But there is no empirical evidence to support this. The annual surveys conducted by the LSLA show that a majority of their members make that complaint. But even that majority is starting to diminish. In 2015, some 91% of members made that complaint. In 2016, the figure was 80%.[11]

7. OVERALL ASSESSMENT

Teething problems. There have undoubtedly been problems with the introduc- 14–046
tion of a new discipline, which was unfamiliar to both judges and practitioners. On the other hand, the system is now settling down. As observed by Sir William Blair, in his lecture on 21 January 2016 entitled "Contemporary trends in the resolution of international financial and commercial disputes":

> "The recently introduced costs budgeting rules introduced following Lord Justice Jackson's report require the court to approve the parties' budgets at an early stage in the proceedings, and are mandatory where the amount of the claim is below £10 million. Despite some teething problems, this seems to be settling down in Commercial Court practice."

Why then do quite a few lawyers dislike cost management? Because it 14–047
means more work and requires people to develop new skills.

Are the views of lawyers the litmus test? No, they are not. The civil justice 14–048
system exists to deliver civil justice to the public at proportionate cost, not to promote the contentment or convenience of lawyers.

Changing attitude of the judiciary. Many judges did not welcome the new 14–049
regime, when it came in. Despite that, there has been a softening of judicial opposition over the last three years, as judges have become more comfortable with the process and more skilful at it. Of course, certain judges still dislike the process and feel no inhibitions about saying so. To some extent this is a generational issue. Traditionally, the Bar, from which many judges are drawn, took no interest in costs. However, attitudes are changing. Younger judges have had experience arguing summary assessments when they were in practice. Some may even have practised at the Costs Bar, a sector which developed in the early years of the 21st

---

[11] See the LSLA's Litigation Trends Survey of June 2016.

century. An increasing number of judges were solicitors and have good background knowledge of costs. Those civil judges appointed since April 2013 must all have demonstrated ability and willingness to costs manage. Otherwise they would not have been suitable for appointment.

14–050   **Changing attitude of the profession.** Many practitioners dislike the process for a variety of reasons. This is especially true of (a) those practitioners who have only done costs management in a few cases, and (b) those who practise in courts where the process has caused delay or where the judges are less enthusiastic. All this is gradually changing. The extent of professional opposition is steadily declining. Many practitioners have spotted that clients like to know what their litigation is going to cost. To some extent, again, this is a generational issue. Younger practitioners are growing up under the new rules and have no difficulty with them.

14–051   **Law Society Gazette article.** On 4 April 2016, the Law Society Gazette published an article entitled "Jackson reforms: counting the cost". The article identified the problems discussed above. It quoted the Chair of the Association of Costs Lawyers ("ACL"):

> "As Master Cook recently pointed out, it seems that costs budgeting is starting to work [in some areas] where it is done properly. It needs to be given more time. You can't just introduce something as radical as predicting costs and expect that to filter through into savings so fast."

The point which the ACL Chair makes about costs management needing to bed down before it delivers benefits is a fair one. Therefore, it is important not to undermine costs management just at the time when the benefits are increasingly being felt.

14–052   **A balanced appraisal.** The same article quoted the President of the Forum of Insurance Lawyers ("FOIL"):

> "Overall budgeting has been a positive change. The courts are getting to grips with it and so are practitioners. The courts are not afraid to cut the budgets – sometimes quite dramatically – and so budgeting is working in that there is starting to be proper control of the costs. But there is still little or no control over incurred costs and there is a trend towards claimants doing a lot more work before they issue proceedings."

The FOIL President makes a fair point about lack of control over pre-issue costs. More judicial control is needed in this area.[12] Nevertheless, there is a great deal of work left to do after the first CMC. The FOIL President is right to say that costs management is an effective procedure for controlling the costs of all that work.

14–053   **What needs to be done now?** The rules governing when courts should undertake costs management require amendment, as discussed in section 6, above.

---

[12] Ideally, recommendation (iv) at the end of FR Ch. 40 should be implemented.

Pre-action costs management. Ultimately, the best way to control costs 14–054
incurred before the first CMC will be to (a) extend fixed recoverable costs, and
(b) introduce pre-action costs management for cases outside the fixed recoverable costs regime. The Final Report proposed that there should be a pilot of pre-
action costs management: see FR Ch. 23, section 6. This would have required the
appointment of an additional Queen's Bench master. In the event, no additional
master was appointed and the pilot did not proceed.

Conclusion. There are three main conclusions to be drawn from this chapter: 14–055

- Costs management may not be popular, but it is slowly bedding down. As
  it does so, the benefits of the process are becoming more apparent.

- It is quite likely that there will be fixed recoverable costs for cases in the
  lower reaches of the multi-track. When that happens, the volume of cases
  requiring costs management will diminish.

- Once the next round of reforms is complete, it will be appropriate to look
  again at pre-action costs management.

APPEALS

1. BACKGROUND

The Bowman Report. In October 1996, a full review of the civil division of **15–001** the Court of Appeal was instituted under the chairmanship of Sir Jeffery Bowman. The review team included Lord Woolf. Its report ("the Bowman Report") was published in September 1997. Its recommendations were along the lines foreshadowed by the Woolf Report, but were much more detailed. The report was backed by statistical research into the manner in which applications and appeals currently arrived at the Court of Appeal: see the "mapping study" at Appendix 7 to the Bowman Report. The review team also surveyed the procedures operated by appellate courts in Ontario, New York, San Francisco and Washington D.C. Those procedures are summarised in Appendix 2 to the Bowman Report.

The regime for appeals introduced in May 2000. The Bowman Report was **15–002** the basis for a completely new regime for appeals, which came into force on 2 May 2000. That regime is contained in CPR Pt 52. The necessary enabling legislation is in the Access to Justice Act 1999, principally at ss. 54 to 56. The following were significant features of the new regime:

- A unified set of rules governing all appeals, subject to specific modifications for particular categories, in particular appeals to the Court of Appeal.

- A permission requirement for almost all categories of appeal, initially to be deal with on paper but subject to oral renewal.

- A particularly strict test for second appeals.

General comments on the new regime. The changes which came into **15–003** effect on 2 May 2000 were described by Brooke LJ in *Tanfern Ltd v Cameron MacDonald (Practice Note)*[2000] EWCA Civ 3023; [2000] 1 WLR 1311 at [50] as "the most significant changes in the arrangements for appeals in civil proceedings in this country for 125 years". The reforms were, broadly speaking, welcomed by Professor Andrews in "A new system of civil appeals and a new set of problems" [2000] CLJ 464. Andrews noted that the Court of Appeal's law-making role would be enhanced; that the changes would reduce the delay, expense and uncertainty of civil proceedings; and that there would be a greater incentive for litigants to "get it right first time round". However, these changes would reduce the chances of rectifying defective decisions. That was the price paid for achieving the impressive benefits of the new system of appeals.

15–004 **Perceptions during the 2009 Costs Review.** Because of the excellent ground-work done by Sir Jeffery Bowman and his team, the general view during 2009 was that the new regime for appeals (then only nine years old) was working sat-isfactorily. There were, however, concerns about costs. One particular problem concerned appeals going up from a no-costs jurisdiction to a costs shifting jurisdiction.

15–005 **Illustration of the problem of appeals from a no-costs jurisdiction.** The problem was illustrated by the Court of Appeal's decision in *Eweida v British Airways plc* [2009] EWCA Civ 1025. The case concerned a claim by Miss Eweida that her employer, British Airways plc, had unlawfully discriminated against her on the grounds of her religious belief. The Employment Tribunal ("ET") dismissed the claimant's claim. The Employment Appeal Tribunal ("EAT") dis-missed her appeal. Both the ET and the EAT were no-costs regimes, so the claim-ant was at no risk as to British Airways' costs in those proceedings. The claimant then appealed to the Court of Appeal. She applied for an order that she should have no liability, alternatively a limited liability, for adverse costs in the event of losing the appeal. The Court of Appeal dismissed her application on the grounds that in the circumstances it did not have power to make either a protective costs order or a costs capping order.

15–006 **Comment.** This was an unsatisfactory state of affairs. Miss Eweida had a prop-erly arguable case. That was obvious, since she had obtained permission to appeal. The policy arguments in favour of letting each side bear their own costs were essentially the same in the Court of Appeal as they were in the EAT. Nevertheless, the Court of Appeal had no power to disapply the costs shifting rules.

2. RECOMMENDATIONS IN THE FINAL REPORT OF JANUARY 2010

15–007 **Chapter 34 of the Final Report.** FR Ch. 34 concluded that it was premature to embark upon any substantive reform of appeals with a view to controlling costs. This was for two reasons. First, the Final Report was recommending a wide range of reforms to the procedures for first instance litigation. It was necessary to await the outcome of those recommendations before overhauling appeals. Secondly, there had been a recent and thorough review of appellate procedures under Sir Jeffery Bowman. It was necessary to allow more time for those reforms to bed in before embarking on another round of appellate reforms.

15–008 **Appeals from no-cost jurisdictions.** Despite that general policy of abstinence, one issue could not be deferred. This was the problem of appeals moving from no-costs jurisdictions to costs shifting jurisdictions. By chance the *Eweida* case, which highlighted the issue, was decided on 15 October 2009. That was during the drafting period for the Final Report.

Proposed solution. Chapter 34 of the Final Report, para. 3.6 proposed the following solution to the problem:

> "Appellate courts should have a discretionary power, upon granting permission to appeal or receiving an appeal from a no-costs jurisdiction, to order (a) that each side should bear its own costs of the appeal or (b) that the recoverable costs should be capped at a specified sum. In exercising that discretion the court should have regard to (a) the means of both parties, (b) all the circumstances of the case and (c) the need to facilitate access to justice for any party which has good grounds to challenge or to support the decision under appeal."

15–009

Qualified one-way costs shifting in appeals. Paragraph 3.10 of FR Ch. 34 proposed that any QOCS regime introduced for first instance cases should also apply to appeals, including the Court of Appeal. That was not a controversial suggestion. Even those who opposed QOCS did not suggest that, if there was to be such a regime, it should be confined to first instance litigation.

15–010

Recommendation for a future review of appeals. Chapter 34 of the Final Report proposed that there should be a review of appeals at some future date, after the reforms recommended for first instance litigation had been implemented and bedded down. The chapter identified a number of issues for future consideration, including procedures for case management of appeals in Victoria.

15–011

Wasn't that ducking the issue? Well, yes and no. Undoubtedly, the Final Report refrained from proposing a broad package of reforms for appeals, similar to the package proposed for first instance litigation. On the other hand, appeals are a second stage in the litigation process. You cannot sensibly design the second stage of the process until you know what the first stage looks like. The proposals for reforming first instance litigation were likely to (and did) generate a storm of controversy. It was uncertain which of the proposals would survive the storm and which would be shipwrecked. In those circumstances it was sensible to defer for future consideration the question of how appellate procedure should be modified in order to promote access to justice at proportionate cost.

15–012

Possibility of a suitors' fund. One specific issue highlighted by Ch. 34 for future consideration was the possibility of establishing a suitors' fund. Paragraph 3.12 stated:

15–013

> "Where a litigant wins at first instance, but loses on appeal, he is likely to be ordered to pay the costs of the other party. It may be thought unjust that a litigant should be saddled with a huge costs bill because of errors made by the judge below. In New South Wales a "suitors' fund" has been established to provide for this contingency. Money for the fund comes out of court fees. Section 5 of the Suitors' Fund Act 1951 provides that money paid into the fund is not to exceed 10% of court fees collected. A party who wins below but loses on appeal may apply for a "suitors' fund certificate". If granted, such a certificate entitles that party to recover part of his costs from the fund."

Sadly, there is no prospect of the MoJ giving up any part of the (now excessive) court fees which it receives in order to establish such a fund. Nevertheless, there does remain a need to do something to alleviate the position of victorious parties at first instance, who may be dragged up to the Court of Appeal and then pay a high price for their Pyrrhic victory below.

3. IMPLEMENTATION

15–014   **Appeals moving up from no-costs jurisdictions.** Dealing with the principal problem identified in FR Ch. 34 was not as easy as it sounded. What about appeals moving up from low costs regimes into the full rigour of judicial costs shifting? At what stage should the restriction upon recoverable costs be set? And upon what criteria? What about test cases? Which appellate courts should the new rule apply to? Initial drafts of the new rule came under close scrutiny from the Rule Committee. The committee rightly sent me away more than once to undertake some re-drafting.

15–015   **CPR Rule 52.9A.** The final product of the drafting process was r.52.9A, which was added to CPR Pt 52 with effect from 1 April 2013. That provides:

> "(1) In any proceedings in which costs recovery is normally limited or excluded at first instance, an appeal court may make an order that the recoverable costs of an appeal will be limited to the extent which the court specifies.
> (2) In making such an order the court will have regard to—
>
>   (a) the means of both parties;
>   (b) all the circumstances of the case; and
>   (c) the need to facilitate access to justice.
>
> (3) If the appeal raises an issue of principle or practice upon which substantial sums may turn, it may not be appropriate to make an order under paragraph (1).
> (4) An application for such an order must be made as soon as practicable and will be determined without a hearing unless the court orders otherwise."

15–016   **Use of the new rule in practice.** There is no statistical evidence as to how often appellate courts are making orders under r.52.9A. In the Court of Appeal, however, I have seen a significant number of cases in which orders have been made precisely in accordance with the intention of that rule.

15–017   **One practical problem.** One practical problem arises from r.52.9A (4). This provision is necessary because any party against whom an order is made under the rule needs to know its position at an early stage. On the other hand, litigants in person may not be aware of the rule or of the need to apply for costs protection at an early stage. Yet litigants in person are the very people who have most need of protection under the rule.

15–018   **The solution.** Rule 3.1A of the CPR came into force on 1 October 2015. This rule requires courts to manage cases with particular regard for the needs of litigants in person ("LIPs"). In the light of that rule, surely any court considering an application for permission to appeal made by a LIP should specifically draw the litigant's attention to the provisions of r.52.9A?

Suggested amendment to Guidelines for LIP cases. The Bar Council, the   **15–019**
CILEx and the Law Society have jointly prepared valuable guidance entitled
Litigants in Person: Guidelines for Lawyers. Might those bodies consider making
an amendment to address the present problem? Should it not be the professional
obligation of lawyers involved in an appeal to draw the attention of any unrepre-
sented party to the provisions of r.52.9A? If the lawyers fail to do so, that should
be a highly material factor when the court is considering whether to reject an
application under that rule on the grounds of lateness.

Qualified one-way costs shifting in appeals. *Parker v Butler* [2016] EWHC   **15–020**
1251 (QB) was a personal injuries action in which the claimant failed at trial
before the circuit judge and failed again on appeal to the High Court judge.
Despite that gloomy result, the claimant's case was not a hopeless one. The fact
that he secured permission to appeal meant that he had a real prospect of success.
Edis J held that the QOCS regime applied on appeal. Accordingly, the costs order
which he made against the claimant was not enforceable. That decision is in
accordance with the intention of the reforms: see section 2, above.

4. THE FUTURE

Recent consultation. In May and June 2016, there was a consultation exer-   **15–021**
cise about a package of reforms designed to reduce the workload of the Court of
Appeal. This exercise was part of Briggs LJ's review and was foreshadowed in
Ch. 9 of his Interim Report. The consultation has come about because the Court
of Appeal is currently overburdened with work. The workload of the court has
increased by 59% over the last five years. The backlog of cases waiting to be
heard is growing. Waiting times for hearings are getting longer. The principal
proposals which were subject to consultation were:

- Raising the threshold for the grant of permission to appeal to the Court of
  Appeal. The suggested criterion is "a substantial prospect of success".

- Removing the right to oral renewal. The suggestion is there should only be
  an oral hearing of a permission application if the lord/lady justice considering the matter on the papers decides that an oral hearing is necessary.

In July 2016, the Rule Committee adopted the second of those proposals. This
again will come into force in October 2016.

Comment. Undoubtedly, measures to reduce the Court of Appeal's backlog are   **15–022**
necessary. It remains to be seen whether the current proposals are too restrictive.
The recent exercise naturally forms part of Briggs LJ's Review of the Structure of
the Civil Courts. The target of that review is different from (but just as important
as) the target of the 2009 Review of Civil Litigation Costs. The objective of the
2009 Review was to find means of reducing costs for litigants, while promoting
access to justice.

15–023   **Not yet time for a comprehensive review of the procedures and costs rules for appeals.** As noted in section 2 above, the Final Report recommended that there should be a future review of appellate procedures and costs rules. Chapter 34 of the Final Report recommended that this review should not take place until the various reforms of first instance litigation had bedded in. This has not yet happened. For example, the rules for costs management are still being tweaked. The introduction of fixed costs as recommended in FR Chs 15 and 16 is still work in progress. The new form bill of costs is still being piloted.

15–024   **Does that mean we can put off the review indefinitely?** No. The Principle of Unripe Time, so eloquently formulated by Professor Cornford,[1] does not apply. The time for a review of appellate procedures and costs rules will come within the next few years.

15–025   **Should there be costs management for appeals?** Whichever future lord or lady justice has the good fortune to undertake that general review may care to consider whether there should be costs management for appeals. There is no reason why a party seeking permission to appeal should not lodge a budget of the anticipated costs of the appeal. The respondent could do the same when lodging its respondent's notice (or when the time for doing so expires). The appellate court could then have a discretion whether to manage the costs of the appeal or simply to leave the budgets on the table for the information of all parties.

15–026   **The first step has already been taken.** The new r.52.9A, which involves controlling costs in advance for a limited category of appeals, is a first step towards introducing costs management for appeals. This may provide some encouragement for any future reformer.

---

[1] In *Microcosmographia Academica.*

Part Five

PARTICULAR CATEGORIES OF LITIGATION

CHAPTER 16

QUALIFIED ONE-WAY COSTS SHIFTING IN PERSONAL INJURY LITIGATION AND POSSIBLY OTHER AREAS

1. BACKGROUND

Costs shifting. Costs shifting is the term used to describe a regime in which **16–001** the losing party in litigation pays the assessed costs of the winning party. England and Wales are a costs shifting jurisdiction. Many US states are not. There has been much academic research on the economics of costs shifting and how the presence or absence of costs shifting affects the conduct of parties. Chapter 9 of the Preliminary Report provides a summary of that research.

What is one-way costs shifting? One-way costs shifting is the term used to **16–002** describe a regime in which one party (usually the claimant) recovers costs if it wins, but does not pay the other party's costs if it loses. That is a very pleasant position for any litigant to be in.

Section 11(1) of the 1999 Act. If a legally-aided person loses an action, s.11(1) **16–003** of the Access to Justice Act 1999 substantially protects him against liability for adverse costs. Section 11(1) provides, so far as material:

> "11(1) Except in prescribed circumstances, costs ordered against an individual in relation to any proceedings or part of proceedings funded for him shall not exceed the amount (if any) which is a reasonable one for him to pay having regard to all the circumstances including:
>
> (a) the financial resources of all the parties to the proceedings, and
> (b) their conduct in connection with the dispute to which the proceedings relate. . ."

Provisions in similar form have protected legally-aided parties ever since the introduction of the Legal Aid and Advice Act 1949. A convenient term for this protection is "the legal aid shield". It is a form of one-way costs shifting.

The position of personal injury claimants up to April 2000. For 50 years, **16–004** legal aid was available for PI cases and the vast majority of PI claimants brought their claims on legal aid. If they won (as most claimants did), they recovered their costs from the defendant's insurers and reimbursed the legal aid fund. If they lost, they were protected by the legal aid shield.

16–005   **The change in April 2000.** In April 2000, legal aid ceased to be available for PI cases. In its place, the Government established the new regime of recoverable ATE premiums and CFAs with recoverable success fees, as discussed in Ch. 5, above. From April 2000, onwards the vast majority of PI claimants proceeded on CFAs with ATE cover. Even wealthy claimants (who would not have qualified for legal aid by reason of the means test) often chose to proceed using CFAs and ATE. There has never been any means test for CFAs and ATE cover. Legal aid remained available for clinical negligence cases between April 2000 and April 2013, but many clinical negligence claimants chose to proceed using CFAs and ATE.

16–006   **The role of recoverable ATE premiums.** The principal function[1] of ATE is to protect the insured party against liability for adverse costs. The policy is normally structured so that if the case is lost no premium is payable, but if the case is won an enhanced premium is payable. The enhancement reflects the fact that no premium would have been paid if the case had failed.

16–007   **The problem with recoverable ATE premiums.** Recoverable ATE premiums achieved a form of one-way costs shifting, but they did so in a most inefficient way. The data collected during Phase One of the Costs Review graphically demonstrated this. Chapter 25 of the Preliminary Report sets out the figures obtained from insurer "X". It can be seen from section 2 of that chapter that during 2008, insurer X paid out about £3 million in ATE premiums on cases which it lost. In the relatively few cases which X won, it recovered costs from the claimants' ATE insurers totalling about £250,000. Self-evidently, X would be better off in a world where (a) X paid out normal costs in cases which it lost (but no ATE premiums on top) and (b) X recovered no costs in cases which it won. Indeed X would have been about £2,750,000 better off. Recoverable ATE premiums are the most expensive form of one-way costs shifting which it is possible to devise.

16–008   **Why is recoverable ATE insurance such an expensive form of one-way costs shifting?** There is no such thing as a free lunch. Defendants pay a high price for the ability to recover costs in the cases which they win. This is because ATE insurers set the premiums at a level to (a) cover their own overheads, salaries, etc, and (b) make a profit. Furthermore, in a regime in which the insured party never pays the ATE premiums, there is no effective control over the level of those premiums. This was a point which the Law Society made in its response to the Final Report (at pp. 21, 22)[2]:

> "There can be no doubt that ATE premiums are a major contributor towards legal costs over which solicitors have no control. . . . There appears to be a substantial lack of transparency in the ATE market.
> . . . The price of ATE insurance is currently prohibitive".

16–009   **The challenge.** The great majority of PI claimants are persons of moderate means, who cannot afford to pay out adverse costs if they lose their claims. In

---

[1] A subsidiary function of ATE is to cover certain disbursements if the insured loses or discontinues.
[2] *Review of Civil Litigation Costs Final Report: response by the Law Society*, October 2010.

those circumstances, one of the challenges for the Costs Review was to find a way of protecting PI claimants against adverse costs, while bringing to an end the prohibitively expensive regime of recoverable ATE premiums.

Analysis in the Preliminary Report. Chapter 25 of the Preliminary Report   **16–010** identified the problem. It invited consultees to consider whether there should be some form of one-way costs shifting for PI claims.

2. RECOMMENDATIONS IN THE FINAL REPORT OF JANUARY 2010

The conflicting views. Chapter 19 of the Final Report summarised the conflict-   **16–011** ing arguments and opinions which consultees had expressed in response to PR Ch. 25. Amongst court users and practitioners, there was a wide spread of views on the question of one-way costs shifting. Some respondents supported the proposal with a variety of qualifications. Others opposed the proposal in principle. Some respondents suggested that there should only be one-way costs shifting in certain categories of case, for example only in CFA cases (as suggested by the Medical Defence Union ("MDU")) or only in claims under £25,000 (as suggested by the Association of British Insurers ("ABI")).

Some respondents, for example the Medical Protection Society ("MPS"),   **16–012** acknowledged that one-way costs shifting would be cheaper than the present regime, but nevertheless opposed it on grounds of principle or pragmatism. The MPS pointed out that not all defendants were insured and that it was harsh for a healthcare professional facing a weak claim to have no prospect of recovering costs. Some respondents feared that one-way costs shifting would encourage unmeritorious claims.

Analysis. There were three problems with "pure" one-way costs shifting.   **16–013** These were:

(i) There must be some costs risk in order to discourage frivolous or hopeless claims.

(ii) Occasionally the defendant may be an uninsured individual and therefore no better off than the claimant.

(iii) Sometimes the claimant may be very wealthy and in no need of protection against the risk of adverse costs.

Conclusion. Chapter 19 of the Final Report reached the following conclusion: **16–014**

"4.1 In my view, the regime of recoverable ATE insurance premiums is indefensible for the reasons set out in chapters 9 and 10 above. On the other hand, most claimants in personal injury cases have for many years enjoyed qualified protection against liability for adverse costs and there are sound policy reasons to continue such protection. The only practicable way that I can see to achieve this result is by qualified one-way costs shifting.
4.2 Despite the arguments of the MDU, the ABI and others, I do not regard it as practicable

to introduce one-way costs shifting for limited categories of personal injury cases, such as low value cases or CFA cases. Either one-way costs shifting is introduced across the board for personal injury cases or, alternatively, two-way costs shifting remains the rule, except for those protected by the legal aid 'shield'. Given that stark choice, I favour introducing qualified one-way costs shifting for all personal injury cases."

16–015   **Proposed rule.** Chapter 19 of the Final Report proposed that QOCS be introduced by making the following rule:

"Costs ordered against the claimant in any claim for personal injuries or clinical negligence shall not exceed the amount (if any) which is a reasonable one for him to pay having regard to all the circumstances including:

    (a) the financial resources of all the parties to the proceedings, and
    (b) their conduct in connection with the dispute to which the proceedings relate."

3. IMPLEMENTATION

16–016   **Acceptance of the recommendation in principle.** After appropriate consultation, the Government accepted that, subject to certain exceptions, recoverable ATE premiums should end. In those circumstances, QOCS was the appropriate way to protect PI claimants against the risk of adverse costs.

16–017   **Rejection of draft rule.** The MoJ did not accept the draft rule set out in FR Ch. 19. There was concern that investigation of the parties' means would be unduly burdensome. In addition, the ABI (whose members would be insuring the defendants in the overwhelming majority of PI cases) were willing to forego costs recovery in those relatively few cases where the claimant was significantly wealthy. On the other hand, the MoJ did accept that claimants should become liable for adverse costs in the event of misconduct in the litigation. The MoJ formulated draft rules on that basis, which the Rule Committee adopted after making appropriate revisions. The new rules came into force on 1 April 2013.

16–018   **The QOCS rules as incorporated into the CPR.** CPR Pt 44 provides:

"Qualified one-way costs shifting: scope and interpretation

    44.13(1) This Section applies to proceedings which include a claim for damages –

    (a) for personal injuries;
    (b) under the Fatal Accidents Act 1976; or
    (c) which arises out of death or personal injury and survives for the benefit of an estate by virtue of section 1(1) of the Law Reform (Miscellaneous Provisions) Act 1934,

but does not apply to applications pursuant to section 33 of the Senior Courts Act 1981 or section 52 of the County Courts Act 1984 (applications for pre-action disclosure), or where rule 44.17 applies.
(2) In this Section, 'claimant' means a person bringing a claim to which this Section applies or an estate on behalf of which such a claim is brought, and includes a person making a counterclaim or an additional claim.

Effect of qualified one-way costs shifting

44.14(1) Subject to rules 44.15 and 44.16, orders for costs made against a claimant may be enforced without the permission of the court but only to the extent that the aggregate amount in money terms of such orders does not exceed the aggregate amount in money terms of any orders for damages and interest made in favour of the claimant.

(2) Orders for costs made against a claimant may only be enforced after the proceedings have been concluded and the costs have been assessed or agreed.

(3) An order for costs which is enforced only to the extent permitted by paragraph (1) shall not be treated as an unsatisfied or outstanding judgment for the purposes of any court record.

Exceptions to qualified one-way costs shifting where permission not required

44.15 Orders for costs made against the claimant may be enforced to the full extent of such orders without the permission of the court where the proceedings have been struck out on the grounds that—

(a) the claimant has disclosed no reasonable grounds for bringing the proceedings;
(b) the proceedings are an abuse of the court's process; or
(c) the conduct of—

(i) the claimant; or
(ii) a person acting on the claimant's behalf and with the claimant's knowledge of such conduct,

is likely to obstruct the just disposal of the proceedings.

Exceptions to qualified one-way costs shifting where permission required

44.16(1) Orders for costs made against the claimant may be enforced to the full extent of such orders with the permission of the court where the claim is found on the balance of probabilities to be fundamentally dishonest.

(2) Orders for costs made against the claimant may be enforced up to the full extent of such orders with the permission of the court, and to the extent that it considers just, where—

(a) the proceedings include a claim which is made for the financial benefit of a person other than the claimant or a dependant within the meaning of section 1(3) of the Fatal Accidents Act 1976 (other than a claim in respect of the gratuitous provision of care, earnings paid by an employer or medical expenses); or
(b) a claim is made for the benefit of the claimant other than a claim to which this Section applies.
(3) Where paragraph (2)(a) applies, the court may, subject to rule 46.2, make an order for costs against a person, other than the claimant, for whose financial benefit the whole or part of the claim was made."

General reaction to the QOCS rules. Despite the reservations expressed **16–019** by some stakeholder groups during the Costs Review, there were no vociferous complaints when the new QOCS rules came into force. In a thoughtful article in *Civil Justice Quarterly*, Dr Andrew Higgins (a commentator who does not pull his punches) broadly welcomed this reform.[3]

---

[3] Higgins, "A defence of qualified one way costs shifting" (2013) 32 CJQ 198–212.

16–020   **Challenge to the QOCS rules.** In *Wagenaar v Weekend Travel Ltd* [2014] EWCA 1105, there was a challenge to the QOCS rules on *vires* grounds. The defendant argued that by reason of amendments made to the Senior Courts Act 1981, the Rule Committee did not have the power to make CPR rr.44.13 to 44.16. The Court of Appeal rejected that challenge. The court then went on to hold that QOCS did not apply to contribution proceedings which the defendant to a personal injury claim might bring against a third party. Both limbs of the Court of Appeal's decision are in accordance with the intention of the reforms.

16–021   **The QOCS rules in practice.** *Questions & Answers*[4] provides an account of how the QOCS rules should be applied in practice. It is not the function of this book to duplicate that detailed guidance. Nevertheless, the decision of HH Judge Freeman in *Zurich Insurance v Bain*[5] is a helpful illustration of what constitutes a "fundamentally dishonest" claim within the meaning of r.44.16(1). In that case, the claimant was involved in a minor road traffic accident, but fortunately suffered no injury. He gave an untruthful account to the doctor who examined him. He maintained at trial an untruthful account of having sustained injury and of subsequently suffering pain. The judge held that this case went beyond simple exaggeration or embellishment. The claimant's dishonesty went to the core of the claim. Therefore the clamant forfeited the protection of QOCS.

16–022   **QOCS in appeals.** As discussed in Ch. 15, above, PI claimants still have the protection of QOCS if their cases go on appeal: *Parker v Butler* [2016] EWHC 1251 (QB).

16–023   **Impact of section 57.** Section 57 of the Criminal Justice and Courts Act 2015 adds a new layer of complication. This section provides, subject to restrictions, that courts will dismiss personal injury cases where the claimant has been fundamentally dishonest. The section also spells out the costs consequences. The courts will have to work out how s.57 of the 2015 Act interrelates with the QOCS rules.[6]

4. SHOULD QOCS BE EXTENDED BEYOND PERSONAL INJURY CASES?

16–024   **The proposal in the Final Report.** The Final Report suggested that QOCS might be considered in other areas of litigation where there is an asymmetric relationship between the parties. Section 5(iv) of FR Ch. 9 stated:

> "(iv) *Other categories of litigation*
>
> 5.10 *Further consultation required if my recommendations are accepted in principle.* The essential thrust of the present chapter is that recoverability of ATE insurance premiums should be abolished and that this should be replaced by qualified one-way costs shifting,

---

[4] Hurst, Middleton and Mallalieu, 2nd edn, at pp. 184–192.
[5] 4 June 2015, discussed in the Law Society Gazette of 23 November 2015.
[6] Kerry Underwood analyses these issues in *Qualified One-Way Costs Shifting, Section 57 and Set-Off*.

targeted upon those who merit such protection on grounds of public policy. The question then arises as to which categories of litigant should benefit from qualified one-way costs shifting. This is a question upon which further consultation will be required, in the event that the recommendations made in this chapter are accepted as a matter of principle.

5.11 *Areas where qualified one-way costs shifting may be appropriate.* In my view qualified one-way costs shifting may be appropriate on grounds of social policy, where the parties are in an asymmetric relationship. Examples of parties who are generally in an asymmetric relationship with their opponents are claimants in housing disrepair cases, claimants in actions against the police, claimants seeking judicial review and individuals making claims for defamation or breach of privacy against the media. If protection modelled upon section 11(1) of the 1999 Act is extended to claimants in such cases, it will not avail those who bring frivolous claims (because unreasonable conduct is taken into account). Nor will it avail those whose resources are such that they can afford to pay adverse costs if they lose.

5.12 I discuss more fully in chapter 19 below how the section 11 model might be adapted and applied to non-legally aided parties, in the event that it is decided to confer upon such parties the benefit of qualified one way costs shifting. See in particular paragraphs 4.5 to 4.11 of that chapter.

5.13 *Professional negligence litigation.* Whether qualified one-way costs shifting should be introduced for any (and if so which) categories of professional negligence litigation should be the subject of consultation. My own view is that this may be difficult to justify outside clinical negligence. Most persons who employ solicitors, accountants, architects etc could afford to take out before-the-event ("BTE") insurance, if they chose to do so.

5.14 *Private nuisance claims.* I accept that private nuisance claims sometimes involve parties in an asymmetric relationship: for example local householders suing a sewage works. However, this is not always the case. Furthermore householders can take out BTE insurance against the costs of such claims, if they choose to do so. I would not positively support qualified one-way costs shifting for private nuisance claims, but others may take a different view. If qualified one-way costs shifting were introduced in the manner suggested in paragraph 5.3 above, it would only in practice avail persons of limited means suing well resourced defendants. Also it would be possible to provide that only human claimants (as opposed to corporate claimants) would benefit from qualified one-way costs shifting in private nuisance cases."

The Government's response. The Government has adopted a cautious   **16–025**
approach to this proposal. In its Response Paper[7] published in March 2011, the
MoJ stated:

"While Sir Rupert suggested that QOCS might be considered for introduction in some non-personal injury claims, the Government is not persuaded that the case for this has been made out at this stage . . . The Government will examine the experience of QOCS in personal injury claims before considering whether it should be extended further."

Defamation and privacy. As discussed in Ch. 18, above, the Final Report rec-   **16–026**
ommended that QOCS should be extended to publication claims. That proposal is

---

[7] "Reforming Civil Litigation Funding and Costs in England and Wales – Implementation of Lord Justice Jackson's Recommendations: the Government Response", Cm 8041, March 2011.

under consideration by the Government, following the conclusion of a consultation exercise.

16–027   **Civil Justice Council working groups.** A working group of CJC chaired by Alastair Kinley produced a report on possible extensions of QOCS in 2016. The report concluded that there were strong grounds for extending QOCS to actions against the police. The group also considered whether QOCS should apply in actions against solicitors for mishandling personal injury claims, but found the arguments to be more finely balanced in this area. Another CJC working group, set up more recently and chaired by Professor Rachael Mulheron, will consider whether QOCS should apply in any other fields of litigation.

16–028   **Formulation of any new QOCS rules.** If the decision is made to extend QOCS beyond the field of personal injury litigation, the formulation of the new QOCS rules will require careful consideration. In the realm of personal injury claims it is practicable to operate QOCS without regard to the parties' means. The defendant is almost always funded by insurers. The claimant is usually a person who cannot reasonably afford to pay adverse costs. In other categories of litigation, however, these comfortable assumptions do not apply so often. What about the millionaire businessman stopped for drunken driving, who chooses to sue the police for wrongful arrest? Or the film star who sues the publishers of a magazine for defamation?

16–029   **Proposed draft.** If QOCS is introduced into fields of litigation other than personal injury claims, the rule makers may perhaps care to consider adopting the formulation suggested in FR Ch. 19, para. 4.7. That reads as follows:

> "Costs ordered against the claimant in any claim for [state relevant field of litigation] shall not exceed the amount (if any) which is a reasonable one for him to pay having regard to all the circumstances including:
>
> (a) the financial resources of all the parties to the proceedings, and
> (b) their conduct in connection with the dispute to which the proceedings relate."

CHAPTER 17

REFERRAL FEES IN PERSONAL INJURY LITIGATION

1. THE STORY UP TO 2009

Historical background. The historical background is as follows. Advertising   **17–001**
or touting for business by solicitors was prohibited until 1987, when the ban was
lifted. Solicitors were prohibited from having arrangements with third parties for
the introduction or referral of business until 1988, when that ban was also lifted.
However, the Law Society retained a ban on "rewarding introducers". In 1991,
the Solicitors Conduct Rules were amended in relation to conveyancing, so as to
permit contractual referrals between lenders and solicitors.

OFT report. In March 2001, the Office of Fair Trading ("OFT") published the   **17–002**
report by the Director General of Fair Trading "Competition in professions". The
Director General set out his approach on p. 3 as follows:

"Indeed, the professions are run by producers largely on behalf of producers. In the
economy generally it is competition that impels producers to act in the interests of
consumers. Restrictions on competition – on the freedom of suppliers of services to
compete with one other – imposed by professions should therefore be subject to close
and careful scrutiny. The aim of the Office of Fair Trading (OFT) is to make sure that
markets work well – for the ultimate benefit of consumers. To that end, we have examined restrictions on competition in the professions selected. The aim has been to identify
significant adverse effects on competition. We have not examined in detail whether or
not every particular adverse effect on competition is justified by countervailing consumer benefits that could not otherwise be achieved. But where restrictions are causing
significant adverse effects on competition, from a policy perspective, they should be
removed unless their proponents can demonstrate strong justifications for them in terms
of consumer benefit. In any event, the professions should not be shielded from the competition laws that apply elsewhere in the economy."

Specific recommendation concerning solicitors' referral fees. In relation to   **17–003**
referral fees paid by solicitors, the Director General stated as follows on p. 14 of
the OFT report:

"Restrictions on receiving a payment for referring a client (Solicitors' Practice Rule 3).
The current regime also prevents solicitors from making payments for work that is
referred to them by a third party. This may be hampering inter alia the development
of an online marketplace that could bring clients and solicitors together. As with

advertising restrictions, there are welcome indications that this restriction may be abolished."

17–004 **Response by the Law Society.** In March 2004, the Solicitors Conduct Rules were amended to allow solicitors to pay referral fees, subject to certain conditions and safeguards.

17–005 **The position in 2009.** By 2009, r.9 of the Solicitors Code of Conduct 2007 governed the referrals of business to and from solicitors. Rule 9.01 provided that, when making or receiving referrals of clients to or from third parties, a solicitor must do nothing which would compromise their independence or ability to act and advise in the best interests of their clients. Rule 9.02 included additional requirements where a solicitor entered into a financial arrangement with an introducer. The agreement between the solicitor and the introducer must be in writing. Before accepting instructions to act for a client referred in these circumstances, the solicitor must give to the client in writing all relevant information concerning the fact that they have a financial arrangement with the introducer and the amount of any payment to the introducer which is calculated by reference to that referral.

2. THE DEBATE DURING THE REVIEW

17–006 **A hot topic.** One of the hot topics during the Review was whether the ban on referral fees should be reinstated. At that time, the principal area of concern was the use of referral fees in PI litigation. Almost all of the debate about referral fees was centred upon PI claims.

17–007 **Arguments for continuing to permit referral fees.** The supporters of referral fees argued:

(i) Referral fees were simply one form of marketing costs and a convenient way for PI solicitors to obtain work.

(ii) The average person does not have the confidence to approach a solicitor. Such a person feels more confident talking to representatives of claims management companies, which in turn depend upon referral fees.

(iii) Claims management companies require high standards from the solicitors to whom they refer claims.

(iv) Referral fees do no harm to claimants, who do not have to pay them.

(v) BTE insurers (like claims management companies) pass PI claims on to solicitors and receive referral fees for doing so. This helps them to keep down the level of insurance premiums charged to the general public.

(vi) Referral fees are now (i.e. by 2009) a fact of life and it is too late to put the clock back.

Arguments for re-imposing a ban on referral fees. The opponents of referral   **17–008**
fees argued:

(i) It is wrong in principle to buy and sell the claims of injured persons. Such
a practice is offensive.

(ii) Referral fees add another layer of costs to the PI litigation process. Very
often, a large part of the costs recovered by claimant solicitors in PI claims
are paid out to the claims management company or BTE insurer who
referred the case.

(iii) The referrers add no value to the process.

(iv) In practice, claims management companies and BTE insurers send work
to the highest bidders. Solicitors compete for work by paying ever higher
referral fees. This drives down the standard of work done by solicitors
(because they have to devote more of their finite resources to buying
claims). The only beneficiaries from the competition are the referrers and it
is the clients who lose out.

(v) Because of market forces, the level of referral fees is slowly rising.
Solicitors are coy about how much they are paying, but unofficial information (e.g. anonymous slips filled in by those attending a seminar on 26 June
2009) suggested some alarmingly high figures. The insidious effect of
referral fees is slowly increasing.

Association of Personal Injury Lawyers debate. On 23 April 2009, APIL   **17–009**
held a debate on referral fees. Although no-one counted the votes, a very substantial majority were in favour of banning referral fees.

Submission by the Personal Injury Bar Association ("PIBA"). During the   **17–010**
consultation period, PIBA sent in particularly cogent submissions on this issue.
They wrote:

"So far as the Bar is concerned, they are not allowed by the Code of Conduct. We can
see no benefit in permitting referral fees for solicitors either. In many cases the referral fee is a substantial proportion of the costs required to conduct a case and it has led
to cost cutting by solicitors and cases being insufficiently prepared to the detriment of
Claimants. Referral fees mean that the solicitor who conducts the case is the highest
payer but not necessarily the best solicitor for the Claimant. The market is driven by
who pays the most, not who provides the best or most efficient or cheapest service.
There is no doubt that referral fees have fuelled the costs war. . .
We can see no public interest in retaining referral fees on competition or economic
grounds. They often result, in our view, in poorer quality service at a greater price and
they do nothing to enhance competence or quality. There are undoubtedly some firms
who pay referral fees and maintain high standards, but this is in spite of not because of
referral fees. There was competition between solicitors prior to the introduction of referral fees. We do not advocate banning of advertising by solicitors and we encourage the
Law Society to advertise a provision of easily accessible information to the public about
services solicitors can provide in every locality."

Conclusion. By then end of the consultation period, it became clear that the   **17–011**
preponderance of informed opinion and the weight of rational argument were in

favour of banning referral fees in PI litigation. The going rate for referral fees in fast track PI claims during 2009 was £600–£900, usually towards the upper end of that bracket. For PI claims above the fast track, referral fees were more bespoke and often linked to profit costs. It was absurd to siphon off such a large part of the "legal" costs to organisations which added no value to the process.

3. RECOMMENDATIONS IN THE FINAL REPORT OF JANUARY 2010

17–012   **Chapter 20 of the Final Report.** FR Ch. 20 set out the arguments on both sides of the debate and summarised the numerous submissions which organisations and individuals had sent in. The chapter noted that both the Bar and the Law Society favoured re-imposing a ban on referral fees. The chapter quoted a letter sent by the OFT to the Civil Litigation Costs Review on 6 August 2009, maintaining its support for referral fees. The chapter gently took issue with that letter.

17–013   **Recommendation concerning personal injury claims.** Chapter 20 of the Final Report recommended that the payment of referral fees for PI claims should be banned.

17–014   **What about referral fees for non-personal injury claims? Shouldn't they be banned as well?** Very possibly they should be banned, but it was not possible to reach any firm conclusion on that issue during the 2009 Review. There was insufficient information concerning the effect of referral fees outside the area of personal injury claims. The Final Report only made recommendations (a) for which there was a proper evidence base and (b) about which there had been full argument.

17–015   **Recommendation concerning other areas of litigation.** The final paragraph of FR Ch. 20 recommended that after PI referral fees had been banned,

> "consideration will have to be given to the question whether referral fees should be banned or capped in other areas of litigation".

4. IMPLEMENTATION

17–016   **Parliamentary process.** Initially, the Government was not minded to accept the FR recommendation to ban PI referral fees. During 2011, however, Jack Straw MP[1] mounted a powerful campaign to secure such a ban. At that stage, the Bill which was to become LASPO was passing through its readings in Parliament. Mr Straw's campaign was successful. The necessary provisions were added to the Bill.

---

[1] Jack Straw MP had been Lord Chancellor during the Costs Review. He was at all times supportive of the FR recommendations, but lost office in the General Election of May 2010.

The legislation as finally enacted. Section 56 of LASPO provides: 17–017

"**Rules against referral fees**

(1) A regulated person is in breach of this section if—

   (a) the regulated person refers prescribed legal business to another person and is paid or has been paid for the referral, or
   (b) prescribed legal business is referred to the regulated person, and the regulated person pays or has paid for the referral.

(2) A regulated person is also in breach of this section if in providing legal services in the course of prescribed legal business the regulated person—

   (a) arranges for another person to provide services to the client, and
   (b) is paid or has been paid for making the arrangement."

Definition of "prescribed legal business". Section 56 goes on to define "pre- 17–018
scribed legal business" as the conduct of PI litigation or any other legal business which the Lord Chancellor may specify by regulations.

Sections 57 and 58 of LASPO. Section 57(1) of LASPO requires the relevant 17–019
regulator to have in place appropriate arrangements for monitoring and enforcing the restrictions imposed by s.56. Section 57(2) enables the regulator to make rules for that purpose. Section 58 provides that the Treasury can make regulations to enable the Financial Services Authority ("FSA") to take action for monitoring and enforcing compliance with s.56. Those regulations have now been made in SI 2013/1635 and give the FSA's successor agency—the Financial Conduct Authority ("FCA")—a broad range of regulatory powers.

The Legal Professional Regulators' Rules. Each of the regulators governing 17–020
the legal professions—the Bar Standards Board ("BSB"), Solicitors Regulation Authority ("SRA") and CILEx Regulation—has had a different approach to implementing the referral fee ban.

Barristers. The BSB and the Bar Council both had a long-standing and 17–021
ingrained hostility to referral fees that pre-dated LASPO. Accordingly, a ban on referral fees was already in place in the Code of Conduct and there was pre-existing guidance on referral fees. That guidance continues to be updated.

Solicitors. The SRA made amendments to its Handbook and inserted new 17–022
provisions into the Code of Conduct to ensure solicitors complied with the ban. Outcomes 6.4 and 9.8 prohibited payment or receipt of a prohibited referral fee. The SRA Handbook is bolstered by practical guidance and information aimed at practitioners.

Enforcement action taken by the SRA. The SRA imposed its first fine for 17–023
breach of the ban on referral fees in December 2015. The solicitor in question had paid £47,000 to a third party for the supply of 38 personal injury cases.[2] The

---

[2] *Law Society Gazette*, 2 December 2015.

SRA is currently pursuing proceedings before the Solicitors Disciplinary Tribunal against two other solicitors for allegedly paying referral fees totalling £75.000.[3]

17–024 **Chartered Legal Executives.** CILEx Regulation has not yet provided for any express rules on referral fees. They have indicated (in response to recent enquiries) that they intend to do so. At the moment, almost all legal executives work in SRA-regulated firms and so the need for dedicated rules for legal executives is not pressing.

17–025 **Claims Management Regulator.** In addition to the FCA and the Legal Professional Regulators, there is a Claims Management Regulator which regulates claims management companies. Their guidance makes clear what business models are non-compliant with the ban and therefore unlawful. In January to March 2014, the Regulator warned 65 claims management companies about their compliance with the ban on referral fees.[4]

17–026 **Consequences of the ban.** Many claims management firms went out of business following the introduction of the ban. Others remained in operation, but changed the ways in which they did business. Likewise, BTE insurers and PI solicitors have changed their business models in order to comply with the ban.

17–027 **Sailing close to the wind.** The SRA has issued guidance to solicitors, warning them about new business models (following the ban on referral fees) which may constitute a breach of their professional duties. In a warning notice dated 11 October 2013, the SRA stated:

> "We know that the ban on referral fees has raised difficult issues in relation to its application and interpretation. We are also aware that, because of the wording of LASPO, it is possible for firms to have arrangements that involve the introduction of personal injury work without being in breach of LASPO. We are concerned, however, that in setting up arrangements in a way that does not breach LASPO, firms are failing to consider their wider duties to their clients and others, and in doing so may be breaching the Principles or failing to achieve the Outcomes. Examples include:
>
> - agreeing with an introducer to deduct money from clients' damages;
> - inappropriate outsourcing of work to introducers;
> - referrals to other service providers which are not in the best interests of clients;
> - failure to properly advise clients about the costs and how their claim should be funded; and
> - lack of transparency about the arrangement."

17–028 **Overall assessment of the effect of the ban.** The ban has been largely, but not totally, successful in eradicating the objectionable conduct highlighted in FR Ch. 20.

---

[3] See the written reasons published by the SRA for their decision to prosecute two solicitors before the Solicitors Disciplinary Tribunal, dated 4 December 2015 and published 20 May 2016, available at: *https://www.sra.org.uk/consumers/solicitor-check/067679.article* [Accessed 1 July 2016].
[4] Legal Futures, 2 July 2014, available at *http://www.legalfutures.co.uk/latest-news/65-cmcs-warned-referral-fee-ban-compliance-first-three-months-2014-2* [Accessed 1 July 2016].

Referral fees outside the field of personal injury. Section 56 of LASPO   **17–029**
contains a mechanism by which the Lord Chancellor can ban referral fees in any
area of litigation. It is reasonable to expect that he or she will do so, as and when
abuses become apparent. The MoJ has recently gone out to consultation on a
proposal to ban the payment of referral fees for publicly funded criminal cases:
see MoJ consultation paper "Preserving and enhancing the quality of criminal
advocacy", October 2015.

Chapter 18

INTELLECTUAL PROPERTY, SMALL BUSINESSES, DEFAMATION/ PRIVACY, JUDICIAL REVIEW, CLINICAL NEGLIGENCE AND OTHER SPECIALIST AREAS

Both the Preliminary Report and the Final Report contain chapters discussing **18–001** individual areas of litigation and how the proposed reforms will impact upon them. These chapters include, but are not limited to, proposals for reform. It is not practicable in this small book to give more than a very brief outline of some of those chapters and the reforms to which they led.

1. Intellectual Property Disputes

Preliminary Report. Section 5 of PR Ch. 29 discussed the position of SMEs **18–002** which need to protect their intellectual property ("IP") rights. Sometimes they found litigation prohibitively expensive and gave up the endeavour. This was a matter of particular concern to the Chartered Institute of Patent Attorneys. The chapter reviewed the history and role of the Patents County Court in dealing with such issues.

Research during the Costs Review. The Strategic Advisory Board for **18–003** Intellectual Property Policy ("SABIP") kindly offered to undertake research for the assistance of the Costs Review. I accepted that offer with alacrity and SABIP carried out three internet surveys in the period August-October 2009. These surveys yielded much valuable information, including the following:

"There was overwhelming support for both a fast track (72.2%) and a small claims forum (78.7%). Furthermore, the survey indicates high levels of potential usage for both these options: respondents indicated their assessment that they would be likely to bring 81 cases in the next year and 287 cases over the next five years to a fast track (cases between £5,000 and £25,000), and 197 cases in the next year and 883 cases over the next five years to a small claims venue (cases of under £5,000).

Given these results, it seems highly likely that high levels of demand exist for both a fast track and a small claims court for copyright and design rights cases. Although it is likely that the survey respondents may have overstated their potential usage of these mechanisms, any proposal to implement these tracks should take into consideration the need to quickly build capacity. Indeed, if the demand implied by our survey were to materialise, there is a risk of the procedures being swamped."

18–004   **High value IP cases.** FR Ch. 2, section 8 and Appendix 3 set out an analysis of the costs of high value IP cases. The adjusted costs incurred on these cases up to first instance judgment or settlement ranged from £196,957 to £1,540,933, with an average cost incurred per case of £696,742. The breakdown showed how much was spent on each of the phases of the litigation.[1]

18–005   **Chapter 24 of the Final Report.** FR Ch. 24 made numerous proposals for procedural reform of IP litigation both in high value and low value cases. Most of these recommendations were implemented, as explained by Mr Justice Arnold in the seventeenth implementation lecture, delivered on 12 February 2013.[2]

18–006   **Fixed recoverable costs for IP cases up to £500,000.** Chapter 24 of the Final Report supported proposals for introducing fixed recoverable costs in respect of IP claims up to £500,000. Those reforms were implemented and have been highly successful, as discussed in Ch. 19, below.

18–007   **Reforms affecting low value cases.** Chapter 24 of the Final Report recommended that a small claims track and a fast track should be established within the Patents County Court, in order to deal with low value IP cases. This recommendation was based upon the SABIP research quoted above.

18–008   **Implementation.** The recommendations concerning low value cases were duly implemented. At the same time, the Patents County Court was re-named the Intellectual Property Enterprise Court. Since then there has been a large flow of cases passing through the small claims track and fast track.[3]

18–009   **The problem of claims for "groundless threats".** Paragraph 5.1 of FR Ch. 24 stated:

> "There is concern amongst practitioners that a legitimate letter before action in respect of infringement may result in a claim for 'groundless threats' by the recipient under section 26 of the Registered Designs Act 1949, section 70 of the Patents Act 1977, section 253 of the Copyright Designs and Patents Act 1988 or section 21 of the Trade Marks Act 1994."

The chapter then discussed ways of alleviating this concern, possibly by means of a pre-action protocol or other guidance.

18–010   **Implementation.** The Law Commission discussed FR Ch. 24 in its 2013 consultation paper *Patents, trade marks and design rights: groundless threats*[4] and proposed legislation to resolve the problem. At the time of writing, the Intellectual Property (Unjustified Threats) Bill is currently before Parliament, sponsored by the Law Commission. The proposed legislation will enable practitioners to engage in appropriate pre-action correspondence without incurring personal

---

[1] The Law Commission examined these figures in its Report No. 346 of 2014 (Cm 8851), at p. 11.
[2] Entitled "Intellectual property litigation: implementation of the Jackson Report's recommendations".
[3] See the figures quoted for the small claims track in Ch. 19, below.
[4] Consultation Paper No. 212 of 2013.

liability. This will facilitate ADR in IP disputes. That is obviously helpful and it fits with the various FR reforms discussed in Ch. 8, above.

2. SMALL BUSINESS DISPUTES

Preliminary Report. Chapter 29 of the Preliminary Report reviewed the role   18–011
of small and medium enterprises ("SMEs") in the UK economy. It highlighted the particular importance of expeditious resolution of small business disputes. The chapter also reviewed the procedures and organisation of the Mercantile Courts, commenting at para. 4.18:

> "The importance of the Mercantile Courts within the civil justice system is very substantial and is sometimes overlooked. Whereas the majority of all litigants in the Commercial Court are overseas companies which have chosen London as their forum, this is not the case in respect of mercantile courts. For a very large number of business disputes which arise in England and Wales, the Mercantile Courts are the natural home. Thus the Mercantile Courts have a pivotal role to play in the smooth running of the economy. Traders and businessmen must know that their contracts will be swiftly and economically enforced and that remedies will be available if their commercial rights are infringed; they must be able to order their affairs against that backdrop."

Lack of central organisation for Mercantile Courts. Chapter 29 of the   18–012
Preliminary Report noted problems arising from the fact that the ten Mercantile Courts existed as separate entities without any central organisation. In this respect, they differed from the TCC and the Chancery Courts in the regions. A related problem was that there was no "Judge in charge of the Mercantile Courts". By contrast, the Judge in charge of the TCC had responsibility for all TCC courts outside London and the Chancellor of the High Court had responsibility for all Chancery Courts outside London.

Survey by the Federation of Small Businesses. The Federation of Small   18–013
Businesses ("FSB") kindly carried out a survey of its members for the assistance of the costs Review. This revealed amongst other things that:

- Members would like the small claims limit raised to at least £15,000 for business disputes.

- The hourly rates for litigants in person should be increased.

- Members would like fixed costs for business disputes up to £500,000.

These views reflected the harsh realities of life for many small businesses. They simply could not afford to litigate disputes with full panoply of court procedures and legal fees.

Final Report. Chapter 25 of the Final Report dealt with small business dis-   18–014
putes. It drew together input from a wide range of court users and other sources. It also summarised the outcome of the "SMEs seminar" on 28 July 2009. The

chapter made a number of recommendations to promote the resolution of small business disputes. They included the following:

(i) A High Court judge should be appointed as Judge in charge of the Mercantile Courts.

(ii) A single court guide should be drawn up for the Mercantile Courts (similar to the court guides for the TCC, Commercial Court and the Chancery Courts).

These two recommendations were accepted. Mrs Justice Gloster (as she then was) became the first Judge in Charge of the Mercantile Courts. Mr Justice Hamblen (as he then was), in liaison with the Mercantile Courts, drew up a court guide for the Mercantile Courts.

18–015   **Small claims limit.** The FSB's wish to increase the small claims limit to £15,000 was more problematic. That would be fine when both parties are businesses, but very often the opposing party is an individual or possibly even a consumer. Chapter 25 of the Final Report therefore concluded:

> "When two businesses are involved in a dispute valued between £5,000 and £15,000, I do accept that such a matter may be suited to the small claims track, so that each side can appear in person. The best way to achieve this would be for both parties to consent at the outset to allocation to the small claims track. Indeed, in such a case the court may well encourage such a course at the first opportunity, if the parties have not thought of it for themselves. Once the claim is allocated (or transferred) to the small claims track the district judge will be more interventionist and thus can promote efficient resolution of the dispute without the assistance of lawyers. No rule change is required to facilitate such consensual allocation to the small claims track: see CPR rules 26.7(3) and 26.8(1)(h)."

18–016   **Litigant in person hourly rates.** The proposal to raise the hourly rate for LIPs raised a host of issues,[5] not just affecting small businesses. Chapter 17 of the Preliminary Report and FR Ch. 14 discussed these issues. The final recommendation (in FR Ch. 14, para. 4.1) was that the hourly rate for LIPs should be increased to £20. The MoJ and the Rule Committee accepted the tenor of this recommendation, but instead chose a figure of £19. Quite why they rejected £20 per hour is not clear—perhaps that would have made the calculations too easy.

3. DEFAMATION AND PRIVACY

18–017   **Definitions.** In this section, "publication claim" means a claim for defamation and/or privacy. "MLA" means Media Lawyers Association.

18–018   **Research by the Media Lawyers Association.** The MLA kindly agreed to collect data for the assistance of the Costs Review. They compiled an anonymised

---

[5] For example, for a stimulating discussion of the issues concerning litigants in person, see Assy, *Injustice in Person*, reviewed at (2016) 132 LQR 505–506.

schedule of all publication claims against MLA members which were disposed of during 2008. That schedule forms Appendix 17 to the Preliminary Report. Quite apart from its utility for the Costs Review, this schedule was also useful material for the academic community.[6]

Chapter 37 of the Preliminary Report. PR Ch. 37 collated the data concern-   **18–019**
ing publication proceedings from many sources including the MLA. It summarised the numbers of claims and the sizes of claims over the preceding six years.
It identified a wide range of issues for debate during Phase Two.

Working group. A working group set up during Phase Two tried to design a   **18–020**
CLAF for publication cases, but was unsuccessful in that endeavour. The group
did, however, identify some important procedural issues.

Chapter 32 of the Final Report. FR Ch. 32 discussed a wide range of issues   **18–021**
concerning publication claims. In particular:

- The chapter noted that the use of juries increased trial costs by 20%–30%.
  It recommended that the use of juries in such cases should be reconsidered.

- The chapter recommended that (following the ending of recoverable
  success fees and ATE premiums) the level of general damages should be
  increased by 10% and QOCS should be introduced for publication claims.

Partial implementation. Some of the recommendations in FR Ch. 32   **18–022**
required primary legislation. There has been partial implementation of the
recommendations:

- The Defamation Act 2013 substantially cut back the use of juries in defamation actions.

- The MoJ went out to consultation in 2013 about the possibility of introducing QOCS for defamation and privacy claims.[7] It has not yet announced its
  decision on the question. For the time being, recoverable success fees and
  recoverable ATE premiums remain in place for defamation and privacy
  claims.[8]

4. JUDICIAL REVIEW

Chapter 35 of the Preliminary Report. PR Ch. 35 noted that some of the   **18–023**
costs issues which bedevil other areas of litigation do not affect judicial review.
Section 2 of that chapter stated:

---

[6] See for example David Howarth's analysis of the Schedule 17 data in "The cost of libel actions: a sceptical note" [2011] CLJ 397–419.
[7] See the MoJ consultation paper "Costs protection in defamation and privacy claims: the Government's proposals" (13 September 2013).
[8] See Ch. 5, above, and the ministerial statement of 12 December 2012.

"2.1 *Effect of permission requirement.* The effect of the permission requirement is that approximately 80% of judicial review claims are weeded out in the early stages. Such claims do not have sufficient prospect of success and they are brought to an end at (usually) modest cost.

2.2 *Less elaborate pleadings.* The claim forms may run to some length, but this is because they contain narrative of the facts. The formulation of the grounds of claim for judicial review ordinarily is, or at least should be, quite concise. Acknowledgements of service contain summary grounds of defence. Although there are exceptions, in the majority of cases the summary grounds of defence are condensed into a few pages or less. The parties do not serve requests for further information or responses to such requests.

2.3 *No disclosure.* The fact that ordinarily there is no disclosure is the overriding feature in relation to costs. The parties simply put forward the documents upon which they rely, subject to any direction by the court that some specific document or group of documents should be disclosed. During the eight years that I sat as an Administrative Court judge, I was not aware of the absence of disclosure becoming a source of injustice. Nor (so far as I can recollect) did counsel ever suggest that this was the case.

2.4 *Written evidence and streamlined procedures.* It would be an oversimplification to say that the facts in judicial review cases are uncontroversial. Very often the judge is called upon to make findings of fact. He or she does so on the basis of the witness statements and the contemporaneous documents. Again I am not aware of concern that injustice is being caused by the absence of oral evidence and cross-examination.

2.5 *Absence of the main costs drivers.* It can be seen from the foregoing that the principal drivers of costs in "heavy" civil litigation are absent from judicial review proceedings. The consequence is that the costs of judicial review proceedings, although beyond the means of many litigants, are substantially reduced."

The general comments in those paragraphs are still valid. Chapter 35 then went on to review protective costs orders, which often generated so much costs that they were counter-productive. The chapter looked at the costs regimes in Canada, where there was a form of one-way costs shifting for judicial review cases, and discussed the options of England and Wales.

18–024   **Chapter 36 of the Preliminary Report.** PR Ch. 36 dealt with environmental claims and, in section 4, discussed the impact of the Aarhus Convention on environmental judicial review claims. Article 9 of that Convention provides:

"2. Each Party shall, within the framework of its national legislation, ensure that members of the public concerned (a) having a sufficient interest or, alternatively, (b) maintaining impairment of a right, where the administrative procedural law of a Party requires this as a precondition, have access to a review procedure before a court of law and/or another independent and impartial body established by law, to challenge the substantive and procedural legality of any decision, act or omission subject to the provisions of article 6 and, where so provided for under national law and without prejudice to paragraph 3 below, of other relevant provisions of this Convention. . .

3. In addition and without prejudice to the review procedures referred to in paragraphs 1 and 2 above, each Party shall ensure that, where they meet the criteria, if any, laid down in its national law, members of the public have access to administrative or judicial procedures to challenge acts and omissions by private persons

and public authorities which contravene provisions of its national law relating to the environment.

4. In addition and without prejudice to paragraph 1 above, the procedures referred to in paragraphs 1, 2 and 3 above shall provide adequate and effective remedies, including injunctive relief as appropriate, and be fair, equitable, timely and not prohibitively expensive."

Directive 2003/35/EC imposes similar obligations on Member States of the EU. This is the Public Participation Directive ("PPD").

Consultation during Phase Two. Phase Two involved wide ranging consul-   **18–025** tation with environmental groups and other bodies concerned with public law issues. Four of the environmental groups coalesced into a group called "Coalition for Access to Justice for the Environment", which presented their collective views to the Costs Review. There was a helpful judicial review seminar, attended by a wide spectrum of stakeholders. There was concern that despite the points made above, litigation was still prohibitively expensive for many who wished to bring properly arguable judicial review claims.

On a separate point, there was general concern about the court's approach   **18–026** to costs in cases where a public authority capitulated at an early stage, often after the grant of permission. Following the guidance in *R (on the application of Boxall) v Waltham Forest LBC* (2001) 4 CCLR 258, courts were frequently making no orders as to costs. This was because the defendants would say that they had conceded on pragmatic grounds and it was not feasible generally to try out the whole case in the context of a costs dispute. Such an approach by the courts was causing real difficulties for claimant solicitors doing public law work.

Chapter 30 of the Final Report. FR Ch. 30 proceeded on the basis that   **18–027** recoverable success fees and ATE premiums would come to an end, as has indeed happened. The chapter proposed that QOCS should be introduced for judicial review claims. If this recommendation is ever accepted, the QOCS will need to be in the form proposed in FR Ch. 19, not in the form of CPR rr.44.13 to 44.16. It would be absurd if claimants who are well resourced could litigate at no costs risk against public authorities. Chapter 30 of the Final Report also recommended that

"if the defendant settles a judicial review claim after issue and the claimant has complied with the protocol, the normal order should be that the defendant do pay the claimant's costs."

This would mean a reversal of the *Boxall* guidance.

Partial implementation. The Court of Appeal has implemented the second   **18–028** of those recommendations by means of judicial decision: see *R (Bahta) v SSHD* [2011] EWCA Civ 895 and *M v Croydon LBC* [2012] EWCA Civ 595; [2012] 1 WLR 2607. Turning to the first recommendation, so far the Government has only implemented QOCS in respect of personal injury claims, leaving open whether it will later extend QOCS to other areas of litigation.

18–029   **How to comply with Aarhus?** That therefore left the problem of how to comply with the Aarhus Convention and the EU Directive. In 2011, the MoJ went out to consultation on a proposal for codification of protective costs orders in Aarhus cases. On 10 January 2012, I sent in a response suggesting a variant of fixed costs, as follows:

> "3.1 *Develop a fixed costs regime.* In my view the proposals in the MoJ consultation paper should be developed as a fixed costs regime and located within CPR Part 45. The label which we apply does matter. First, as critics of every reform always say, the devil is in the detail. I believe that the details will be much easier to work out if we formulate the new regime within the framework of fixed costs rather than develop the scheme as a special sort of PCO. Secondly, the way a costs regime is classified affects the culture or the mindset of practitioners and judges who deal with cases under that regime.
>
> 3.2 *The detail.* The new regime could be added to the Pantheon of Part 45. It would become "Part 9: Fixed Costs for Environmental Judicial Review Cases". Such cases could be defined as all judicial review cases falling within Aarhus or the PPD. A set of rules for such cases could then be developed broadly similar to that set out in CPR rules 45.41 to 45.43 and section 25C of the Costs Practice Direction."

18–030   **Implementation.** The MoJ and the Rule Committee adopted the Pt 45 approach. A special costs regime for Aarhus cases was added at the end of CPR Pt 45. This limits the costs liability of an individual claimant to £5,000 and the costs liability of any other claimant to £10,000. The costs liability of the defendant is limited to £35,000.

5. Clinical Negligence

18–031   **Preliminary Report.** PR Ch. 11 and Appendices 12, 21 and 22A–22D contained extensive data concerning the costs of clinical negligence litigation. The analysis at PR pp. 139–142 highlighted the particular problem of late settlement of meritorious clinical negligence claims. Any culture of late settlement is to be deplored, especially in the field of clinical negligence.

18–032   **Final Report.** FR Ch. 2, section 6 and Appendix 2 set out the details of 1,000 clinical negligence cases which were closed or settled by the NHSLA in the year ended 31 March 2009. The analysis of this material in conjunction with the statistics in the Preliminary Report provided a firm basis for reviewing clinical negligence and making reform proposals.

18–033   **Chapter 23 of the Final Report.** FR Ch. 23 proposed amendments to the clinical negligence protocol and the NHSLA's procedures, which were duly adopted in 2010, as discussed in Ch. 8, above. These reforms were specifically designed to promote early settlement and to tackle the problems identified in PR Ch. 11. Chapter 23 of the Final Report also made proposals for harmonisation of case management directions in clinical negligence cases. These proposals have generally been adopted. The chapter discussed a number of pre-action problems, including access to medical records and failures by defendants to instruct lawyers promptly about notified claims. The chapter also proposed:

"The NHSLA, the MDU, the MPS and similar bodies should each nominate an experienced and senior officer to whom claimant solicitors should, after the event, report egregious cases of defendant lawyers failing to address the issues."

The NHSLA, the MPS and the MDU implemented that recommendation. They each nominated appropriate individuals for that role.

Unimplemented recommendations. Some of the recommendations in FR   **18–034**
Ch. 23 were unimplemented, in particular the proposal for a special pilot of costs management in clinical negligence litigation and for the appointment of an extra Queen's Bench master. These omissions were unfortunate and may account for the problems which subsequently arose in the costs management of clinical negligence cases.

Twelfth implementation lecture. The twelfth implementation lecture,[9] deliv-   **18–035**
ered on 23 March 2012, discussed the FR reforms to clinical negligence litigation in much greater detail. This can be accessed on the Judiciary website.

6. OTHER SPECIALIST AREAS

The Preliminary Report and the Final Report contained individual chapters dis-   **18–036**
cussing chancery litigation, housing claims, commercial disputes, TCC litigation, nuisance claims and collective actions. Some, but only a minority, of the recommendations in these chapters have been implemented. In particular, the procedure for homelessness appeals has been revised as proposed in FR Ch. 26. The procedure for *Beddoe* applications has been revised as proposed in FR Ch. 28.

---

[9] Entitled "The reform of clinical negligence litigation".

Part Six
QUANTIFYING COSTS

Part Six
QUANTITATIVE COSTS

FIXED RECOVERABLE COSTS

1. BACKGROUND

Definitions. In this chapter, "fixed costs" is used as an abbreviation for a regime of scale or fixed costs, under which the amount recoverable is prescribed by the rules or can be calculated arithmetically in accordance with the rules. "RTA" means road traffic accident.   **19–001**

The state of play after Woolf. Lord Woolf recommended that there should be a comprehensive scheme of fixed costs for all stages of litigation in the fast track. Powerful vested interests resisted that proposal and they were successful. Lord Woolf only managed to secure a grid of fixed costs for fast track trials. The costs of almost all pre-trial work remained at large. Nevertheless, Lord Woolf had let the genie was out of the bottle and the idea was not going to go away.   **19–002**

The RTA scheme. In 2003, the Supreme Court Act 1981 (a statue later renamed the Senior Courts Act 1981) was amended to pave the way for a new scheme in respect of uncontested, low value PI claims arising out of road traffic accidents ("the RTA scheme"). The RTA scheme[1] provided fixed costs for PI claims up to £10,000, which were settled before issue.   **19–003**

Kerry Underwood's prediction. In 2006, Kerry Underwood published the second edition of his book entitled *Fixed Costs*. Chapter 1 began with the bold statement: "Fixed costs represent an opportunity to rescue a civil justice system that, like most public services, is in terrible trouble." Chapter 1 predicted that fixed costs would spread quickly from the RTA scheme to other areas of litigation.   **19–004**

What was the position in 2009, when the costs Review began? The position was essentially the same as described in Underwood's book.   **19–005**

---

[1] Explained by Simon J in *Butt v Nizami* [2006] EWHC 159 (QB).

(i) Section I of Pt 45 of the CPR set out fixed costs for certain items of work.

(ii) There was the RTA scheme.

(iii) There were fixed fast track trial costs.

19–006   *(i) Section I of CPR Part 45.* Section I of CPR Pt 45 set out the amounts which were recoverable in respect of solicitors' charges in specified categories of case, which the defendant did not contest. Generally speaking, section I applied to:

(a) money claims where, *inter alia*, judgment in default was obtained or summary judgment was given;

(b) claims where the court gave a fixed date for the hearing when it issued the claim and judgment was given for the delivery of goods; and

(c) uncontested claims for possession of property and similar matters.

19–007   *(ii) The RTA scheme.* The RTA scheme provided fixed costs for RTA claims up to £10,000, which included PI damages and which settled before issue of proceedings. The fixed costs (excluding success fee) were £800 + 20% of the agreed damages up to £5,000 + 15% of any agreed damages between £5,000 and £10,000.

19–008   *(iii) Fast track trial costs.* Part 46 of the CPR governed the costs which the court may award as the costs of an advocate for preparing for and appearing at the trial of a claim in the fast track (excluding other disbursements or VAT). Part 46 defined such costs as "fast track trial costs". The amount of fast track trial costs prescribed by CPR Pt 46 is set out in the table below:

Value of the claim	Amount of fast track trial costs which the court may award
No more than £3,000	£485.00
More than £3,000 but not more than £10,000	£690.00
More than £10,000 but not more than £15,000	£1,035.00
For proceedings issued on or after 6th April 2009, more than £15,000	£1,650.00

If the case settles at the door of the court, the fast track trial costs are still payable: *Mendes v Hochtief (UK) Construction Ltd* [2016] EWHC 976 (QB).

19–009   **Proposed fixed costs regime for the Patents County Court.** During 2009, work was in progress to develop a fixed costs regime for the Patents County Court. Mr Justice Arnold had assembled some convincing evidence to show that that was what court users wanted. Furthermore the Patents County Court was then facing competition from courts elsewhere in the EU, where fixed costs at modest levels were the norm. In IP litigation (unlike most other fields), the parties often had a choice as to the jurisdiction in which they would litigate.

Issues for the Costs Review. Against that background, an obvious question for the Costs Review was whether to extend fixed costs, and if so how far. It was necessary to consider (a) whether there should be fixed costs for some or all pre-trial work in fast track cases; and (b) whether there should be fixed costs for any cases above the fast track.   **19–010**

2. DEBATE DURING THE COSTS REVIEW

The position of the assessors. One of the few issues upon which all the assessors were agreed was that there should be a serious attempt to achieve a fixed costs regime for all stages of fast track litigation. We therefore sought the assistance of an experienced group of district judges and practitioners in producing the first draft of such a scheme.   **19–011**

Proposals in the Preliminary Report concerning fast track fixed costs. Chapter 22 of the Preliminary Report outlined Lord Woolf's earlier proposal for fixed costs. The chapter noted that the reasons why fixed costs had not been introduced were "complex and in part political".[2] The chapter asserted that the time had come to resurrect the proposal. Table 22.2 on p.205 set out a draft grid of fast track fixed costs for consideration. The grid was stated to be an illustration.   **19–012**

Proposals in the Preliminary Report concerning fixed costs above the fast track. Chapter 23 of the Preliminary Report identified the policy considerations for and against fixed costs in the multi-track as follows: **19–013**

"1.2 *Policy arguments in favour.* The policy arguments in favour of a fixed cost regime above the fast track have previously been mentioned. They include the following:

(i)   Some litigants (e.g. small businesses) may regard the risk of incurring indeterminate costs liability to the other side if they lose as worse than the risk of failing to recover all their own costs if they win. A party can control the costs which he incurs. A party cannot control the costs which the other side may be running up. Nor can a retrospective detailed assessment achieve such control.

(ii) Such a regime achieves certainty in those categories of civil litigation where it is impracticable to establish type 1 fixed costs. Certainty is a commodity which many litigants (especially commercial litigants) crave and which is singularly lacking in civil litigation.

(iii) If both parties know that, win or lose, they will be paying at least part of their own costs, there will be an incentive for economy on both sides.

1.3 *Policy arguments against.* The policy arguments against a fixed costs regime above the fast track have also been mentioned previously. They include the following:

---

[2] PR Ch. 22, para. 1.6.

> (i) It is unjust that the party who is vindicated should bear part of his own costs. The claimant, if successful, should keep all of his damages intact. The defendant, if successful, should walk away from the courtroom no poorer than when he arrived.
>
> (ii) In a fixed costs regime a wealthy party can generate much expense by procedural manoeuvres and thus grind down the other side, which will never recover all of its costs."

19–014   **Information about fixed costs regimes overseas.** In the Preliminary Report, Chs 23, 55, 58, 59 and 62 described in detail the fixed costs schemes or similar regimes in Germany, certain Australian states, New Zealand and the East Caribbean. The Preliminary Report invited consideration of whether we should adopt some similar scheme in England and Wales.

19–015   **Debate during Phase Two.** The PR proposals concerning fixed costs provoked much lively debate during Phase Two, the consultation period. Chapters 15 and 16 of the Final Report summarise that debate. Suffice it to say that all possible viewpoints were articulated and each of the stakeholder groups defended their corner with gusto. There was a seminar on 22 July 2009, specifically focused on fixed costs.

19–016   **Conclusion in respect of the fast track.** It became clear during the course of Phase Two that, at the very least, there must be a regime of fixed costs for all fast track cases. I therefore sought the help of the CJC in working out the details.

19–017   **Work to develop fixed costs for fast track cases.** During the autumn of 2009, the CJC hosted a series of five facilitative meetings (a) between claimant representatives and defendant representatives in relation to PI claims, and (b) between landlord representatives and tenant representatives in relation to housing disrepair claims. The meetings were chaired by Michael Napier QC, who was one of the Costs Review assessors. A substantial quantity of data was assembled and provided by Professor Paul Fenn, another of the assessors, for the assistance of all present. Tim Wallis of the CJC acted as mediator, when required. His Honour Judge Nic Madge assisted Mr Napier in chairing the housing disrepair meetings. Bob Musgrove, Chief Executive of the CJC, was the overall organiser.

19–018   **Proposals for fixed costs for fast track personal injury cases.** Although the facilitative meetings did not reach agreement on figures for fixed costs, they exposed the issues and brought the competing arguments into sharp relief. On the basis of all that material, it was possible to draw up sensible grids of fixed costs for most categories of PI cases. Those grids appear as Tables A and B on FR pp. 538–539.

19–019   **Intellectual property cases.** During the summer of 2009, the Intellectual Property Court Users Committee was developing a scheme of fixed costs for IP claims up to £500,000. This scheme fitted perfectly with the emerging proposals of the Costs Review. The labours of the IP Court Users were much appreciated. Their timing was perfect and they were doing all the work.

What about the rest of the multi-track? This wasn't so easy, as views were   **19–020**
sharply divided. Two partners of CMS Cameron McKenna LLP put forward an
interesting proposal[3] for proportionate fixed costs in all claims up to £250,000.
Despite the attraction of this proposal, it seemed best to let the other reforms bed
in before embarking upon such an ambitious scheme.

3. RECOMMENDATIONS IN THE FINAL REPORT OF JANUARY 2010

Fixed costs for fast track personal injury cases. Chapter 15 of the Final   **19–021**
Report was one of the longest chapters in the Final Report. It reviewed the issues
concerning fast track fixed costs in detail. The chapter proposed that a regime of
fixed costs be introduced for personal injury claims in accordance with tables A
and B, set put on pp. 538–539.

Fixed costs for medical reports. Paragraph 5.22 of FR Ch. 15 proposed that   **19–022**
there should be fixed costs for medical reports and for obtaining medical records in
fast track personal injury cases. This would not be difficult to achieve, in view of the
agreements which had already been reached with medical reporting organisations.

Fixed costs for fast track non-personal injury cases. Section 6 of FR Ch. 15   **19–023**
set out proposals for fixing the costs of all non-PI claims. In relation to RTA
claims not involving personal injury (sometimes called "bent metal" claims), the
proposal was (a) if resolved pre-issue: £626 + 4% of damages; (b) if settled post-
issue: £1,583 + 9% of damages; (c) if the case went to trial: the same as (b) + fast
track trial costs. In relation to most other fast track non-PI claims, the proposal
was for caps in respect of pre-trial costs plus the fast track trial costs as already
established. The supporting evidence for all these proposals is to be found in the
Preliminary Report, the Final Report and their appendices.

Need for regular reviews. In any fixed costs scheme, the figures must be kept   **19–024**
under regular review. Chapter 15 of the Final Report emphasised the importance
of such reviews.

Intellectual property claims up to £500,000. Chapter 24 of the Final Report,   **19–025**
building on work done by the Intellectual Property Court Users' Committee, supported the proposal for a fixed costs regime for IP claims up to £500,000. Such
claims .would proceed in the Patents County Court, which was subsequently
renamed the Intellectual Property Enterprise Court. The total recoverable costs
in those cases would be £50,000 in respect of patent or infringement claims and
£25,000 in respect of other claims.

The lower reaches of the multi-track generally. Chapter 16 of the Final   **19–026**
Report considered the possibility of introducing a fixed costs regime in the
lower reaches of the multi-track generally. Chapter 16 reached the following
conclusions:

---

[3] See FR p.171, para. 2.8.

"2.9 Having considered the competing arguments advanced during Phase 2, I think that it would be premature to embark upon any scheme of fixed costs or scale costs in respect of lower value multi-track cases for the time being. The top priority at the moment must be (a) to achieve a comprehensive scheme of fixed or predictable costs in the fast track and (b) to introduce a scheme of capped scale costs for lower value multi-track IP cases. These proposals are set out in chapters 15 and 24 respectively.

2.10 Once the necessary reforms have been implemented in the fast track and in multi-track cases in the Patents County Court (the 'PCC'), there must be a period of evaluation. Following that period of evaluation, I recommend that further consideration should be given to the possibility of introducing a scheme of fixed costs or scale costs into the lower reaches of the multi-track. . . .

2.11 If, following that future consultation process, any scheme of fixed costs or scale costs is to be adopted, there will be a variety of models for consideration. One model would be a system of scale costs subject to an overall cap, such as that which is planned for the PCC. Another model would be the CMS scheme.[4] A third model would be a scheme of fixed costs of the kind operated in Germany. The German costs regime is described in PR chapter 55. Since the German civil justice system is structured differently from our own, the German costs rules could be a general guide but not, of course, a template."

4. IMPLEMENTATION

19–027   **Intellectual property claims.** The proposed fixed costs scheme for IP claims up to £500,000 was duly implemented in 2011. The relevant rules are in CPR Pt 45 at rr.45.30–45.32 and in PD 45, section 3.

19–028   **Was this scheme a success?** Yes, it was. Court users liked it.[5] The number of new claims in the Intellectual Property Enterprise Court increased following the introduction of fixed costs. According to a Freedom of Information request, the figures are as follows:

Time Period	Small Claims Track	Multi Track Claims
1 January – 31 December 2011	0	116
1 January – 31 December 2012	2	186
1 January – 31 December 2013	61	226
1 January – 31 December 2014	113	195
1 January – 6 August 2015	50	133

---

[4] The CMS scheme covered cases up to £250,000.

[5] See the seventeenth implementation lecture delivered by Mr Justice Arnold on 12 February 2013, entitled "Intellectual Property Litigation: Implementation of the Jackson Report's Recommendations", in particular at para. 3.7.

Fast track personal injury cases. The MoJ and the Rule Committee originally   19–029
rejected the FR proposals for fixing the costs of fast track PI cases. In late 2012,
however, there was a change of heart. In 2013, they implemented a scheme of
fixed costs for most PI fast track claims in accordance with the recommendations in FR Ch. 15 and Tables A and B, subject to modest adjustments. It was not
possible to complete the exercise by 1 April 2013. These fixed costs rules were
incorporated into CPR Pt 45 and came into force on 31 July 2013 (four months
after the general implementation date).[6]

Did the introduction of fixed costs deter people from bringing fast track   19–030
personal injury claims? No, it didn't. According to the statistics from the
online claims portal, the introduction of fixed costs does not seem to have had
any deterrent effect on claims being launched. Inevitably, there was a spike of
claims issued in March 2013, as solicitors launched actions in a rush to avoid the
new rules, with a consequent decline in the following months. If one ignores that
abnormal period, however, the number of claim notification forms sent through
the online claims portal has remained reasonably static both before and after the
introduction of fixed costs. Some 833,170 claims were launched in 2012, as com-
pared to 876,532 in 2015.

Fixed costs for medical reports in fast track personal injury cases. With   19–031
effect from 1 October 2014, CPR Pt 45 was amended to prescribe fixed costs
for medical reports and for obtaining medical records in soft tissue injury claims
under the RTA Protocol. Rule 45.19(2A) allows the following:

"(a) obtaining the first report from any expert permitted under 1.1(12) of the RTA
    Protocol: £180;
 (b) obtaining a further report where justified from one of the following disciplines—

    (i) Consultant Orthopaedic Surgeon (inclusive of a review of medical records
       where applicable): £420;
    (ii) Consultant in Accident and Emergency Medicine: £360;
    (iii) General Practitioner registered with the General Medical Council: £180; or
    (iv) Physiotherapist registered with the Health and Care Professions Council: £180;

 (c) obtaining medical records: no more than £30 plus the direct cost from the holder
    of the records, and limited to £80 in total for each set of records required. Where
    relevant records are required from more than one holder of records, the fixed fee
    applies to each set of records required;
 (d) addendum report on medical records (except by Consultant Orthopaedic Surgeon):
    £50; and
 (e) answer to questions under Part 35: £80."

---

[6] It was a historical accident that fixed costs were not introduced in 2013 for fast track employers'
liability disease cases where liability was disputed. For further explanation, see Jackson LJ's lecture
to the Westminster Legal Policy Forum entitled "The future for civil litigation and the fixed costs
regime" on 23 May 2016. It is available on the Judiciary website.

5. THE FUTURE

19–032   **Non-personal injury fast track cases.** The MoJ has not yet implemented the FR recommendations for fixing the costs of non-PI fast track cases. Informal indications have been that the MoJ is sympathetic to the proposal for fixing those costs, but other matters have taken priority. It is hoped and indeed expected that this will soon be addressed.

19–033   **The lower reaches of the multi-track.** It is now five years since fixed costs were introduced in the Intellectual Property Enterprise Court and three years since fixed costs were introduced into the fast track for PI cases. Experience of those regimes has been satisfactory. Indeed there has been an increase in the number of IP cases brought under the fixed costs regime. We now have three years' experience of costs budgeting and costs management, which has sharpened everyone's appreciation of costs issues. Therefore, the time has now come to take forward the proposals in FR Ch. 16, namely fixing costs in the lower regions of the multi-track. The case for doing so was addressed in the IPA Annual Lecture on 28 January 2016.[7] Following the lecture, ministers have indicated that they are now considering the introduction of fixed costs into the lower reaches of the multi-track.[8]

19–034   **What are the benefits of introducing fixed costs into the lower reaches of multi-track?** Two obvious benefits are (i) proportionality and (ii) certainty.

(i) *Proportionality.* Fixing costs is an effective way of ensuring that a party's recoverable costs and its adverse costs risk are proportionate to the subject matter of the litigation in every case (depending, of course, upon the figures which are chosen). This will apply unless the party's conduct is such as to attract an order for costs assessed on the indemnity basis.

(ii) *Certainty.* A fixed costs regime provides certainty and predictability. This is something which most litigants desire and some litigants desperately need. A fixed costs regime is easier for solicitors to explain to clients than the current costs rules. Also a fixed costs regime dispenses with the need for costs budgeting and costs assessment. This will achieve (a) a substantial saving of process costs for the parties and (b) a substantial reduction in the demands made upon the resources of the court.

19–035   **Survey by the Federation of Small Businesses.** During 2009, for the assistance of the Costs Review, the FSB carried out a survey of their members on a number of issues. Among other matters, this survey revealed a preference for fixed costs in business disputes up to £500,000: see FR Ch. 25, para. 2.8. Most members of the FSB are, or at least were at the time of the survey, "micro-businesses", which simply dared not run the risk of an open-ended liability for adverse costs. They

---

[7] Available at *https://www.judiciary.gov.uk/wp-content/uploads/2016/01/fixedcostslecture-1.pdf* [Accessed 1 July 2016].
[8] e.g. the keynote speech by Lord Faulks at the APIL Annual Conference on 4 May 2016.

were therefore willing to make only a partial (but certain) costs recovery if they won.

In areas such as this, the views of the clients matter. Obviously, the submissions of the profession are important as well. But those submissions must not be allowed to drown out the voices of the actual court users.

How can a scheme of fixed costs be devised for the multi-track? It will be **19–036** possible to build on the new "proportionate costs" rule in order to establish a grid of fixed costs. In the first instance, it will be sensible to limit this exercise to the lower reaches of the multi-track. CPR r.44.5(3) (which implements FR Ch. 3, para. 5.15) sets out five factors to consider in determining whether costs are proportionate, namely:

(a) the sums in issue in the proceedings;

(b) the value of any non-monetary relief in issue in the proceedings;

(c) the complexity of the litigation;

(d) any additional work generated by the conduct of the paying party; and

(e) any wider factors involved in the proceedings, such as reputation or public importance.

Demands for amplification of the proportionate costs rule. Ever since **19–037** work began on implementing the FR reforms, there has been much pressure from the profession for provisions to supplement the new "proportionate costs" rule. Unfortunately, any attempt to draft a practice direction which supplements those five general rules with another set of general rules, albeit more specifically focused, is doomed to fail. This is for the reasons set out in Ch. 3, above. The only way to satisfy the requests for amplification is to convert the five identified factors into hard figures: in other words, to create a fixed costs regime.[9]

How can you convert the five factors in r.44.3(5) into a fixed costs grid? **19–038** This will involve two principal stages:

(i) Determining for each level of claim (e.g. £25,000 to £50,000; £50,000 to £100,000, etc) what amount of costs would be proportionate for such litigation.

(ii) Then devising a set of rules for adjusting those costs in order to take into account factors (c), (d) and (e). This could be done by means of specifying a percentage addition to the costs established at the first stage.

There may then be a need to add an escape clause or some other provision to deal with exceptional circumstances.

---

[9] See Hurst, Middleton & Mallalieu, *Questions and Answers* at pp. 42–43:
"Those seeking certainty are, in effect, wishing for something akin to a form of fixed fee regime for all cases. . . . Be careful for what you wish."

19–039   **An illustration of how that might be done.** The IPA Annual Lecture delivered on 28 January 2016 was a first attempt at that exercise. As made clear at the time, the lecture was an illustration of how one might set about devising a grid of fixed costs. The lecture was not setting out a set of final figures to be incorporated as they stood into CPR Pt 45. On the contrary, the lecture proposed a programme of facilitative meetings under the aegis of the CJC in order to discuss the figures and develop the rules for adjustment. A lecture at the Westminster Legal Policy Forum on 23 May 2016 supplemented the IPA Annual Lecture.[10]

19–040   **Should there be a special fixed costs scheme for clinical negligence cases?** There has been some discussion over the last year or so about the possibility of introducing a special fixed costs scheme for clinical negligence cases in October 2016. This would appear to be an unwise course. Clinical negligence cases are not so different from all other claims that they should have their own separate regime established in advance. Such an approach would lead to an unwelcome Balkanisation of civil litigation. Clinical negligence cases will in due course benefit from whatever general fixed costs regime the Government may decide to introduce. In late May 2016, the Department of Health stated that they were postponing their fixed costs plans.[11] From the point of view of the integrity of civil justice, this decision is to be welcomed.

---

[10] Both lectures were by Jackson LJ and are available on the Judiciary website.
[11] "*Litigation Futures*, 31 May 2016, available at: *http://www.litigationfutures.com/news/government-admits-defeat-bid-introduce-fixed-costs-clinical-negligence-1-october* [Accessed 1 July 2016].

DETAILED ASSESSMENT

1. BACKGROUND

Nineteenth century. The Judicature Acts 1873–1875 established the Supreme **20–001**
Court of Judicature, which included the Court of Appeal and the divisions of
the High Court. The RSC regulated the procedure of those courts. From 1883
onwards, RSC Order 65 r.29 provided:

> "On every taxation the Taxing Master shall allow all such costs, charges and expenses as
> shall appear to him to have been necessary or proper for the attainment of justice or for
> defending the rights of any party, but, save as against the party who incurred the same,
> no costs shall be allowed which appear to the Taxing Master to have been incurred or
> increased through over caution, negligence or mistake or by payment of special fees to
> counsel or special charges or expenses to witnesses or other persons, or by other unusual
> expenses."

Twentieth century. In the second half of the twentieth century, the rules gov- **20–002**
erning "taxation" or assessment of costs underwent successive revisions, but the
format of bills of costs remained broadly similar. It was based on the style of a
Victorian account book.

The three stages. Ever since the nineteenth century, the process of determin- **20–003**
ing the amount of costs to be paid has involved, essentially, three stages. First, the
receiving party lodges its bill of costs. Secondly, the paying party identifies which
costs it is disputing and why. Thirdly, there is a hearing before a taxing master
(re-styled as costs judge after the Woolf reforms) to decide the issues.

Issues for the Costs Review. One of the many issues for consideration in the **20–004**
2009 Review was whether and how the process of detailed assessment of recoverable costs should be modernised.

The form of bills of cost. The current form bill of costs has a long and distin- **20–005**
guished pedigree. It is based upon the style of a Victorian account book. Despite
those historic virtues, the format is neither helpful nor appropriate in the twenty

first century. The current form of bill makes it relatively easy for a receiving party to disguise or even hide what has gone on. What is required is a bill which (a) gives relevant information to the court and to the paying party, and (b) is transparent. Chapter 53 of the Preliminary Report highlighted these issues and invited consultees to give their views.

20–006   **Views during the Costs Review consultation.** Most of those consulted endorsed the criticisms set out above. The current bill of costs is cumbersome, time consuming and expensive to produce. It is opaque, giving no clear information to the reader as to why costs were incurred or even the underlying work done. The information about time spent on documents is particularly difficult to decode. The current form of bill is an anachronism that makes no use of time-recording software.

20–007   **Procedure for detailed assessment.** A second cause for concern was the somewhat cumbersome procedure for detailed assessment. Points of dispute and points of reply tended to be prolix and formulaic. The rules governing settlement offers were unduly restrictive.

20–008   **Procedure disproportionately expensive for lower value bills.** A third, but pressing, problem was that in respect of lower value claims the whole process was unduly expensive. An oral hearing, with representatives instructed to appear on both sides, generated disproportionate cost. Some people looked enviously at the system of provisional assessment which the Hong Kong courts have developed.

2. RECOMMENDATIONS IN THE FINAL REPORT OF JANUARY 2010

20–009   **Requirements for a bill of costs.** Chapter 45 of the Final Report set out the three requirements which any new bill would need to meet:

(i) It must provide a transparent explanation about what work was done and why.

(ii) It must provide a user-friendly synopsis of the work done, how long it took and why.

(iii) It must be inexpensive to produce.

20–010   **Use of modern IT.** Paragraphs 5.4–5.8 of FR Ch. 45 argued that a new bill of costs should be developed which was capable of being automatically generated from time-recording software. It would contain all the necessary information required for the paying party—or a judge—to understand the receiving party's costs in a clear, transparent and intelligible way while producing considerable savings in time.

20–011   **Recommendations in respect of bills of costs.** Chapter 45 of the Final Report made two recommendations in respect of bills of costs:

"(i) A new format of bills of costs should be devised, which will be more informative and capable of yielding information at different levels of generality.

(ii) Software should be developed which will (a) be used for time recording and capturing relevant information and (b) automatically generate schedules for summary assessment or bills for detailed assessment as and when required. The long term aim must be to harmonise the procedures and systems which will be used for costs budgeting, costs management, summary assessment and detailed assessment."

Procedure for assessing costs. Paragraphs 5.10–5.16 of FR Ch. 45 recom-   **20–012**
mended that the procedure for assessing costs be reformed as follows:

"5.10 *Interim payments.* The Costs PD should provide that whenever the court makes an order for costs to be assessed, the court shall also order an interim payment on account of costs, unless there is good reason not to do so. It would be going too far for the rules to make an order for interim payment automatic. For example, there may be doubt about the right to any further costs or there may be a real prospect of a set off at a later stage.

5.11 *Points of dispute and points of reply.* Both points of dispute and points of reply need to be shorter and more focused. The practice of quoting passages from well known judgments should be abandoned. The practice of repeatedly using familiar formulae, in Homeric style, should also be abandoned. The pleaders on both sides should set out their contentions relevant to the instant cases clearly and concisely. There should be no need to plead to every individual item in a bill of costs, nor to reply to every paragraph in the points of dispute.

5.12 In order to achieve the required approach to points of dispute and points of reply I propose that sections 35 and 39 of the Costs PD be amended as set out in appendix 10 to this report.

5.13 *Compulsory offers.* PP [paying party] should be required to make an offer when it serves its points of dispute. The offer may be contained in the points of dispute or in a separate document. The sum offered may be more or less than the amount of the interim payment ordered by the court.

5.14 *Offers.* The Part 36 procedure should apply to detailed assessment proceedings. The '14 day' provision in Costs PD paragraph 46.1 should be repealed.

5.15 *Costs of detailed assessment proceedings.* The default position should remain as set out in CPR rule 47.18. However, if PP makes an offer which RP [receiving party] fails beat, then the normal consequence should be that RP pays PP's costs after the date when the offer expired. Likewise RP should be rewarded for making a sufficient offer, which PP rejects. The reward should be enhanced interest and indemnity costs in respect of the assessment proceedings.

5.16 *Time for appeal.* Time for appeal should start to run from the conclusion of the final hearing, unless the court orders otherwise. There will be some occasions when it would be appropriate for the court to order otherwise. For example, it may be sensible for an appeal against a decision on preliminary issues to proceed before the full detailed assessment takes place."

Provisional assessment. Paragraph 5.17 of FR Ch. 45 recommended that a   **20–013**
system of provisional assessment should be piloted. In respect of lower value bills, the costs judge should assess the amount of costs recoverable on the papers. There should be no oral hearing unless either party was so dissatisfied with the decision that it wanted such a hearing. That party would pay both sides' costs, unless it achieved a substantially better outcome as a result of the hearing.

3. Procedural Reforms Implemented in April 2010

(i) *Full detailed assessment*

20-014   **Reforms to the procedure for detailed assessment.** A working group chaired by Senior Costs Judge Peter Hurst prepared a series of amendments to the CPR and the Costs Practice Direction which would give effect to the package of reforms proposed in FR Ch. 45, paras 5.10–5.16 (quoted above). This was a massive exercise and involved rewriting the Costs Practice Direction. All of those reforms came into force on 1 April 2013.

20-015   **And how are the new procedures for detailed assessment working in practice?** They are working well. One can say this with some confidence, because there has been a resounding silence from court users. If practitioners disliked the new rules about offers or the new form points of dispute or any of the other innovations, we would have heard about it soon enough. Lack of audible protest is the most that any civil justice reformer can realistically hope for.

20-016   **Is there any place for ADR in the detailed assessment of costs?** Yes, there certainly is. Chapter 9, above, has emphasised the general merits of ADR. The same principles apply when the parties are in dispute about the quantum of costs. Colin Campbell, a former costs judge, has identified the benefits in his article "Mediating the costs of the action – ADR's alternative to detailed assessment".[1] The benefits include that a mediator, knowing the offers on both sides and using his costs expertise, can help the parties to bridge the gap. An effective mediation is substantially cheaper than going through the full process of detailed assessment.

(ii) *Lower value bills which go to provisional assessment*

20-017   **Pilot of provisional assessment.** A pilot of provisional assessment began at Leeds, Scarborough and York on 1 October 2010 and completed its first year on 30 September 2011. The pilot continued for a second year, but monitoring was less intense after 1 October 2011 because of other pressures on court staff. From the outset, more pilot cases proceeded at Leeds than at the other two court centres. The two regional costs judges conducting the pilot were DJ Bedford and DJ Hill.

20-018   **Procedures adopted in the pilot.** The procedures adopted in the pilot were set out in PD 51E. In essence any bill of costs, in which the base costs claimed were £25,000 or less, was assessed on paper by the district judge, who then produced a provisional assessment of the amount of costs due to the receiving party. If either party was dissatisfied, it could request an oral hearing. If that party achieved a result at the oral hearing which was better by 20% (or more) than the provisional assessment, it could recover (subject to any offers that had been made) the costs of the oral hearing. If it failed to achieve that degree of success, it paid the costs of the oral hearing.

---

[1] This forms Ch. 12 of *Costs Law: an Expert Guide,* edited by Laura Slater.

Results from the first year of the pilot. The great majority of all provisional   **20–019**
assessments were carried out at Leeds. Therefore, data collection and analysis
centred on that court. A total of 119 cases entered the pilot at Leeds. Out of those
119 cases, 19 settled at an early stage and 100 proceeded to provisional assessment.
Out of those 100 cases, there were 17 requests for an oral hearing, but only two
cases actually proceeded to an oral hearing. In neither of those two cases did the
party who sought a hearing achieve an improvement in its position of 20% or more.

Benefits of provisional assessment. On the basis of the pilot, the principal   **20–020**
benefits of provisional assessment appeared to be the following:

(i) The process was quick and simple. It thus enabled many parties, who
would normally be put off by the expensive and convoluted process of
detailed assessment, to obtain a judicial assessment of bills. Thus, the
process addressed one major complaint about detailed assessment which
was repeatedly raised during the Costs Review.

(ii) The figures which were assessed (or agreed following provisional
assessment) were likely to be fairer than settlements negotiated in circumstances where neither party could face going through the process of normal
detailed assessment.

(iii) The process was far cheaper for the parties than traditional detailed assessment, because (save in rare cases) they avoided the costs of preparing for
and attending a hearing. Indeed, unlike traditional detailed assessment, it
was cost effective. DJs Hill and Bedford estimated that the savings for the
parties were at least £4,000 per case.

General introduction of provisional assessment. With the help of DJ Hill, I   **20–021**
drafted rules for provisional assessment, which took account of certain glitches in
the pilot and lessons learned. The Rule Committee approved the draft rules and
they now appear as CPR r.47.15 and section 14 of the Costs Practice Direction.
The provisions apply to bills of costs up to £75,000. They came into force on 1
April 2013.

4. REFORMS TO BILLS OF COSTS – STILL WORK IN PROGRESS

Work undertaken by the Association of Costs Lawyers. In 2010, the   **20–022**
Association of Costs Lawyers ("ACL") set up a "Jackson Working Group" in
order to take forward FR recommendations 106 and 107. That group did some
excellent and detailed work. In October 2011, the ACL published its report entitled *Modernising Bills of Costs* as part of the implementation of those recommendations. The report recommended investigating whether the Uniform Task-Based
Management System ("UTBMS") operated by Legal Electronic Data Exchange
Standard ("LEDES") could be adapted for use in producing a new Bill of Costs.
The UTBMS consists of standard time recording codes for litigation. US law
firms, including those based in the UK, use this system. Some of the Magic Circle
firms also use UTBMS.

20–023   **Hutton Committee.** Senior Costs Judge Peter Hurst asked Jeremy Morgan QC to set up a working group, known as the "Jackson Review EW-UTBMS Development Steering Committee" to take forward the proposal in the ACL Report. That committee is now chaired by Alexander Hutton QC. It is known as "the Hutton committee" and includes Costs Judge Colum Leonard. The Hutton Committee carried out a detailed review. It then recommended adapting the codes in the existing UTMBS into new "J-Codes",[2] which were formulated for an UTMBS code set for use in England and Wales (EW-UTBMS).

20–024   **Formal request of 30 July 2014.** On the 30 July 2014, Lord Dyson MR, Senior Costs Judge Peter Hurst and I sent a written request to the Hutton Committee to move on to the next stage of their work. That was one of Peter Hurst's last acts as Senior Costs Judge. The 30 July 2014 was the occasion of his—hugely well attended—valedictory hearing in the Royal Courts of Justice.

20–025   **Production of a new form bill.** The Hutton Committee, after a considerable amount of effort and hard graft, produced a new format bill of costs which was built on three integrated pieces of work.

20–026   **The J-Codes.** First, they have created J-Codes: a standardised way of capturing time-recorded information adapted from the UTBMS. The J-Codes work by identifying the Precedent H phase in which work is undertaken (e.g. Pre-Action), what task is being worked on (e.g. Investigation of the facts or law) and the type of activity being undertaken (e.g. Planning, researching or drafting). The J-Codes were endorsed by the Master of the Rolls, Senior Costs Judge Peter Hurst and myself in the written request dated 30 July 2014. They have now been ratified by the body with oversight of the UTBMS, the LEDES Oversight Committee.

20–027   **The electronic spreadsheet.** Secondly, there is a multi-purpose electronic Excel spreadsheet. This allows for a firm's time-recording data to be fed into it automatically and to create a bill of costs from it. It is possible to sort the data in a number of ways (by phase, by date or by the type of work being done). From this base you can generate a bill showing the full amount of the actual costs, which the client must pay. You can also generate a bill showing the costs recoverable from the other side. This requires adjustments, to strip out items payable by the client but not permissible as recoverable costs. The electronic spreadsheet can produce a bill for either detailed or summary assessment.

20–028   **The finished bill.** Thirdly, there is the finished version of the bill—this condenses all the information contained in the spreadsheet into a clear and legible format. It makes it possible for the judge or the paying party to examine the bill in varying levels of generality and with ease of comparison with the costs budget. Although the full bill will be in electronic form only (as it will have too many columns to print in A4) and it is designed primarily for use on screen, a shortened printed version can easily be made from it. Both will need to be served. A finished

---

[2] The committee felt that "J" was a suitable letter, because it was the initial of Jeremy or Jackson or Judicial.

version of the print bill, including example data, is available as Precedent AA, attached to PD 51L (White Book 2016, pp. 1627–1645) and available on the MoJ website.

Consultation and criticism. The Hutton Committee conducted a consultation **20–029** on their proposals and received a number of critical responses. Four key strands of criticism have emerged from them, namely:

(i) The proposed system is too expensive to implement.

(ii) The proposed system is too complex to work with.

(iii) The requirement to use J-Codes is too prescriptive.

(iv) It would be too time-consuming to transfer work done before J-codes into the new format.

Comment. For reasons explained in a recent lecture, it is not accepted that **20–030** those criticisms are valid.[3] In any event, the first three criticisms are really directed to J-Codes, rather than to the concept of the new form bill and accompanying electronic spreadsheet. The fourth criticism could be met by only using the new system for future work.

Supporters of J-Codes. Having identified the criticisms, it is only fair to say **20–031** that there are many strong supporters of J-codes. Those who have the necessary IT find that the procedures are extremely efficient and cost effective. Deborah Burke, Chair of the Law Society Civil Litigation Section Committee, states that J-Codes have the following benefits:[4]

"1. Within the costs management regime, J-codes make the processes of budget construction and monitoring quicker and cheaper. J-codes work with Precedent H and Precedent Q, and they will work with the new e-bill format.
2. For all cases, costs negotiations and costs assessments can be made more effective and less costly.
3. Costs information is transparent, efficient, and informative both for firms and their clients.
4. Data that has been recorded thematically can be analysed in many different ways for many different purposes.
5. J-codes are part of the UTBMS code set family which is already present in many time recording/PMS and they map to other existing code sets.
6. J-codes map to the grid of fixed recoverable fees suggested by Lord Justice Jackson and can be used to help firms decide whether and how they will work with fixed recoverable fees when they are introduced."

Decision of the Rule Committee. The Rule Committee established a voluntary **20–032** pilot for the proposed new bill of costs, commencing in October 2015. Practice Direction 51L sets out the rules governing the voluntary pilot. The original plan was that the voluntary pilot would end in April 2016 and that a mandatory pilot would start. However, at their December 2015 meeting, the Rule Committee

---

[3] See *The new form bill of costs*, 21 April 2016, available on the Judiciary website.
[4] *Costs Law: an Expert Guide*, Ch. 3, "J-Codes and the new bill of costs".

decided to extend the lifespan of the voluntary pilot until December 2016. It was agreed that the proposals warranted "careful further consideration" and "that it was too soon for any decision to be taken".

20–033   **The present position.** At the time of writing, the new form bill of costs is still subject to the voluntary pilot set out in PD 51L. Some firms are using J-Codes and the new form bill of costs. Others are not.

5. SUGGESTED WAY FORWARD FOR BILLS OF COSTS

20–034   **A practical solution.** There is a practical solution to the present quandary. A sensible way forward would be to revise the current proposals, preserving the work of the Hutton Committee while allowing for greater flexibility in the new bill.

The Hutton Committee's proposed version of the bill should be adopted as the new bill format, albeit with the references to the J-Codes removed. The CPR should allow practitioners to prepare that bill in any manner of their choosing; whether with the assistance of J-Codes, automatically generated by an Excel spreadsheet or by hand.

A digital copy of this should be served on the court and the paying party along with an electronic spreadsheet, which clearly and accurately details the work done in the course of litigation, following the Precedent H stages. This should be in the same format of phase/task/activity and adopt the Precedent H guidance for what work falls in a given phase. Time entries can either be generated automatically by time-recording software or inputted manually by those who prefer to record their work done on paper. For those using J-Codes, the Hutton Committee spreadsheet provides an excellent tool for preparing the bill.

20–035   **Advantages of this approach.** This proposal has three key elements to commend it:

    (i) There is a new format bill which meets the three criteria set out in section 2, above, and the recommendations in the Final Report. The new format bill integrates with costs budgeting and Precedent H. It can be generated automatically by time-recording software. It provides a framework for software providers to create tools for the professions.

    (ii) It makes good use of the excellent work of the Hutton Committee. While revising the proposals will mean that the current version of the spreadsheet and the J-Codes are not an essential part of the scheme, their value will be preserved for those who adopt J-Codes.

    (iii) It sidesteps much of the criticism which gave rise to the present delays. The print version and the accompanying spreadsheet are not radical innovations. Nor do they involve significant cost. They require only a basic level of computer literacy and an understanding of how to present information clearly.

Lecture on 21 April 2016. I put forward the above proposals in a lecture at the   **20–036**
Law Society's Civil Litigation Conference on 21 April 2016.[5] Alexander Hutton
QC was present and supported the proposals.

Action taken by the Rule Committee. At its meeting on 13 May 2016, the   **20–037**
Rule Committee considered the proposals made in the lecture of 21 April and set
up a sub-committee to take the matter forward. As an interim measure, the Rule
Committee extended the present voluntary pilot until 30 September 2017.

Conclusion. It is hoped that the above proposals or a variant of them will find   **20–038**
favour and that in the near future we shall have intelligible bills of costs, which
(a) make full use of modern IT and (b) are much quicker and cheaper to produce.
This will be very much in the public interest.

---

[5] *The new form bill of costs.* This lecture is available on the Judiciary website: *https://www.judiciary. gov.uk/.*

CHAPTER 21

SUMMARY ASSESSMENT

1. BACKGROUND

Woolf reforms. One of Lord Woolf's many successful innovations was to introduce summary assessment for a wide range of hearings. With effect from 26 April 1999, the normal practice was for the court summarily to assess the recoverable costs at the end of any hearing which lasted for a day or less.   **21–001**

A shock for the profession. This reform came as a something of a shock, because up till then the normal practice was to send all costs off for detailed assessment at a later date. Suddenly, all litigators were required to understand the rules and principles governing costs assessments and actually to argue about them. For the first time—*horribile dictu*—even barristers were required to pay attention to costs. There were murmurings in the Inns of Court that such distasteful matters were hardly fit to be debated by members of the Bar.   **21–002**

And a good thing too. Although unwelcome to many, it was highly beneficial for all litigators (both barristers and solicitors) to be forced to confront the realities of costs. For the first time, the costs consequences for their clients of what the lawyers were doing unfolded before their eyes. In the years following 1999, all those involved in the litigation process gained an increasing understanding of how costs were calculated and what should be allowed as recoverable costs. Indeed it was because of that increased understanding that the profession (not without some grumblings) has been able to take on the new discipline of costs management.   **21–003**

Impact on the judiciary. Many judges are ex-barristers. In 1999, they too found the introduction of summary assessment to be an unwelcome intrusion into their normal work. Neverthelessm over the years they have adapted to the process well. The more recent appointees generally have extensive experience of arguing summary assessments at the Bar.   **21–004**

Concerns at the time of the 2009 Costs Review. At the time of the Costs Review, summary assessment was still a relatively new discipline. There were concerns about (a) lack of consistency by the courts in carrying out summary assessments, and (b) lack of relevant detail which the courts needed to carry out the process properly. There were also concerns about the guideline hourly rates ("GHRs") used   **21–005**

in summary assessments. It was the practice of the Master of the Rolls to set the GHRs, acting on the advice of the Advisory Council on Civil Costs. That was a body operating under the aegis of the MoJ and chaired by an eminent Oxford professor. Many maintained that there was no satisfactory evidential basis for the GHRs.

2. RECOMMENDATIONS IN THE FINAL REPORT OF JANUARY 2010

21–006 **Chapter 6 of the Final Report: proposal for a Costs Council.** FR Ch. 6 proposed that the Advisory Council on Civil Costs should be disbanded and that a Costs Council should be set up. This body should be chaired by a High Court judge and it should have a number of functions. One important function would be to set GHRs and keep them under review.

21–007 **Composition of the Costs Council.** Turning to the composition of the Costs Council, para. 2.4 of Ch. 6 stated:

> "If a Costs Council is set up, it should be chaired by a judge or other senior person, who has long experience of the operation of the costs rules and costs assessment. It is appropriate for the Costs Council to include representatives of stakeholder groups. However, its membership should not be dominated by vested interests. It is important that all members be of high calibre and appropriate experience, so that the recommendations of the Costs Council will be authoritative.
> The Costs Council, like the Civil Procedure Rule Committee, should include a consumer representative. It should also, in my view, include an economist and a representative of the MoJ. It is unrealistic to expect the Costs Council to act on the basis of consensus, because of the conflicting interests which will be represented within it. The chairman will sometimes act as mediator and sometimes as arbitrator between opposing views, so as to ensure that fair and consistent recommendations are made on costs levels."

21–008 **Structure of Costs Council.** The Final Report proposed at Ch. 6, paras 2.15 and 2.16 that the Costs Council should either be a free standing body or, alternatively, an adjunct of the Civil Justice Council. Those paragraphs also proposed that the Costs Council should report to the Master of the Rolls, who had responsibility for setting GHRs.

21–009 **Chapter 44 of the Final Report.** FR Ch. 44 noted that some judges still felt uncomfortable undertaking "heavy" summary assessments. The chapter also noted that form N260 (the schedule lodged by parties before a hearing at which summary assessment is anticipated) was insufficiently informative. In particular, both the paying party and the court needed more information about work done on documents. This was often a large sum, about which no relevant information was provided. Chapter 44 concluded with two recommendations

> "(i) If any judge at the end of a hearing within Costs PD paragraph 13.2 considers that he or she lacks the time or the expertise to assess costs summarily (either at that hearing or on paper afterwards), then the judge should order a substantial payment on account of costs and direct detailed assessment.
> (ii) A revised and more informative version of Form N260 should be prepared for use in connection with summary assessments at the end of trials or appeals."

3. IMPLEMENTATION

Establishment of Costs Committee. The MoJ accepted the recommenda-   21–010
tions made in FR Ch. 6. It disbanded the Advisory Council on Civil Costs and
established a "Costs Committee" as a sub-committee of the Civil Justice Council.
A High Court judge was appointed to chair the committee. Members of the committee included judges and senior members of the profession from all sides. Two
distinguished economists were available to attend meetings when required.

The current position. The big problem which the Costs Committee faced was   21–011
that it did not have the resources to carry out proper empirical research, although
it undertook such surveys as it could. Also the profession was less than forthcoming in providing relevant information. Despite those handicaps, the committee
submitted its recommendations for new GHRs in June 2014. The Master of the
Rolls did not accept those recommendations because they lacked a sufficient evidential base. Thus the GHRs remain as they were in 2010.

Oh yes. What next? It must be admitted that, so far, this has not been a hugely   21–012
successful reform. Nevertheless, two points should be made on the positive side:

(i) In the new "proportionate" approach to costs, GHRs matter less than they
used to, although they still form a material part of the first stage test of the
reasonableness of the costs claimed.

(ii) The Costs Committee still exists. It can and should return to work. There
will be a new Master of the Rolls in October 2016. Sooner or later, the next
Master of the Rolls will have to grapple with the issue of GHRs and the
Costs Committee will be his first port of call.

Rules governing when courts should undertake summary assessment.   21–013
Paragraph 9.2 of PD 44, which came into force on 1 April 2013, follows the same
approach as the former Costs Practice Direction. It provides:

"The general rule is that the court should make a summary assessment of the costs—

(a) at the conclusion of the trial of a case which has been dealt with on the fast track,
in which case the order will deal with the costs of the whole claim; and
(b) at the conclusion of any other hearing, which has lasted not more than one day, in
which case the order will deal with the costs of the application or matter to which
the hearing related. If this hearing disposes of the claim, the order may deal with
the costs of the whole claim,

unless there is good reason not to do so, for example where the paying party shows
substantial grounds for disputing the sum claimed for costs that cannot be dealt with
summarily."

New form N260. A working group of district judges took forward recommen-   21–014
dation (ii) of FR Ch. 44. They produced a new version of form N260, which came
into force on 1 April 2013. A distinctive feature of the new version was that it contained a schedule of work done on documents. The receiving party was required to
set out details of all such work, including the time spent and grade of fee earner.

21–015   **An initial problem: no-one took any notice.** One problem which besets civil justice reformers is that sometimes people take no notice of their efforts and go on as before. Initially, this was the case with form N260. Practitioners continued turning up to hearings with the old form and judges could hardly refuse to assess their costs. The 2014 White Book contained the following plea:

> "In April 2013 a new version of form N260 was introduced, providing detailed information concerning work on documents, as recommended in chapter 44 of the *Final Report*. One problem, however, is that many practitioners remain blissfully unaware of this development and continue to use the old form. The new form N260 is printed para 48GP.56. Please would practitioners use it?"

Surprisingly, this plea was effective and practitioners started to use the new form.

21–016   **Beneficial effect of costs management on the process of summary assessment.** Chapter 44 of the Final Report identified that training in costs management and the subsequent experience of costs management would be likely to improve the consistency and skill of judges in carrying out summary assessment. Despite all the criticisms made of the initial judicial training for costs management, that prediction has been born out. There has been a marked improvement in the standard of summary assessments since the introduction of costs management. There has also been an increased willingness to carry out summary assessment in cases where the judge might previously have been tempted to order detailed assessment.

21–017   **Survey by London Solicitors Litigation Association.** The observations in the previous paragraph may be impressionistic, but they are supported by a survey which the LSLA carried out in June 2016. The LSLA's Litigation Trends Survey stated: "summary assessment of costs by a trial judge receives surprisingly positive backing in our survey."

4. The Future

21–018   **The three types of summary assessments.** There are three principal situations in which courts make summary assessments of costs. They are: (i) at the end of interim applications, (ii) at the end of appeals lasting less than a day, and (iii) at the end of trials.

21–019   **Is the new form N260 fit for all types of summary assessment?** Form N260 is generally satisfactory for situations (i) and (ii). It is also generally satisfactory for making a summary assessment at the end of a fast track trial. That is the only type of trial specifically referred to in PD 44 para. 9.2. Nevertheless, there is an increasing tendency for some courts (for example, the Leeds TCC and the Birmingham Mercantile Court) to carry out summary assessments at the end of multi-track trials. This is practicable because previously approved or agreed costs budgets are available. Form N260 is not really suitable for the assessment of costs at the end of any substantial trial.

Proposal for summary assessment bill for use at the end of trials. It is   **21–020**
therefore suggested that, once the new form bill of costs discussed in the previous chapter has been finalised, a "mini-version" should be developed for use in
summary assessments at the end of trials. Once technology is in place for generating the new form bill of costs, there should be no difficulty in generating mini-
versions for the purpose of summary assessment. Indeed, even in fast track cases,
that form of bill would be more helpful than form N260.

The Rolls Building leads the way. The Shorter and Flexible Trials Pilot   **21–021**
Scheme is now proceeding in the Rolls Building under PD 51N. Paragraph 2.58
of the PD provides for the judge summarily to assess costs at the end the trial, save
in exceptional circumstances. Paragraph 2.58 of the PD requires the parties' costs
schedules to follow the format of Precedent H, not form N260.

Part Seven
CONCLUSION

LESSONS FROM THE PROCESS

1. FIRST LESSON: CIVIL LITIGATION ISSUES ARE INTRACTABLE

Issues are multi-faceted. Most of the issues in this field are multi-faceted and admit of no perfect solution. Reformers are looking not for a perfect solution, but for the least bad option. For example, costs shifting promotes access to justice because it is a means of funding parties who are proved right (and therefore deserve to be funded). But it also inhibits access to justice, because the adverse costs risks deters many people from pursuing meritorious claims or defences. The least bad option is to preserve costs shifting but with severe restrictions, such as the new proportionality rule and fixed costs where possible.   **22–001**

Everyone perceives the public interest as residing in a state of affairs which coincides with their own commercial interest. This doesn't mean that all the stakeholder groups who send in submissions or speak up at seminars are being disingenuous. Far from it. They are being honest and usually have powerful points to make from their own perspective. The proposition on which this paragraph is based is simply a fact of human nature. It is therefore necessary to examine critically every submission from every source, however eminent the author may be.   **22–002**

Quot homines tot sententiae. The number of opinions which exist on civil justice issues is bewilderingly large. Any quest for consensus is therefore hopeless. Even if reformers win sufficient support for their package of reforms as a whole to secure implementation, it is highly unlikely that any individual will agree with them on every single point. Turning to the present project, those who supported the FR reforms inevitably had reservations about this point or that. But there was no consensus whatsoever about which proposals needed trimming or quietly dropping.   **22–003**

Listen to clients as well as lawyers. Lawyers and their clients often have different perspectives on the issues. For example, clients are much more likely than lawyers to support fixed costs and costs budgeting. If you are canvassing issues at a large meeting organised by major solicitors, take votes *separately* from the solicitors and the clients present. The voting figures may be very different.   **22–004**

2. SECOND LESSON: ONE PERSON IS MORE EFFECTIVE THAN A COMMITTEE

22–005   **A committee will seldom agree on major issues.** The second lesson really follows from the first lesson. Lawyers tend to be articulate and opinionated. They all have their own views on civil justice issues. Any committee of lawyers and other professionals with an interest in the law will have difficulty in reaching agreement on any serious package of reforms. The Evershed Committee illustrates the point. The members were all top lawyers and judges, fizzing with legal knowledge and experience. They deliberated for six years and produced three reports. The Committee recommended many wise revisions and amendments to the rules. But, in the words of Sorabji, "the Evershed Committee avoided fundamental questions or issues of principle".[1] The final result of the Evershed Committee's labours was the new RSC 1965. The RSC 1965 first appeared in the White Book 1967. The White Book preface stated that the new rules constituted "revision, not reform".[2] These comments are in no sense a criticism of the eminent members of the Evershed Committee. This is simply an illustration of the difficulty which any committee of that calibre will have in reaching agreement on controversial issues.

22–006   **The only solution is to appoint one person.** If those setting up a review or inquiry want to receive firm conclusions on controversial issues and firm recommendations, the only option is to entrust the task to one person. That is what the Lord Chancellor did in 1994, when appointing Lord Woolf to carry out his Access to Justice Inquiry. Lord Woolf had the benefit of various assessors and working groups to proffer advice, but in the end he alone made up his mind. His task would have been impossible if his various advisers and assessors had been required to agree on every point. Sir Henry Brooke's report on the question of unifying the civil courts was also a one-person project, although of course he consulted widely. The Briggs review in 2015–2016 was likewise a one-person project.

22–007   **Should that person be a judge?** Not necessarily. Sir Jeffery Bowman, who is not a judge, produced an excellent report on the reform of appeals, as discussed in Ch. 15, above. If the appointee is a judge, he or she has the advantage of detailed knowledge and experience of the civil justice system. But, set against that obvious advantage, there is the disadvantage of being steeped in the culture of the legal profession. Writing a report which will dismay some of your friends and former colleagues, or perhaps reduce their earnings, is not easy.

3. THIRD LESSON: ANY PROPOSALS FOR REFORM SHOULD BE EVIDENCE-BASED

22–008   **Collating evidence should start as soon as possible.** Amassing statistical and financial evidence from all possible sources is a vital part of the exercise and should start as early as possible. The material gathered during the Costs Review is to be found principally in the appendices to the Preliminary Report and the Final

---

[1] John Sorabji, *English civil justice after Woolf and Jackson*, p. 17.
[2] *Supreme Court Practice 1967*, preface, p. x.

Report, but some of the more important statistical and survey evidence is set out in the chapters. Chapters 6 and 11 of the Preliminary Report consist entirely of statistical material, surveys and costs data.

Making use of the evidence. Once data have been collected, it is necessary to   **22–009**
analyse the figures and the evidence objectively to see where they lead. The data gathered in the Costs Review provided an empirical basis for many of the recommendations made. The accountant judicial assistant produced valuable analyses of the figures for internal use during Phase Two and Phase Three.

Examples. The following are examples of how the statistical and financial data   **22–010**
fed into the conclusions and recommendations of the Final Report):

- The figures in FR Appendix 1 graphically demonstrated how recoverable success fees and recoverable ATE premiums drove up costs and distorted incentives. This supported the case for ending the recoverability of those items.

- The judicial survey conducted during Phase One of the Costs Review revealed (amongst much else) that in PI litigation, for every £1 which liability insurers paid out to claimants in damages, they paid out £1.80 in claimants' costs. This was part of the basis for a raft of recommendations concerning personal injury litigation.

- The Internet surveys carried out during August–October 2009 (referred to in Ch. 18, above) demonstrated the need for a small claims track and a fast track in the Patents County Court (now the Intellectual Property Enterprise Court). Subsequent experience confirmed the conclusions drawn from the initial research: see the large number of low value cases brought on those tracks, once they were established.[3]

- Professor Fenn's analysis of 63,998 PI cases showed that the package of FR reforms would make 61% of PI claimants better off and 39% of PI claimants worse off. This analysis supported the package of recommendations to (a) end recoverable success fees, (b) end recoverable ATE premiums, (c) increase damages by 10%, and (d) introduce QOCS.

- The survey of small businesses undertaken by the FSB (referred to in Ch. 18, above) demonstrated a need for fixed costs in the lower reaches of the multi-track.

- The details of a large block of defamation cases set out in PR Appendix 17 made it possible to assess to what extent the concerns of the MLA recorded in section 3 of PR Ch. 10 were justified.

- The data collected from a number of separate sources[4] demonstrated that the majority of meritorious clinical negligence cases did not settle until after the

---

[3] See section 3 of Ch. 19, above.
[4] In particular, data from the Legal Services Commission, the NHSLA and the MPS. The data are set out in PR Chs 6 and 11, Graphs A1-A16 in Appendix 21, and Appendices 22A, 22B, 22C and 22D.

issue of proceedings. This supported the proposal for a raft of amendments to the pre-action process and the clinical negligence pre-action protocol.

22–011   **Overseas procedures.** The experience of overseas jurisdictions is, self-evidently, valuable evidence of how a range of different procedures work out in practice. You can get feedback from judges, practitioners and court users—which may or may not be the same. The following are examples of overseas procedures which the FR reforms drew upon:

- The experience of concurrent expert evidence in Australia showed that such a procedure can work effectively and lead to a saving of trial costs. It was particularly significant that practitioners endorsed the views of judges about the utility of the procedure. The new rules for concurrent expert evidence in England drew upon, but did not replicate, the Australian rules.

- The experience of using fixed costs in Germany demonstrated the practicality and the benefits of such a regime. The data collected by the Soldan Institute showed how the fixed costs regime impacted upon (a) hourly rates and (b) the take-up of BTE insurance.[5]

- Hong Kong's experience of provisional assessment showed that such a procedure worked satisfactorily.

- Singapore's experience during the 1990s showed the benefits of enforcing compliance with rules and court orders more robustly.[6]

Without wishing to state the obvious, it is always necessary to take account of the different contexts, before adopting any foreign procedures lock, stock and barrel into our own CPR.

4. FOURTH LESSON: IMPLEMENTING A REPORT IS HARDER THAN WRITING IT

22–012   **The difference between writing and implementing.** Writing a report is essentially a matter of analysing the evidence and choosing between conflicting arguments. A panel of assessors is hugely valuable for the purpose of discussion and debate. The Costs Review assessors brought to bear a vast range of experience gained from different viewpoints over their professional lifetimes. It is no part of the assessors' function, however, to seek unanimity on any issue. Nor, during the course of the review, is the reviewer trying to persuade anyone about anything. The task is essentially one of listening with an open mind. All that changes in the implementation phase. It suddenly becomes necessary to win a sufficient degree of support for all of the key proposals.

22–013   **The author of a civil litigation report must stick with it and not walk away.** Any serious report on how to reform civil procedure or the funding mechanisms is

---

[5] See PR Ch. 55.
[6] See section 2 of the fifth implementation lecture.

bound to be controversial. All reforms have winners and losers. Those who stand to lose out—however deservedly—will mount sustained campaigns to demolish the report. They are, of course, highly articulate. (Otherwise they wouldn't be at the top of their profession.) They will recruit sympathetic academics and will fight their corner with vigour. It behoves the reformer to respond to criticism, acknowledging good points and exposing bad ones. No-one else knows to the same degree (a) the details of the underlying evidence or (b) which elements of the package can safely be abandoned. If the author says in lordly style "I have written my report – do what you want with it",[7] there is a danger that the package of reforms will lose its coherence or possibly fall to pieces during the implementation process. It will be recalled that Lord Woolf was closely involved with the implementation of his own report. In this respect (as in many others), Lord Woolf set a good example to follow.

Déjà vu. The debates and seminars during the implementation period are **22–014** essentially a re-run of the debates and seminars during the course of the review. In the present case, it is difficult to think of any argument or point of view put forward during the implementation period which had not previously been deployed during the course of the Costs Review. There is, however, one important difference. During the review, the warring parties concentrate on attacking one another. During the implementation period, they concentrate their fire on the reviewer. Whoever has lost out on this issue or that will show no mercy to the author of the offending report.

The implementation is long drawn out and stressful. Any package of civil **22–015** justice reforms is likely to require both primary and secondary legislation. That means a long drawn out implementation process. The reformer should therefore expect to come under heavy gunfire for several years. Incidentally, it is curious how often people are charming to you at meetings and seminars, but write acerbic articles afterwards.

Anyone who wants quiet life should not try to reform the civil justice system.

Presenting draft rules to the Rule Committee. However carefully you may **22–016** labour over drafting, your efforts will have shortcomings. The Rule Committee is a formidable body with a large pool of talent. They will pick holes in every draft and expose its shortcomings. In respect of the rules or rule amendments which I drafted, the Rule Committee invariably sent me away to do some re-drafting— sometimes more than once before the final version was approved.

Piloting the reforms. The inevitable delay in securing primary legislation is a **22–017** benefit, not a drawback. It provides an opportunity to pilot some of the reforms which do not depend upon legislation. As discussed in earlier chapters, some of the FR reforms were piloted at designated court centres. Each of the pilots threw up unexpected teething problems and enabled at least some of the glitches to be

---

[7] That approach of stepping back is obviously appropriate if the judge has written a report on a "political" issue (such as press regulation). The comments in this paragraph are only relevant to reports about detailed reforms to the civil justice system. Such matters are very much the concern of the Judiciary.

put right before the general implementation date. To take just one example: the provisional assessment pilot demonstrated shortcomings in the format of points of dispute. It was possible to deal with these shortcomings during 2012 and to draw up a new form of Precedent G,[8] which assisted both provisional assessment and the full detailed assessment process. The new precedent G came into force on the general implementation date. Many points of this character emerged during the pilots and were dealt with before April 2013. It would be foolish to suggest that the pilots eliminated all teething problems, but they certainly assisted.

22–018   **Implementation lectures.** Another benefit of the time lag (while primary legislation is going through) is that this gives a chance to explain the reforms, as they are emerging. In the present case, it was possible to deliver a series of implementation lectures. As and when draft rules were approved by the Rule Committee, it was possible to annexe the drafts to implementation lectures.

5. FIFTH LESSON: COLLATERAL ATTACK IS INEVITABLE

22–019   **Events after Woolf.** In April 2000, 11 months after the Woolf reforms came in, the Government made substantial cuts to legal aid. At the same time, it introduced a new regime of recoverable success fees and recoverable ATE premiums. None of these reforms had any connection with the Woolf report. The cutbacks in legal aid reduced access to justice. The new rules for CFAs and ATE massively drove up costs, thus leading to the "costs war" described in PR Ch. 3. Many commentators, quite unjustifiably, appeared to treat these matters as a consequence of the Woolf reforms.

22–020   **Events after Jackson.** On the very day that the FR reforms were introduced, the Government made deep cuts in legal aid. Subsequently, there were substantial increases in court fees. Both these measures reduced access to justice and generated higher litigation costs. On top of that, as a result of "austerity", extensive staffing cuts were made at regional court centres, just when the reforms were bedding in. All these developments were contrary to my recommendations, but many commentators treated them as part and parcel of the "Jackson reforms".[9]

6. AND FINALLY: ARE THE COSTS REVIEW REFORMS A SUCCESS?

22–021   **No-one should be judge in his own cause.** This principle has obvious application here. Any opinion ventured in this book might be criticised for lack of objectivity.

---

[8] See *White Book*, 2016, pp. 1443–1444.
[9] For example, the Litigation Trends Survey published online by the LSLA and New Law Journal in June 2016 reads as if the recent increases in court fees were part of the Jackson reforms.

Nevertheless some points can properly be made. In particular: **22–022**

(i) Some of the Jackson reforms have unquestionably reduced the costs of litigation[10]: in particular, the ending of recoverable success fees and recoverable ATE premiums, the introduction of fixed costs for fast track PI cases, the banning of referral fees and the new rules about proportionate recoverable costs.

(ii) Views differ on whether costs management reduces costs, but the procedure certainly gives parties a better understanding of their financial position. Also, as many commentators accept, the process is now bedding down. Both judges and practitioners are becoming more familiar with budgeting.

(iii) Some of the reforms are directed to the litigation process: in particular, changes to case management and the disclosure rules, control of written evidence, concurrent expert evidence, more effective compliance and similar matters. Once the flurry of litigation about relief from sanctions had died down, these new rules (when used) have worked smoothly.

(iv) The proposals for making effective use of IT in the civil courts were not taken forward when the other reforms were introduced. But there are good prospects that this will now happen, following the work of Lord Justice Briggs.

(v) Some of the reforms are directed to the funding of civil litigation: in particular, permitting DBAs, promoting TPF, encouraging the spread of BTE, proposals for a CLAF, reforming CFAs and increasing general damages by 10%. Insufficient use is made of DBAs and this will remain the case until the DBA Regulations 2013 are revised. There has been a welcome increase in the use TPF, but that only assists certain classes of litigation. The Bar, the Law Society and the CILEx have set up working groups to take forward the proposals for a CLAF.

(vi) Some of the reforms are directed to the process of assessing recoverable costs. These reforms include changes to summary assessment, introducing provisional assessment and revising the procedures for detailed assessment. None of those matters have proved controversial in the three years since their introduction. The new procedures are working well.

(vii) The proposal for a new form bill of costs, which takes advantage of modern IT, is still in the implementation phase. The proposed new form bill is currently the subject of a pilot. Concerns raised during the first part of the pilot are being addressed by the Hutton Committee and a subcommittee of the Rule Committee. It can be predicted with reasonable confidence that we shall end up with a new form bill of costs which (a) is a considerable improvement on the old one and (b) makes effective use of modern IT.

---

[10] See, for example, the report dated 19 January 2015 by the Institute and Faculty of Actuaries. This shows that legal costs for whiplash-type claims have dropped by 65%.

(viii) The reforms are interconnecting and form a coherent package. The intention was that they should all be introduced on the same date. For the most part that was achieved, with 1 April 2013 being the general implementation date.

22–023   **Specific areas of litigation.** Some of the FR reforms are directed to specific areas of litigation, such as: intellectual property, small business disputes, defamation/privacy, judicial review, clinical negligence, personal injury, chancery, housing, large commercial actions. This book deals collectively (and briefly) with those topics in Ch. 18. In so far as the recommendations have been implemented in those areas, they do not appear to be the subject of criticism.

22–024   **Commentators ignore reforms which are working well and hunt out whatever they can criticise.** That is absolutely fair game and no civil justice reformer can object to that. But anyone who is making an overall assessment should, perhaps, take into account those reforms which are working well.

22–025   **Conclusion.** All of the FR reforms are intended, one way or another, to promote access to justice at proportionate cost, so far as that is possible within the constraints of an adversarial common law system. It is for others to judge the extent to which the reforms achieve that objective.

CHAPTER 23

WHERE NEXT?

1. SUCCESSIVE WAVES OF CIVIL JUSTICE REFORM

Painting the Forth Bridge. The reform of civil procedure, like the apocryphal painting of the Forth Bridge, is a never ending task. New forms of IT revolutionise what the courts can do, how judges work and how professionals work.[1] These developments determine what court users expect and what overseas jurisdictions may be achieving. Therefore, they challenge as well as assist the courts. As the world changes, so do the demands which society makes upon the civil courts.
    23–001

A state of flux. Therefore the civil justice system is constantly in a state of flux, as one reform project follows another.[2] Sometimes the reforms are gradual and incremental. Sometimes they come in a block. The reforms may be the product of one mind (after consultation); they may be the product of a committee or working group. Implementation may be the product of orderly debate within the Rule Committee or the result of a more haphazard Parliamentary process. Lord Justice Briggs has recently reviewed a cluster of civil justice issues. It is probable that his Final Report will lead to a package of reforms and substantial improvements.
    23–002

The Beach. No package of civil justice reforms lasts for ever. New reformers appear with their own ideas. When the tide comes in, it sweeps away yesterday's sandcastles.
    23–003

The Woolf reforms. Despite the previous comments, Lord Woolf's reforms are a significant milestone and they will endure for many years. Even so, his two monumental reports did not spring out of the ether. On the contrary, Lord Woolf built upon and developed much excellent work which had been done by his predecessors. In particular, the Report of the Review Body on Civil Justice (Cm 394
    23–004

---

[1] For a stimulating discussion of what may lie ahead, see R. and D. Susskind, *The future of the professions*.
[2] Sir Jack Jacob discussed "the need for continual reform" in *The reform of civil procedural law*, at p. 5.

of 1988) contained a raft of proposals for improving the management of civil litigation by the parties and by the court. The subsequent Heilbron-Hodge report,[3] published by the Bar Council and the Law Society, made 72 further proposals directed to the same end. Lord Woolf's Final Report, however, unlike many earlier reports was followed up by a general implementation programme.

23–005   **The reforms proposed by the Civil Litigation Costs Review Final Report.** As noted in Ch. 1, above, the reforms proposed in the Review of Civil Litigation Costs Final Report take their place in a long line of similar exercises. The FR proposals, like Lord Woolf's proposals, were followed up by a general implementation programme.

23–006   **Overlap with the Woolf reforms.** It is not uncommon for there to be a degree of overlap between successive reform programmes. In the present case, the Final Report:

- picks up the unimplemented proposals of Lord Woolf for fixed costs in the fast track;

- builds on Lord Woolf's theme of proportionality;

- proposes modest improvement to pre-action protocols, in order to build on Lord Woolf's concept;

- seeks to make case management conferences more effective, precisely as Lord Woolf intended;

- seeks to make disclosure of documents more focused and less costly, which was one of Lord Woolf's objectives;

- promotes alternative dispute resolution ("ADR"), which was a major theme of Lord Woolf's proposals;

- builds on Lord Woolf's proposals in respect of summary assessment;

- repeats the pleas made by Lord Woolf for proper IT systems within the civil courts.

23–007   **Overlap with the Briggs reforms.** Lord Justice Briggs' review focused on the structure of the civil courts. Nevertheless it can be seen from Briggs LJ's reports that there is some overlap with the Final Report. In particular, Briggs LJ's reports:

- support the fixed costs proposals;

- support the FR recommendation to make costs management a discretionary process, rather than mandatory in every case;

---

[3] *Civil justice on trial – the case for change*, report by the Independent Working Party set up jointly by the General Council of the Bar and the Law Society, June 1993. The chairman was Hilary Heilbron QC and the vice-chairman was Henry Hodge OBE, later Mr Justice Hodge.

- support the recommendations made by Lord Woolf and myself in respect of court IT;

- seek to promote ADR, making full use of modern technology through ODR.

The Online Court. The online court proposed by Briggs LJ is an innovation,   **23–008**
which builds on the work of Professor Richard Susskind and others. It is a far-sighted proposal, which should bring access to justice for lower value claims within the reach of many litigants in person, who currently feel shut out of the system. This will be the next "big event" in civil justice reform.

2. UNFINISHED BUSINESS FROM THE REVIEW OF CIVIL LITIGATION COSTS FINAL REPORT

The implementation process is never a neat and tidy affair. In an ideal world,   **23–009**
any major report would be followed by a period for drafting and preparation. Then all the recommended reforms would come into force on the same day. In the real world, that never happens:

- In Lord Woolf's case, some of his recommendations were never implemented: for example, his recommendations for fast track fixed costs and court IT. Others of his reforms were delayed for many years after the general implementation date of 26 April 1999: for example, transferring all of the former Rules of the Supreme Court ("RSC") and County Court Rules into the new Civil Procedure Rules ("CPR").[4]

- In the case of the Review of Civil Litigation Costs Final Report (as noted in earlier chapters), some of the recommendations were implemented early, some were implemented late and some have not yet been implemented.

Work in progress. As Briggs LJ noted in Ch. 3 of his Interim Report, some   **23–010**
of the FR reforms should be regarded as work in progress. Final Report reforms which have a good prospect of implementation and may therefore be character-ised as work in progress include:

- The new form bill of costs, which is currently the subject of a voluntary pilot.

- The fixed costs recommendations, in so far as not yet implemented. The Government has indicated that it is now giving serious consideration to taking forward those matters.

- Revising the Damages-Based Agreements Regulations 2013, so as to make damages-based agreements workable.

---

[4] The 2016 White Book still contains one or two Rules of the Supreme Court and County Court Rules, which—17 years after the introduction of the Woolf reforms—have not yet been transposed.

- Developing a Contingent Legal Aid Fund ("CLAF"). The Bar Council, the Law Society and the Chartered Institute of Legal Executives ("CILEx") have set up a working group to take forward the proposals for a CLAF.

- Reforms to Intellectual Property ("IP") law, so that practitioners sending proper pre-action correspondence do not face claims for claims for "groundless threats".

- Provision of proper court IT, as proposed in Lord Woolf's Final Report and subsequently in the Review of Civil Litigation Costs Final Report.

23–011   **Guideline hourly rates.** As noted in Ch. 21, above, the review of guideline hourly rates ("GHRs") has been parked. This matter cannot stay in the car park for ever. Even in the new age of proportionality GHRs have a role. So does the Costs Committee of the Civil Justice Council ("CJC"). Perhaps, therefore, that committee should get back to work. Furthermore practitioners should co-operate with the Costs Committee in providing the evidence which it needs.

23–012   **What about recoverable success fees and recoverable ATE premiums?** As discussed in Ch. 5, above, the Final Report recommended that success fees and after-the-event insurance ("ATE") premiums should be cease to be recoverable in any circumstances. The Government accepted the general recommendation, but carved out four exceptions. One of those exceptions, namely that relating to insolvency proceedings, has now been terminated. The other three exceptions remain in place. It is submitted that some other way of dealing with the subject matter of each of those three exceptions must be found, as discussed in Ch. 5, above.

23–013   **Need for simplification of costs law.** A large body of case law has accumulated around the recoverability regime (i.e. the rules governing recoverable success fees and recoverable ATE premiums). Additionally, the recoverability rules themselves are quite complex. One of the incidental arguments in favour of ending recoverable success fees and recoverable ATE premiums was that this would lead to a welcome simplification of the law of costs. That goal is now in sight. But it will not be possible to achieve the desired simplification until the last vestiges of recoverable success fees and recoverable ATE premiums have been swept away.

23–014   **Civil Justice Council working party.** A CJC working party chaired by Professor Rachael Mulheron is currently reviewing several aspects of the FR reforms, some three years after the general implementation date. Those aspects include:

- Before-the-event insurance ("BTE") and how this might become more effective;

- Qualified one-way costs shifting ("QOCS") and whether that might be extended to private nuisance claims;

- Concurrent expert evidence.

It is likely that the CJC working group will make recommendations about how to build on those reforms. It is quite possible that the working group will look at other FR reforms as well. This is a constructive and beneficial project. No civil justice reformer should regard their own pronouncements as the last word upon any topic.

Future review of appeals. The reforms of Briggs LJ will cut down the work-   **23–015**
load of the Court of Appeal and reduce the present unacceptable delays in the hearing of appeals. As a separate matter, however, consideration will have to be given in due course to controlling the costs of appeals, as discussed in Ch. 15, above.

Other work necessary to follow up the FR reforms. Earlier chapters have   **23–016**
identified other work which will be necessary to follow up the FR reforms. In particular:

- More must be done to promote BTE insurance, as discussed in Ch. 7, above.

- A close watch needs to be kept on the operation CPR Pt 36, to ensure that it does not become a means of circumventing costs budgets or fixed costs by parties who are "playing the system", rather than genuinely trying to settle.

- The costs management rules may require amendment along the lines suggested in Ch. 14, above.

- Possibly QOCS can be extended into some of the areas identified in Ch. 16, above.

- In view of the increased use of summary assessment at the end of substantial trials, a new form of summary assessment bill (following Precedent H format) should be developed, as discussed in Ch. 21.

Promotion of ADR. There is still more work to be done in relation to ADR.   **23–017**
Many people remain unaware of what ADR has to offer and still think of "court" as the only way of progressing their disputes. It is still the case, as stated in the Final Report six years ago, that there needs to be a serious campaign to alert people to the existence of ADR and to what it can offer. If *The Archers* and one or two other popular radio or TV programmes were to include a successful mediation, this would give a welcome boost to ADR generally.

Increased number of litigants in person. The retraction of legal aid has led to   **23–018**
a massive increase in the number of litigants in person ("LIP"). The courts are still adapting to this change and to the requirements of the new CPR r.3.1A. Chapter 15, above, suggests one way of assisting LIPs to benefit from the recent reforms. All procedures must now be reviewed with the needs of LIPs in mind. The increased co-operation between the courts and organisations such as the Citizens' Advice Bureaux and the Personal Support Unit is to be welcomed.[5]

---

[5] A scheme which has been set up for pro bono representation of LIPs on applications to the High Court and the Court of Appeal is an example of such co-operation. The Specialist Bar Associations, the Law Society, the Citizens' Advice Bureau at the Royal Courts of Justice, court staff and judges have co-operated to make this work.

23–019   **Referral fees.** Subject to resources, consideration should be given to whether there is a need to ban referral fees in areas outside personal injury litigation. This can readily be done by means of regulations under s.56 of the Legal Aid, Sentencing and Punishment of Offenders Act 2012 ("LASPO"). But it will be necessary to consider competition issues and whether the harm done by such referral fees is such as to warrant a ban. The evidence available in the Costs Review did not make it possible to reach a decision on this issue in 2009.

23–020   **Pre-action costs management.** Once costs management has bedded in fully, serious consideration will have to be given to extending the process to the pre-action period. Chapter 23 of the Final Report proposed that there be a pilot of pre-action costs management[6] in clinical negligence cases, subject to the appointment of one more Queen's Bench master. That did not happen. The issue will not go away, especially as there is an increasing tendency for some practitioners to load costs into the pre-action period. Pre-issue costs management may in the future become necessary for cases which fall outside fixed costs regimes.

3. THE EFFECTS OF EVER-INCREASING COURT FEES

23–021   **An issue that cannot be avoided.** One issue which policy makers will have to consider is the current level of civil court fees, which many believe to be excessive. This is now emerging as a source of real concern.

23–022   **Litigation Trends Survey.** The Litigation Trends Survey published by the London Solicitors Litigation Association ("LSLA") in June 2016 dwelt at some length on the issue of court fees. The LSLA stated:

> "There is little doubt that for lower value claims, the substantial hike in court fees has already deterred many clients from issuing proceedings. Not only do clients now have to bear front-loaded costs before issuing proceedings, but now a significant proportion of their litigation spend will have to be devoted to paying the court issue fee. For those cases which ultimately run through to trial, an increased fee may turn out to be a reasonable price to pay for using the courts, yet this doesn't take into account the fact that the vast majority of cases settle early on in the proceedings. For those cases, the court fee is likely to be disproportionate to the services provided, according to respondents to our survey."

23–023   **Costs Review Preliminary Report.** My own Preliminary Report expressed similar concerns. Chapter 7 of the Preliminary Report dealt specifically with court fees and included detailed analysis of the court fee levels in 2009. Paragraph 5.2 stated:

> "I see considerable force in all of the submissions that have been made in this regard. For the reasons set out in chapter 4 above, the civil courts play a vital role in the maintenance of social order and the functioning of the economy. The maintenance of the civil justice system and the proper resourcing of the courts is the function of the State.

---

[6] In accordance with a procedure suggested by Master Yoxall.

Subject to any arguments which may be advanced during Phase 2, I would suggest it is wrong in principle that the entire cost or most of the cost of the civil justice system should be shifted from taxpayers to litigants. This is now particularly pertinent, given that court fees have increased in the last ten years substantially in excess of inflation."

The position now. In the seven years since publication of that report, court fees   **23–024**
have continued to rise at a rate in excess of inflation. Whilst it is not appropriate for a judge to "campaign" about court fees (or any other form of indirect taxation), there is a serious point of principle here, which those responsible for the civil justice system will have to confront.

4. Should We Tear Up the Civil Procedure Rules and Start Again?

No.

A dose of realism. It is a common *crie de Coeur* that the CPR are now so   **23–025**
complicated that the best thing to do is to tear them all up and start again. Sadly, that will not work. Anyone who settles down to draft a new, simple procedural code will soon find that things get out of hand. They must deal with the numerous vicissitudes of civil litigation and the burgeoning statutes requiring special civil remedies. They will soon discover that their sparkling new rules are becoming convoluted. Matters will not stop there. Ingenious lawyers will circumvent or challenge the new rules. They will bring test cases on appeal. Before you know where you are, the new rules will have encrusted upon them a mass of case law. Then the commentators and academics will set to work. Every new rule will have its own accompanying commentary.

Look at what happened last time. The hope in the 1990s was that the new   **23–026**
CPR would be shorter and clearer than the old RSC. It was envisaged that new case law could be absorbed into practice directions, so that there would be no need to look at the law reports for glosses on the rules. Alas that did not happen. The opposite was the case. The new technical terms invented were usually longer than their predecessors. Writs became "claim forms". Pleadings became "statements of case". Garnishee orders became "third party debt orders"—and so forth. New rules drafted in plain English were generally longer than their tersely expressed predecessors. New statutes came along, all requiring their own "Parts" in the CPR. A new body of case law grew up around most of the CPR. Occasionally, the old authorities gained a new lease of life and became attached to the new rules, the classic example being *Ladd v Marshall* [1954] 1 WLR 1489. There is then scope for interesting arguments about how influential the old authorities are when attached to the new rules. None of these developments were the "fault" of the Woolf reforms. They are inevitable features of any procedural code in a common law jurisdiction.

Prediction. If anyone decides to tear up the CPR and start all over again, they   **23–027**
will have the same experience.

5. CONCLUSION

23–028   **An incremental process.** Civil justice reform and civil procedure reform are a continuous process. Occasionally it becomes possible to knock out identified areas of complexity. The Rule Committee should seize any such opportunity with both hands.[7] But wholesale re-writing of the procedural code should not be attempted too often. About once per century would seem to be sufficient. There have been major re-writes[8] of our procedural rules in 1883 and 1999. For the foreseeable future, the reform of civil procedure must be gradual and incremental.

23–029   **A modest contribution for others to build upon.** It is hoped that the reforms which bear my name are making a modest contribution to promoting access to justice at proportionate cost. Others will develop and build upon those reforms in order to achieve the same objective.

23–030   **The future.** Even now, while the recent reforms are bedding in, new issues are confronting the civil justice system and further reforms are coming forward. This book has attempted to put the matters for which I am responsible into their proper context and to identify some of the likely future developments.

---

[7] For example, it may now be possible to do away with the rules on costs capping and all the case law encrusted upon those rules.
[8] The preparation of the RSC 1965 was not an exercise on the same scale as the preparation of the RSC 1883 and the CPR 1998.

APPENDIX A

APPENDIX A

DIAGRAM ILLUSTRATING THE RELATIONSHIP BETWEEN SOME OF THE REFORMS PROPOSED IN THE REVIEW OF CIVIL LITIGATION COSTS FINAL REPORT
A SCHEME DESIGNED TO PROMOTE ACCESS TO JUSTICE AND THE FAIR RESOLUTION OF DISPUTES AT PROPORTIONATE COST

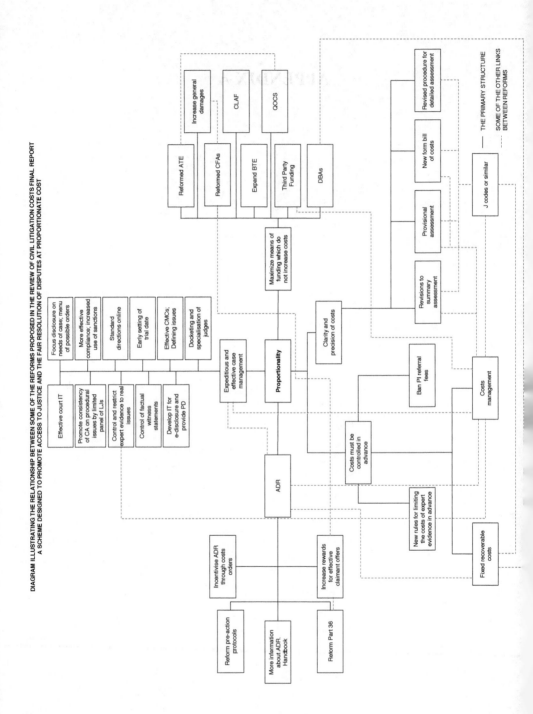

APPENDIX B

APPENDIX B

LORD JUSTICE JACKSON'S RESPONSE TO MINISTRY OF JUSTICE CONSULTATION PAPER CP 13/10

INDEX

1. INTRODUCTION

1.1   **The Consultation Paper and this Response.** I welcome the Government's Consultation Paper CP 13/10 and the detailed consideration which has been given to the proposals advanced in my Final Report ("FR"). The purpose of this Response is (a) to engage with some of the important issues raised by the Government and (b) to address the formidable arguments being publicly deployed against the FR proposals. Also I am concerned to prevent errors occurring in the process of translating the FR proposals into primary legislation, not least because I shall carry some personal responsibility for the reforms. This Response sets out further information gathered over the last year. It also sets out my final views on the issues which are the subject of consultation, in the light of the analyses and debates which have taken place since publication of the FR. This Response is intended to be constructive and I hope it will assist the Government in reaching decisions on civil justice issues.

1.2   This response is being placed on the Judiciary website for two purposes: first, so that the dialogue between the Ministry of Justice and myself is conducted in an open and transparent manner; secondly, so that other consultees, especially those who take a different view, can see what I am saying and consider it before the 14th February deadline for consultation responses.

1.3   **Abbreviations.** In this response:
"ATE" means after-the-event insurance.
"CFA" means conditional fee agreement.
"Consultation Paper" means the Ministry of Justice's Consultation Paper CP 13/10 (November 2010) "Proposals for Reform of Civil Litigation Funding and Costs in England and Wales".

"FR" or "Final Report" means Review of Civil Litigation Costs Final Report.

"Legal Aid Consultation Paper" means the MoJ's Consultation Paper CP 12/10 (November 2010) "Proposals for the Reform of Legal Aid in England and Wales".

"MoJ" means Ministry of Justice.

"PR" means Review of Civil Litigation Costs Preliminary Report.

"QOCS" means qualified one-way costs shifting.

"Recoverability" means the ability to recover success fees and ATE premiums from opposing parties.

Citation of PR and FR. In citing paragraphs of the Preliminary Report or the **1.4** Final Report I shall use the convention of chapter number followed by paragraph number. Thus "PR para 5.3.5" means Preliminary Report chapter 5, paragraph 3.5; "FR para 10.4.17" means Final Report chapter 10, paragraph 4.17.

My role since publication of FR. The Final Report was published on 14th **1.5** January 2010. Since then I have served as a member of the Judicial Steering Group, which oversees implementation of the FR proposals on behalf of the judiciary.[1] Contrary to my original intention, I have remained immersed in costs issues throughout 2010 and my sitting commitment has been slightly reduced to allow time for work on implementation. I have also attended innumerable conferences, seminars and meetings, in order to give lectures on particular aspects of the proposals, to answer questions and to listen to the views of others. Many of these debates have been robust, to say the least.[2] As the debates have proceeded and further evidence has accumulated, my views on the main issues have become firmer.

Further calculations of Professor Fenn. Since publication of the Final Report **1.6** Professor Fenn has done further calculations re the effect of the package of reforms proposed. These calculations have been put onto the Judiciary website[3] and were presented in my lecture to the Legal Action Group on 29th November 2010. These calculations are set out at Appendix 1, paras 1 to 3.

2. CONDITIONAL FEE AGREEMENTS AND SUCCESS FEES
(CONSULTATION PAPER, SECTION 2.1, PAGES 18–29)

The rationale for recoverable success fees. The theory underlying recover- **2.1** ability is that in any cohort of cases where the claimants' solicitors are acting on CFAs, there will be some winners and some losers. The success fees recovered from defendants in successful cases will cover the claimants' costs in unsuccess-

---

[1] See para 264 of the Consultation Paper.

[2] For example, at a conference organised by the Law Society's Civil Litigation Section on 23rd February 2010 my report came in for strong criticism from some quarters. A solicitor in the audience (to some applause) castigated my proposed reforms as "tyrannical". Throughout 2010 there have been forceful attacks on the FR, both at meetings and in articles, sometimes emanating from those with a vested interest in the present arrangements. However, no rational argument has been put forward to dissuade me from the FR recommendations.

[3] See *http://www.judiciary.gov.uk/media/speeches/2010/jackson-lj-handout-29112010.*

ful cases. Thus the defendants will end up paying the entirety of the claimants' costs in every single case, regardless of outcome, and the claimants will pay nothing in any case (win or lose).[4] This regime has many flaws,[5] some of which have become more starkly apparent over the last the year.

2.2   **The theory is flawed.** First, why should defendants collectively have to pay not only the costs of claimants who win but also the costs of claimants who lose? No other country in the world has such an unusual system. This regime can be, and is, used by all manner of litigants, who have no conceivable need for such bounteous support from their adversaries. In addition to the examples cited in FR chapter 10, I would now add (a) international finance companies suing the Civil Aviation Authority, (b) large contractors suing public authorities in procurement disputes (c) construction companies in ordinary commercial disputes. It is inappropriate that bodies such as these should be able (indirectly and through the mechanism of recoverable success fees) to have their litigation costs paid by the other side in every case, regardless of who wins. Such organisations can well afford to pay their own costs when they lose.

2.3   **The practice is flawed.** Secondly, as pointed out at FR para 10.4.17, the present CFA regime presents lawyers with an irresistible temptation to cherry pick. Of course, there are some lawyers who honourably ensure that they take on enough losing cases in order to "spend" the success fees gained from successful cases. But there are many lawyers who do not. Over the last year I have heard numerous accounts of solicitors or counsel who run safe cases on CFAs and make a handsome profit from the process. For example, a solicitor from a claimant firm doing mainly employers' liability cases recently admitted to me that his firm wins about 98% of cases in which proceedings are issued. A London QC recently stated that he had done 10 CFA cases and won all of them. A partner in one city firm tells me that the firm does CFA work because it sees this as a means of generating substantially increased profits, not charged to its own clients. Many similar accounts (always non-attributable) have reached me. The experience of the Association of Law Costs Draftsmen is to the same effect.[6] This state of affairs is hardly surprising, because in any sector work tends to follow the most remunerative path. Obviously the financial records of solicitors and counsel are confidential. However, from all the information which has come to me over the last year, I deduce the following. First, the present regime is being used (perfectly lawfully) to generate disproportionate profits for a significant number of CFA lawyers.[7] Secondly, and in consequence, this imposes an excessive costs burden on the general public.

2.4   Thus the elegant balance, which is assumed by the model described in para 2.1

---

[4] There is a modification in large commercial cases, where the CFAs often provide for "no win/low fee". These arrangements can be even more lucrative for lawyers.

[5] See FR chapter, chapter 10.

[6] "The whole CFA regime has been a disaster . . . Many solicitors filter out risky cases and take on safe ones with, nevertheless, attractive success fees. Many solicitors have made substantial profits out of the CFA regime, at the expense of the man in the street." PR para 10.14.6.

[7] It would be helpful to know whether, after enquiry, either the Chairman of the Bar or the President of the Law Society seriously dispute this proposition.

above, is not achieved in practice. In a typical cohort of claimant cases run on CFAs, the defendants end up paying *substantially more than* the claimants' costs of every case, regardless of outcome. The inflationary effect of CFAs upon costs can be seen from FR paras 2.2.8, 2.2.14 and 2.2.17.[8]

At a time when public funds are scarce, it may be thought inappropriate to impose upon the National Health Service, local authorities, government departments, police authorities, other public authorities, small companies, motorists and many others the huge burden of paying "success fees" on top of the proper costs of litigation. **2.5**

The Government's proposal to abolish recoverability of success fees. I therefore welcome the provisional view indicated by the Government that recoverability should be abolished. **2.6**

Areas of concern indicated in the Consultation Paper. The Government identifies in paras 69–70 of the Consultation Paper three areas of concern where some element of recoverability might be retained, namely (i) judicial review; (ii) housing disrepair, (iii) complex personal injury or clinical negligence claims. I shall address these three areas separately. **2.7**

(i) Judicial review. There is no need for recoverable success fees in this area. First, legal aid will remain available for the most important judicial review cases.[9] Secondly, as long as provision is made for the adverse costs risk[10] solicitors will be willing and able to take on meritorious judicial review cases on CFAs without recoverable success fees.[11] The solicitors will either charge no success fee or they will agree a success fee which is within the client's means. I have sat for many years as a judge in the Administrative Court and do not accept the proposition that judicial review claimants generally are unable to make any contribution to their own costs. Although special provision must be made[12] for genuinely impecunious claimants, in most judicial review claims it is desirable that both parties should have a financial stake in the litigation. This serves to deter frivolous claims and promote responsible litigation conduct. **2.8**

(ii) Housing disrepair. The majority of housing disrepair claims are brought on legal aid, not CFAs.[13] Legal aid will remain available for the most important housing disrepair cases.[14] Where legal aid is not available, CFAs could still be viable without recoverable success fees. The tenant's main concern is to secure that repairs are carried out. If the solicitors insist upon receiving a success fee in addition to the proper costs of the litigation, that could (by agreement between solicitor and client) be capped at a percentage of any general damages recovered. **2.9**

---

[8] The figures are in FR appendix 1, tables1 to 8. For cases which settled, see table 10.
[9] See paras 4.95 to 4.99 of the Legal Aid Consultation Paper.
[10] As to which see below.
[11] See PR para 36.3.8, FR paras 30.2.18, 30.3.1 to 30.3.3, 30.4.10.
[12] And can be made – see above.
[13] See the submissions of the Housing Law Practitioners' Association quoted in FR para 26.4.1.
[14] See para 4.78 of the Legal Aid Consultation Paper.

2.10   *(iii) Complex personal injury or clinical negligence claims.* Many complex personal injury claims present little or no risk on liability, so there is no need for a success fee at all in such cases.[15] So far as quantum is concerned, there is no reason why the Part 36 risk should be borne by the defendant. On any view, that should be a matter between the claimant and his own solicitors.[16] Where there is genuine need for a CFA, I adhere to the view that a scheme whereby (a) general damages are increased, (b) the rewards for effective claimant offers are increased and (c) the client has a limited liability to pay a success fee out of damages is the best way forward. Another option for complex personal injury or clinical negligence cases will be contingency fees, as discussed in FR chapter 12. I do not accept that these arrangements will either (a) deny access to justice for claimants who have strong claims or (b) make it uneconomic for solicitors to act in such cases.

2.11   An argument which has been urged at many meetings over the last year is that solicitors will stop taking on "risky" cases. I view this argument with scepticism because (with certain honourable exceptions) claimants with risky cases are already unable to find CFA solicitors. Indeed one of the arguments which is repeatedly urged in support of the present regime is that ATE insurers see to it that only very strong cases are pursued on CFAs. One substantial claimant clinical negligence firm examined its records over the period April 2004 to June 2009 for the purposes of the Costs Review. It found that there was not a single CFA case which had been lost at trial or dropped at a late stage. When one looks at the various statistics,[17] it can be seen that the vast majority of claims recorded as "unsuccessful" are dropped at a very early stage.

2.12   Traditionally, the more risky clinical negligence cases have been supported by legal aid. According to the NHSLA statistics, cases supported by legal aid have a lower success rate than those funded by any other means.[18] The question whether legal aid should be retained for clinical negligence is the subject of a separate consultation, upon which it is not my function to comment in this paper.

2.13   *Conclusion.* The reality is that the present CFA regime incentivises the bringing of strong claims, but at disproportionate cost and in an environment where the claimant has no interest in controlling costs. The reforms proposed in the FR will also incentivise the bringing of strong claims, but at proportionate costs and in an environment where the claimant has an interest in controlling costs.

2.14   In my view, recoverable success fees are the worst possible way to tackle the problem of funding litigation, for all the reasons set out in FR chapter 10. Furthermore, the existence of recoverable success fees adds a layer of complexity (and therefore cost) to the civil process. The mass of rules and case law which surround recoverable success fees form a jungle, which should be cut down and cleared. The alternative course which is advocated by some, namely to keep recoverable success fees with sundry restrictions and qualifications, will simply make matters worse. There is now a pressing need to simplify civil procedure, rather than weave in yet more complexity.[19]

---

[15] See e.g. *Pankhurst v White* [2010] EWCA Civ 1445.
[16] See FR paras 10.5.18 to 10.5.21.
[17] For example, those in PR appendices 12, 22 and 23, discussed in PR chapter 11.
[18] See PR para 11.4.2.
[19] See FR paras 4.3.2 to 4.3.6 at pages 43–45.

In so far as particular categories of litigant need financial support in order to **2.15**
bring or defend claims, other measures should be taken which are (a) simpler, (b)
less expensive and (c) targeted upon those who merit support. Those measures are
set out in the Final Report and further addressed in this paper.

Answers to questions. Accordingly my answers to the questions posed on pages **2.16**
28–29 of the Consultation Paper are:
Q. 1: Yes.
Q. 2: Not applicable.
Q. 3: No.
Q. 4: This would be better than the present regime, but I could not endorse it.
Q. 5: No.
Q. 6: Not applicable.
Q. 7: Yes, provided that it is not recoverable from the other side.
Q. 8: Yes.
Q. 9: 25%.
Q. 10: It should be binding in all cases.

3. AFTER-THE-EVENT INSURANCE PREMIUMS (CONSULTATION PAPER, SECTION 2.2, PAGES 30–35)

The principal purpose of ATE – protection against adverse costs. The principal **3.1**
purpose of recoverable ATE premiums is to protect the insured party (usually but
not always the claimant) against liability for adverse costs. The claimant recovers
costs[20] if he/she wins, but has no liability for costs if he/she loses. If the claimant
wins, the defendant pays an enhanced premium;[21] if the claimant loses, the insurer
picks up the tab. Thus, the theory runs, in any cohort of cases where the claimants
have ATE cover, the defendants will end up meeting the claimants' liability for
adverse costs in every case, regardless of outcome.

This is about the most inefficient and expensive form of one way costs shift- **3.2**
ing that it is possible to devise.[22] In any cohort of cases where claimants have
ATE, the defendants are in a far worse position than they would be if they
were never entitled to recover costs from the other side – win or lose. The
inefficiency of this form of one way costs shifting is illustrated by the Personal
Injury Bar Association's submissions, which ironically were advanced in
support of the current regime.[23] It is also illustrated by the Law Society's recent
Response.[24]

---

[20] Generally a multiple of his/her costs, because there will also be a CFA.
[21] Enhanced, because nothing is payable to insurers if the case is lost; ie the premium is itself insured.
[22] This is graphically illustrated by (i) the figures provided by the Medical Protection Society (FR paras 19.2.6 to 19.2.7) and (ii) the figures supplied by insurer X (PR paras 25.2.3 to 25.2.7).
[23] See FR paras 9.3.4 and 9.3.5.
[24] *Review of Civil Litigation Costs Final Report: Response by the Law Society*, October 2010: "There can be no doubt that ATE premiums are a major contributor towards legal costs over which solicitors have no control. . . . There appears to be a substantial lack of transparency in the ATE market" (page 21); "The price of ATE insurance is currently prohibitive" (page 22) Despite these observations, the Law Society seeks to support the present regime.

3.3   Furthermore, there is the anomaly that well resourced parties are entitled to take out ATE insurance and conduct risk free litigation against their adversaries. The "super claimants" referred to in FR para 10.2.9 are one example. [25] Also construction practitioners tell me that this practice is becoming increasingly common in their field, sometimes with ATE premiums approaching 100%. There is no reason why, in litigation between (say) two contractors, one side should be at no risk of adverse costs and the other side should be at massively increased risk.

3.4   I therefore welcome the Government's indicated intention to abolish recoverable ATE premiums and to replace these by a more rational form of one way costs shifting in appropriate cases.

3.5   *The subsidiary purpose of ATE – paying disbursements.* The second function of recoverable ATE premiums is to protect the insured party (usually but not always the claimant) against liability for his/her own disbursements. If the claimant wins he/she recovers disbursements from the other side. If the claimant loses, the insurer pays the disbursements plus an enhanced ATE premium.[26]

3.6   The Government suggests as a possible refinement of the proposed reforms that ATE premiums should continue to be recoverable in so far as they relate to the claimants' disbursements. In my view this should be rejected for three reasons:

(i) The basic premise that losing claimants should collectively have their disbursements paid by defendants is questionable. Why should the Birmingham City Council or the Ministry of Defence or the National Health Service (to take just three examples of bodies whose overstretched resources have recently been in the news) not only pay the disbursements of claimants who win but also pay the disbursements of claimants who lose? No other legal system in the world imposes such an odd requirement. Losing claimants comprise (a) those who abandon their claims before issue and (b) those who issue proceedings and subsequently discontinue or fail. It is a gross waste of public money that these claimants – however wealthy they may be – should collectively have their disbursements met by the tax payer or council tax payer.

(ii) There is a strong case for saying that losing claimants[27] or their solicitors should meet their own disbursements – as happens in Scotland and indeed in every other jurisdiction outside England and Wales. Personal injury cases seem to be causing particular concern in the present consultation. But disbursements in the vast majority of unsuccessful personal injury cases are well within the means of claimants and their solicitors: see FR paras 19.5.3 to 19.5.8.

(iii) If contrary to my view, the Government decides that losing claimants should still have their disbursements paid out of public funds, then the present ATE regime is an extremely inefficient and expensive way of achieving that result. Under the present regime defendants pay (a) the

---

[25] Commercial organisations who perfectly lawfully exploit the present rules to crush their opponents.
[26] Enhanced, because nothing is payable to insurers if the case is lost; ie the premium is itself an insured disbursement.
[27] Or their trade unions (as always happened before 2000 in union cases) or legal expenses insurers.

claimants' disbursements in respect of unfounded claims and (b) the profits and administration costs of the ATE insurers, their agents and any other middlemen who may be involved. A much better and cheaper way of achieving the policy objective would be to provide legal aid for such disbursements. The legal aid authority would (a) control the level of disbursements[28] more effectively than ATE insurers and (b) focus this resource on those claimants who really merit such support.

Para 90 of the Consultation Paper refers to the retraction of legal aid. At the **3.7** present time, however, legal aid is still available for clinical negligence cases. The MoJ is currently consulting on a proposal to exclude clinical negligence from the scope of legal aid.[29] May I suggest that consideration be given to retaining legal aid for reasonable pre-litigation disbursements in clinical negligence cases? This would at least establish whether the claimant has a case worth pursuing. If it turns out that there is a good case, then the legal aid fund would have a first charge upon any damages and costs recovered. I do not have the means to cost this proposal, although no doubt the MoJ can do so. I doubt that it would make a significant inroad on the savings to be achieved by withdrawing legal aid from clinical negligence claims.

Section 30 of the Administration of Justice Act 1999: Membership Organisations. **3.8** There is a helpful summary of this regime in paras 92 to 94 of the Consultation Paper. I agree with the Government's view that any changes to the recoverability of ATE premiums ought to apply equally to the arrangements for Membership Organisations.

Answers to questions. Accordingly my answers to the questions posed on page **3.9** 35 of the Consultation Paper are:
  Q. 11: Yes.
  Q. 12: Not applicable.
  Q. 13: Not applicable.
  Q. 14: No.
  Q. 15: Not applicable.
  Q. 16: Not applicable.
  Q. 17: See paras 3.6 and 3.7 above.
  Q. 18: Yes.

4. THE 10% INCREASE IN GENERAL DAMAGES (CONSULTATION PAPER, SECTION 2.3, PAGES 36 TO 39)

The Government indicates acceptance of the recommended 10% increase in **4.1** general damages for personal injury, nuisance and other civil wrongs to individuals, but raises a number of issues for consideration.

---

[28] By providing scales of remuneration under regulations.
[29] See paras 4.163 to 4.169 of the Legal Aid Consultation Paper.

4.2   *Method of achieving the adjustment.* The Consultation Paper states at para 97: "adjustments to the level of general damages have hitherto been regarded as a judicial issue for the courts rather than the Government". I agree and have not included this item in the list of reforms requiring legislation.[30] It will be recalled that in so far as the Law Commission's recommendations[31] for increasing personal injury damages were accepted, those increases were implemented by means of a guideline judgment handed down by a five member Court of Appeal, presided over by the Master of the Rolls: see *Heil v Rankin* [2001] QB 272. The same procedure could be adopted for implementing any future increase in the level of general damages.

4.3   *Possible refinement.* The Government proposes as a possible refinement that the 10% increase in general damages should apply only in CFA cases and that it should be paid as success fee to the solicitors. Whilst I understand the thinking behind this refinement, I would be strongly opposed to it and would see this as undermining the whole structure of my reforms. I say this for four reasons, as set out in paras 4.4 to 4.8 below.

4.4   First, there is a strong argument to the effect that general damages are already too low.[32] The present reform project provides a golden opportunity to raise the level of general damages by 10% across the board. It is significant that the Association of British Insurers (whose members will be paying the increased damages) accepts the appropriateness of an across the board 10% increase as part of a balanced package.[33] In the ABI's view, the beneficial effect of the total package of reforms upon litigation behaviour makes the (otherwise unwelcome) damages increase acceptable. So this recommended reform has the unusual feature of both being beneficial to claimants and acceptable to defendants.

4.5   Secondly, an across the board increase of 10% in general damages will (despite the abolition of recoverability) leave the great majority of personal injury claimants better off. See Appendix 1, which comprises Professor Fenn's calculations plus my analysis. This was presented in the Legal Action Group 2010 Annual Lecture.[34] On the other hand, if the Government's proposed refinement is adopted, (a) no claimant will be better off, (b) some claimants will be worse off and (c) all the extra money will go straight to lawyers.

4.6   The fact that the majority of claimants will be better off under my proposals is an important feature of the package. This fact also makes it surprising that claimant representatives are so strongly opposed to the recommendations.

4.7   Thirdly, it is wrong in principle that claimants should recover more by way of damages **or** costs, because they choose to fund their litigation by means of CFAs rather than some other method. This creates perverse incentives. It sets England and Wales on a different course from the rest of the world. It means that instead

---

[30] See FR page 472.
[31] Contained in Law Commission Paper No 257 "Damages for Personal Injury: Non-pecuniary Loss" (1999).
[32] See e.g. PR para 10.15.2.
[33] At a number of conferences this year the ABI's representative has made it clear that they accept the 10% increase in general damages, subject to the proviso that the rest of the FR proposals are implemented as a package and in full.
[34] See *http://www.judiciary.gov.uk/media/speeches/2010/jackson-lj-handout-29112010.*

of getting rid of the conceptual carbuncle of recoverable success fees we retain it with additional complications.

Fourthly, one of the vices of the present regime (which has resulted in unaccep- **4.8** table levels of costs) is that CFA claimants have no financial stake in the litigation and no interest in the costs being incurred on their behalf. My proposed package of reforms will put an end to this state of affairs. The Government's proposed refinement will not.

Is a 10% increase high enough? It has been suggested that in some instances **4.9** a 10% increase in general damages will not be sufficient to cover an appropriate success fee (see Consultation Paper para 101). The example cited is that of catastrophic personal injury cases. The first point to note is that many catastrophic injury cases involve no risk whatsoever on liability. There may be a Part 36 risk if the defendant makes an adequate settlement offer which the claimant rejects, but there is no rational justification for making the defendant pay any success fee referable to that risk.[35] I do accept, however, that some personal injury cases (primarily clinical negligence) involve complex issues on liability. I will focus on these cases in the next paragraph.

There are many clinical negligence cases in which, despite their complexity, **4.10** the claimant has a good case on liability.[36] Solicitors conducting such cases will (under my proposals) be able to deduct from damages success fees of up to 25% of general damages + past special damages. I do not accept that that this regime (a) makes it uneconomic for solicitors to conduct such cases or (b) would be unacceptable to claimants. This was precisely the regime that prevailed before April 2000 and was regarded as satisfactory for non-legally aided cases. This has been confirmed by well informed claimant representatives.[37]

Success fees will be highest in those few cases which proceed to trial. In those **4.11** cases, however, the claimant can dramatically improve his position by making a Part 36 offer, reflecting the true value of his claim. If the defendant does not accept that offer, the claimant will make a substantially enhanced recovery[38] and will be well placed to pay the success fee.

The 100% per cent principle. The "principle" that damages are sacrosanct **4.12** and that claimants must retain 100% of their damages without any deduction for costs is discussed and rejected at Consultation Paper paras 102 to 108. I agree with the reasoning set out in those paragraphs. Interestingly, this issue was discussed at a well attended conference of the Law Society's Civil Justice Section on 23rd February 2010, after there had been some debate on the Costs Review Final Report, but before I had left the meeting. The Chairman took a vote on the question: "As a matter of public policy should a successful claimant have his/her damages reduced in order to pay their own solicitor's costs incurred as a result

---

[35] See FR paras 10.5.18 to 10.5.22.

[36] I have encountered such cases at the Bar and they generally settled at an early stage.

[37] See PR paras 16.3.1 to 16.3.2. See also the submissions of Association of Personal Injury Lawyers to Lord Woolf as recorded in para 25 of chapter 2 of Lord Woolf's Final Report on Access to Justice: *http://www.dca.gov.uk/civil/final/index.htm.*

[38] If my recommendations for reforming Part 36 are accepted.

of the negligence or other wrongdoing of a tortfeasor?" In response, 58% of the audience voted "yes" and 42% voted "no".

4.13 *Trade unions.* The position of trade unions should not be overlooked in this kaleidoscope of conflicting interests. Prior to April 2000 trade unions funded personal injury litigation by their members, recovering their costs in successful cases and meeting both sides' costs in unsuccessful cases. Since April 2000, however, the position has been reversed.[39] Trade unions, instead of funding personal injury litigation, now make a substantial profit out of the process.[40] No policy justification has ever been advanced for this substantial subsidy of trade unions by the general public through the mechanism of recoverability. The only justification which has been suggested to me informally is that it frees up more funds to spend on employment tribunal proceedings. If recoverability is abolished, unions will resume their historic function of supporting members' personal injury claims. This will further increase the number of "winners" from the package of reforms, because claimants who are union members will recover general damages enhanced by 10%, whilst having legal costs covered by their unions. This will particularly apply to employers' liability cases (the first of Professor Fenn's graphs).

4.14 *Answers to questions.* Accordingly my answers to the questions posed on page 39 of the Consultation Paper are:
   Q. 19: Yes.
   Q. 20: No.

5. PART 36 OFFERS (CONSULTATION PAPER, SECTION 2.4, PAGES 40–45)

5.1 *Increasing the rewards for successful claimant offers.* Paras 111 to 114 of the Consultation Paper provide a helpful summary of my proposal to increase the reward for claimants, when defendants reject claimant offers but subsequently fail to beat such offers at trial.

5.2 Para 115 of the Consultation Paper raises a concern that this measure may not be effective because only a low percentage of multi track claims are resolved at trial. I do not share this concern, because once a claimant offer has been rejected, any subsequent settlement negotiations will be conducted under the shadow of that unaccepted offer. In other words, if the claimant's offer was well judged his/her subsequent negotiating position will be strengthened.

5.3 Having listened to debate about Part 36 at numerous seminars and meetings over the last year, I support both the modifications discussed in para 116 of the Consultation Paper. I would suggest the following scale:

---

[39] See FR para 10.4.4.
[40] Obviously the figures are confidential to the unions concerned. However, some interesting information was recently provided by a union solicitor, who (at his request) came to brief me about personal injury issues from a claimant perspective. He cited the example of a trade union of modest size which used to spend about £250,000 per year in supporting members' personal injury claims. Now, however, through a combination of direct and indirect benefits that union makes a profit of about £200,000 per year out of the process.

Total damages + value of non-monetary award	Percentage increase
Up to £500,000	10%
£500,001 to £1 million	£50,000 + 5% of excess over £500,000
Above £1 million	£75,000 (with no further increase)

The court must retain a discretion to award less than this sum, if it would be unjust to award the full amount (i.e. the same test as governs the existing rewards for successful claimant offers).[41]

Concern is expressed at para 117 of the Consultation Paper that the proposed **5.4** standard uplift may not sufficiently encourage early settlements; the claimant could gain the same benefit by making an effective offer just before trial. Whilst I understand this concern, there are already other incentives for early settlement. Furthermore, even in the run up to trial there are still savings (in terms of costs and judicial resources) to be achieved from settlement, so that settling continues to be desirable. Finally, if the claimant is on a CFA, the success fee will be highest in cases that go to trial, so the increased sum awarded will assist the claimant to meet that success fee, if his/her reasonable settlement offer is rejected.

A separate point is raised in para 117 of the Consultation Paper, namely that **5.5** the increased reward may not be appropriate if the claimant's offer relates only to liability. This is a difficult point, which has not been discussed at the various meetings that I have attended over the last year. My present tentative view is that where the claimant makes an offer on liability which is not accepted but is subsequently vindicated (e.g. to settle on the basis of 25% contributory negligence), the increased reward should still be given. However, the views expressed in consultation by claimant and defendant representatives will be important on this issue.

It should be noted that in each of the situations discussed in the two preced- **5.6** ing paragraphs the court will retain a discretion to award less than the prescribed uplift if, in all the circumstances, it would be unjust to award the full amount.

Reversal of Carver v BAA plc. There is a helpful discussion of this proposal **5.7** at paras 119 to 124 of the Consultation Paper. The Government notes the arguments for reversing the effect of *Carver*, but is concerned that this may be seen as endorsing the principle that parties can press on to trial even where their positions are very close. I do not share this concern. If the parties' positions are close there is already a strong incentive to settle, because whichever party is vindicated will gain a substantial reward under Part 36, at the expense of the other party.[42]

---

[41] See CPR rule 36.14 (3) and (4).
[42] This will be even more the case if my recommendation is accepted for enhancing the rewards for successful claimant offers.

The risks of pressing on in that situation are almost invariably perceived as overwhelming.[43]

5.8   A possible refinement is suggested at paras 125–127 of the Consultation Paper. I can see the logic of this proposal (indeed it was canvassed in my Preliminary Report) but I do not believe that it should be adopted, essentially for two reasons:

(i)   It introduces further complexity into the rules, at a time when we should be looking for greater simplicity.[44]

(ii)   The simple approach of penalising whichever party fails to beat the other's offer, creates certainty and provides more than sufficient incentive to settle. No-one is going to risk a massive financial penalty in the hope of obtaining a few more £s in damages, alternatively in the hope of shaving a few more £s off the settlement, as the case may be.

5.9   One important point to note, which is not specifically picked up in the Consultation Paper, is that if there is to be any free standing supplement to the claimant's damages or other award, legislation will be required. The Rule Committee cannot amend substantive law. See item 9 in the list of legislation required.[45]

5.10 *Answers to questions.* Accordingly, my answers to the questions posed on page 45 of the Consultation Paper are:

Q. 21: Yes.
Q. 22: Yes, for the reasons set out above and in my Final Report.
Q. 23: Yes, for the reasons set out above.
Q. 24: Yes, as set out in para 5.3 above.
Q. 25: Yes.
Q. 26: Yes.
Q. 27: No.

6. QUALIFIED ONE-WAY COST SHIFTING (CONSULTATION PAPER, SECTION 2.5, PAGES 46–57)

6.1   There is a helpful summary of the FR proposals for qualified one way costs shifting ("QOCS") at paras 128 to 137 of the Consultation Paper, followed by discussion of a number of specific issues to which those proposals give rise. I shall address those issues separately.

6.2   *QOCS and Part 36.* The difficulty suggested at para 140 of the Consultation Paper does not arise. If the defendant makes a derisory offer and subsequently wins on liability, the claimant will still be protected by the proposed QOCS rule. He will not have received any damages out of which he could meet an order for costs. The "modification" suggested in para 141 of the Consultation Paper

---

[43] I say that having often at the Bar advised clients on settlement negotiations, during a period when no-one was cushioned by recoverable ATE premiums.
[44] See FR paras 4.3.1 to 4.3.5.
[45] FR page 472.

is already inherent in the draft rule proposed at FR para 19.4.7. The damages received by the claimant form part of his "financial resources". The claimant cannot be treated as having acquired any larger sum when the court comes to apply QOCS.

Insufficient certainty? Concern is expressed in para 142 of the Consultation **6.3** Paper that claimants will have insufficient certainty under the proposed QOCS rule and might still feel the need for ATE insurance. I do not agree. Precisely this form of words has been in use for legal aid cases over the last half century and it has always been regarded as providing sufficient certainty, even when the financial limits for legal aid were more generous than in recent times. I do accept, however, that my proposed rule will need to be backed up by regulations, as is the case with section 11(1) of the Administration of Justice Act 1999 and its predecessor provisions. The drafting of such regulations will be a matter for detailed work, if and when the recommendation for QOCS is accepted in principle.[46]

The refinement suggested at para 143 of the Consultation Paper. I understand **6.4** the thinking behind this proposal for an early costs setting hearing. My concern, however, is that it will generate much satellite litigation – in other words that the extra costs generated by the process will outweigh the benefits. At the outset of litigation there will be a strong temptation for the parties respectively to make and oppose such applications, even though most cases will ultimately settle without any costs being sought from the claimant.[47] A further difficulty is that it is impossible to foretell at the outset of litigation what conduct issues will arise. There is therefore a danger of two separate "costs" hearings taking place, which would cause even more expense.

The suggested refinements at paras 144 to 146 of the Consultation Paper. **6.5** These paragraphs suggest a number of refinements which may have some merits in isolation, but collectively they will add too much complexity. The proposed rule contains sufficient flexibility to deal with all these matters. In my view, both the rule and the supporting regulations must be kept as simple as possible.

Parents and spouses/partners. I agree with the approach suggested in para 148 **6.6** of the Consultation Paper.

Should QOCS be limited to CFA cases? This issue is explored in para 150 of **6.7** the Consultation Paper. In my view QOCS should definitely not be so limited. First, CFAs (unlike legal aid) are not means tested. Some immensely wealthy individuals and indeed some prosperous companies take out CFAs. So the presence of a CFA is not a badge which identifies litigants who merit special protection. Furthermore, any restriction of QOCS to CFAs would simply incentivise the use of CFAs. Finally, there is no need for any such restriction. The proposed QOCS rule as drafted provides protection for those who need it, but not for

---

[46] Colin Stutt (my former assessor, who was closely involved with drafting the existing regulations) would be willing to assist the MoJ with the detailed drafting work.
[47] According to experienced practitioners, this is what has happened with protective costs orders in judicial review cases: see FR paras 30.2.10 and 30.3.1.

others. I accept that, as with any rule, there will be difficult borderline cases. It will be the function of regulations to produce as much clarity as possible in this area. Nevertheless, the "borderline" problems which will be caused under QOCS pale in comparison with the difficulties which the present ATE regime creates.

6.8 *Low value cases.* I agree with the statement in para 152 of the Consultation Paper that QOCS should not be limited to low value cases.

6.9 *QOCS in types of litigation other than personal injury.* Paras 153 to 167 of the Consultation Paper contain a helpful discussion of which areas outside personal injury litigation might merit QOCS. This raises wide policy considerations, which must be a matter for Government. My own opinion on these questions (which are pre-eminently matters for ministers rather than judges to assess) are already set out in FR chapter 9 and in the chapters dealing with individual categories of litigation. This is an area where the responses to consultation will be particularly important, as indicated in FR para 9.5.10.

6.10 *Should QOCS be confined to individuals?* The Government inclines to the view that QOCS should be confined to individuals, but notes the problem that some organisations are not well resourced. My own view is that QOCS should not be expressly limited to individuals. The formulation of the proposed QOCS rule automatically has the effect that well resourced organisations will have no protection against adverse costs.

6.11 *Answers to questions.* Accordingly, my answers to the questions posed on pages 56 and 57 of the Consultation Paper are:
Q. 28: Yes.
Q. 29: Yes.
Q. 30: Yes, to the extent indicated in my Final Report.
Q. 31: As set out in my Final Report.
Q. 32: QOCS should apply to all claimants, however funded.
Q. 33: No.
Q. 34: No.
Q. 35: Not applicable/ No.

7. OTHER ISSUES THE SUBJECT OF THIS CONSULTATION

7.1 On the other issues raised in the Consultation Paper, I have little to add to my Final Report.

7.2 *Alternative recommendations on recoverability.*[48] I agree with the Government's view[49] that these issues do not arise, because the primary recommendations are the way forward. The practical difficulties which the Government identifies only

---

[48] Consultation Paper paras 175–210.
[49] Consultation Paper para 175.

serve to emphasise the necessity for a radical and uniform approach, namely abolition of recoverability.

Proportionality.[50] I see good sense in the Government's suggested refinement.[51]   **7.3**

Contingency fees.[52] I see the force of the Government's argument that contin-   **7.4**
gency fee agreements require no greater regulation than CFAs. This point has
been made at a number of meetings over the last year. It will be interesting to see
the outcome of consultation on questions 46 and 47.

Litigants in person.[53] The point has been made at a number of recent meetings   **7.5**
that my figure of £20 per hour for litigants in person is too high. I see force in the
Government's arguments for £16.50.

8. OTHER PARTS OF THE FINAL REPORT

There is obvious good sense in the Government's decision to tackle the issues   **8.1**
identified in section 2 of the Consultation Paper first. The Government touches
upon other parts of the Final Report in section 3 of the Consultation Paper, without
posing any questions. I hope it will assist if I comment briefly on these matters.

Referral fees.[54] On this issue I am in agreement with the Law Society, whose   **8.2**
views are quoted in Appendix 1. I am also in agreement with the Bar Council,
which issued a similarly trenchant statement on 23rd December 2010.[55] The fact
that such huge referral fees are paid, even in low value personal injury claims,
is indicative of the surplus funds which have been sucked into such litigation,
without being used actually to prosecute the cases. An important part of any
reform package must be to cut out middlemen who add no value to the process.

Fixed recoverable costs.[56] I welcome the Government's indication that this is   **8.3**
currently under serious consideration. Professor Fenn has done a great deal of
detailed work which underlies the recommendations in FR chapter 15. It is important to make use of this work whilst the data, on which that chapter is based, are
still fresh. I have not done the further work foreshadowed in FR paras 15.5.30 and
15.6.15, in view of the MoJ's indication that fast track fixed costs were not to be
included in the first stage of the implementation process.

If the Government adopts the package of recommendations for reforming   **8.4**
CFAs, recoverable success fees must of course be removed from the present
matrix of fixed costs and from any future extended matrix of fixed costs. See FR

---

[50] Consultation Paper paras 211–219.
[51] Consultation Paper para 219.
[52] Consultation Paper paras 220–237.
[53] Consultation Paper paras 248–252.
[54] Consultation Paper paras 255–258.
[55] "Referral fees represent an unwarranted and unjustifiable threat to the public interest in the efficient and effective provision of legal services to consumers. They should be prohibited."
[56] Consultation Paper paras 259–260.

chapter 17, which deals with the integration of (a) fast track fixed costs and (b) ending recoverability.

8.5   *Costs management and case management.*[57] The judiciary is taking the lead on these matters, as indicated in para 263 of the Consultation Paper. In addition to the pilots mentioned in that paragraph, the proposals for docketing and specialisation of judges[58] have been the subject of a pilot at the Leeds Court Centre since 1st November 2010. Also work is now being put in hand under the direction of HH Simon Grenfell on the development of standard form case management directions, to be available on line.[59] I express my gratitude to the MoJ and HMCS for the support which they are giving to these various initiatives.

8.6   *Clinical negligence.*[60] I welcome the decision of the NHSLA to obtain independent expert evidence on contested claims at an earlier stage, in accordance with the recommendation made in FR chapter 23. It should also be noted that a recommendation in that chapter for amendments to the Pre-Action Protocol for the Resolution of Clinical Disputes was implemented on 1st October 2010.

8.7   In relation to the late provision by health authorities of medical records required for litigation, I understand from the Information Commissioner that (contrary to the suggestion in para 277 of the Consultation Paper) this is not the kind of matter which his office would handle, or indeed could handle within a realistic time scale.[61] Perhaps, therefore, my recommendation in relation to this aspect might be given further consideration.

8.8   *Intellectual property.*[62] In relation to para 282 of the Consultation Paper, it should be noted that the limit which has been recommended (but not yet implemented) for financial remedies in the Patents County Court is £500,000. In relation to para 283 of the Consultation Paper, a sub-committee of the Patents County Court Users Committee has recently put forward proposals for dealing with small claims and fast track cases in the Patents County Court.[63] The Judicial Steering Group will discuss these proposals with the MoJ.

8.9   *Matters requiring legislation.* In addition to the matters identified in the Consultation Paper or discussed above, the following recommendations will require legislation, if they are to be implemented:[64]

    (i) Abrogation of the common law indemnity principle (a matter about which the Government is not "currently persuaded").

---

[57] Consultation Paper paras 263–264.
[58] Contained in FR chapter 39.
[59] As recommended in FR para 39.5.3.
[60] Discussed in paras 277–280 of the Consultation Paper.
[61] This kind of situation is not one for which the Commissioner's civil monetary powers were intended.
[62] Consultation Paper paras 281–283.
[63] As recommended in FR chapter 24.
[64] See the list of primary legislation required on page 472 of the Final Report.

(ii) Permitting pre-action applications in respect of breaches of pre-action protocols.

(iii) Permitting pre-action costs management by the court.

(iv) Permitting the proposed reconstitution of the Patents County Court.

(v) Amending section 68 (1) of the Senior Courts Act 1981 to enable district judges to sit in the Technology and Construction Court.

If legislation is going to be promoted this year to deal with the main reforms **8.10** arising from the Final Report, it may be sensible for the Bill to include other matters which depend upon primary legislation, in so far as those recommendations are accepted. I doubt that Parliamentary time would be found for a second bill on civil justice reform to pick up residual matters.

Rupert Jackson   14th January 2011

I have read through this Response written by Lord Justice Jackson and I agree with it.

Peter Hurst, Senior Costs Judge   14th January 2011

APPENDIX 1
RUPERT JACKSON'S HANDOUT FOR THE LEGAL ACTION GROUP ANNUAL LECTURE ON 29TH NOVEMBER 2010

Professor Fenn's analysis
Following publication of the Civil Litigation Costs Review Final Report, Professor Fenn has done some further calculations re the cumulative effect of the following reforms:

- End recoverability of success fees and ATE premiums.
- Introduce one way cost shifting
- Increase general damages by 10%.

Professor Fenn has analysed a sample of 63,998 personal injury cases. These range from low value fast track claims to high value multi-track claims. However, the majority of all PI claims and therefore the majority of claims in Professor Fenn's sample are lower value.

It can be seen from Professor Fenn's graphs on the following pages that 61% of claimants will be better off and 39% of claimants will be worse off, if the above reforms are implemented.

My analysis of combining the above measures with other reforms recommended in the Final Report

The next question to consider is what will be the consequence of two further reforms, viz (i) de-regulating success fees and (ii) banning referral fees.

At the moment success fees in PI cases are fixed at the levels set out in CPR Part 45. If those success fees are (a) de-regulated[65] and (b) payable by the clients rather than opposing parties, the effect will be to create competition between solicitors on the basis of which firms charge the lowest success fees. The effect will be to drive down success fees below their present levels.

The Law Society strongly recommends that the payment of referral fees should be banned. At page 31 of its Response to my Final Report the Law Society states:

> "The Law Society's view is that referral fees should not have a place in legal work for the reasons that Jackson LJ indicates in his report. We believe that they add costs and place incentives on solicitors to provide a lower level of service to their clients. The Society believes that they should be prohibited for all involved in the process, including solicitors, other legal service providers and anyone else involved in the claims process. The Society relaxed the rules under pressure from the OFT and remains uncomfortable with that decision."

At the moment a large part of the costs paid to PI claimant solicitors (sometimes more than 50%) are sucked up in referral fees. This is not a sensible proportion of gross income to devote to marketing. The referrers add no discernible value to the claims process. Once solicitors are freed from the burden of paying referral fees, funds will be freed up enabling them to charge lower success fees. Thus the beneficiaries of competition between solicitors will be the injured claimants, rather than referrers (claims management companies, BTE insurers etc) as at present.

In my view, the combined effect of all the proposals in the Final Report will be to drive down success fees to significantly lower levels than those prescribed in CPR Part 45.[66]

Thus if the whole package of recommendations in the Final Report is implemented, far more than 61% of all PI claimants will benefit as a result of the reforms and far fewer than 39% will lose out as a result of the reforms.

Rupert Jackson   29th November 2010

---

[65] Subject to an upper limit of 25% of damages, excluding damages referable to future losses.
[66] See the reasoning in chapter 17 of the Costs Review Final Report.

Gains and Losses arising from the combination of an additional 10% on damages, one way cost shifting, and non-recoverable success fees/ATE premiums[67]

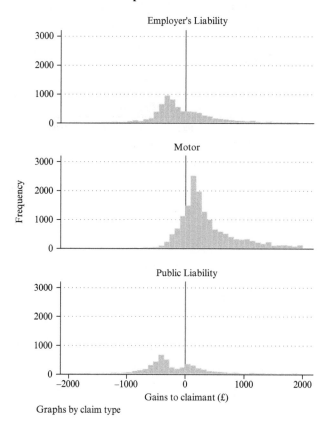

Graphs by claim type

---

[67] ATE premiums for disbursements only (estimated).

Total RTA, EL and PL combined

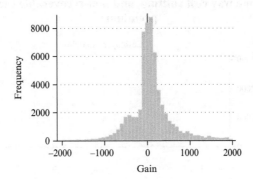

BIBLIOGRAPHY

Books

Andrews, Neil, *Andrews on Civil Processes* (Intersentia, 2013), Vol 1 "Court Proceedings".

Aristotle, *Nicomachaean ethics* (book 5), *Eudemian ethics* (book 6).

Assy, Rabeea, *Injustice in Person* (Oxford University Press, 2015).

Bentham, Jeremy, *Introductory view of the rationale of judicial evidence* (1810).

Bentham, Jeremy, *Principles of judicial procedure* (Tait, 1843).

Betancourt, J. and Crook, J., *ADR, Arbitration and Mediation* (Chartered Institute of Arbitrators, 2014).

Blackstone, Sir William, *Commentaries on the laws of England*, 1st edn (Clarendon Press, 1765).

Blake, S., Browne, J. and Sime, S., *The Jackson ADR Handbook*, 1st edn (Oxford University Press, 2013); 2nd edn (Oxford University Press, 2016).

Cornford, F.M., *Microcosmographia Academica* (Bowes & Bowes, 1908).

Englard, Izhak, *Corrective and distributive justice: from Aristotle to modern times* (Oxford University Press, 2009).

Genn, Dame Hazel, *Judging civil justice – The Hamlyn Lectures, 2008* (Cambridge University Press, 2009).

Hart, H.L.A., *The concept of law*, 2nd edn (Oxford University Press, 1994).

Hibbert, Peter, *The Electronic Evidence and E-disclosure Handbook* (Sweet & Maxwell, 2016).

Hodges, Vogenauer and Tulibacka, *The Costs and Funding of Civil Litigation* (Hart Publishing, 2010).

Holdsworth, Sir William, *A history of English law* (Methuen & Co and Sweet & Maxwell, 1982).

Hurst, P., Middleton, S. and Mallalieu, R., *Costs & Funding following the Civil Justice Reforms: Question & Answers*, 2nd edn (Sweet & Maxwell, 2016) [*"Questions & Answers"*].

Jacob, Sir Jack, *The reform of procedural law* (Sweet & Maxwell, 1982).[1]

Justinian, *Institutes.*

Legg, Michael, *Case Management and Complex Civil Litigation* (Federation Press, 2011).

Lord Justice Jackson (Editor-in-Chief), *The White Book* (Sweet & Maxwell, 2016).

Rawls, John, *A theory of justice* (Oxford University Press, 1972).

Sime, S and French, D, *Blackstone's guide to the civil justice reforms 2013* (Oxford University Press, 2013).

Slater, Laura (ed), *Costs Law: An Expert Guide* (ARK Group, 2016).

---

[1] This contains all of the lectures and papers by Sir Jack Jacob cited in this book.

Sorabji, John, *English civil justice after the Woolf and Jackson reforms* (Cambridge University Press, 2014).

Susskind, Richard and Daniel, *The future of the professions* (Oxford University Press, 2015).

Underwood, Kerry, *Fixed Costs*, 2nd edn (LexisNexis Butterworths, 2006).

Underwood, Kerry, *Qualified One-Way Costs Shifting, Section 57 and Set-off* (Law Abroad Publishers 2016).

Zuckerman, Adrian, *Zuckerman on Civil Procedure: Principles of Practice*, 2nd edn (Sweet & Maxwell, 2006); 3rd edn (Sweet & Maxwell, 2013).

Reports

ACL, *Modernising bills of costs* (2011).

Brooke, Sir Henry, *Should the civil courts be unified?* (Judicial Office, 2008).

CEDR, *Seventh mediation audit* (May 2016).

Civil Justice Council, *The damages-based agreements reform project: drafting and policy issues* (2015).

Civil Justice Review, *Report of the Review Body on Civil Justice* (Cmd 394, 1988).

General Council of the Bar and the Law Society, *Civil Justice on trial – the case for change: Report of the Independent Working Party set up jointly by the General Council of the Bar and the Law Society* (1993).

Law Society, *Review of Civil Litigation Costs Final Report: response by the Law Society* (2010).

Lord Justice Briggs, *Civil Courts Structure Review: Final Report* (July 2016).

Lord Justice Briggs, *Civil Courts Structure Review: Interim Report* (December 2015).

Lord Evershed, *Final Report of the Committee on Supreme Court Practice and Procedure* (1953).

Lord Evershed, *Interim Reports of the Committee on Supreme Court Practice and Procedure* (1949 and 1951).

Lord Woolf, *Final Report on Access to Justice* (HMSO, 1996) (available online).

Lord Woolf, *Interim Report on Access to Justice* (Lord Chancellor's Department, 1995) (available online).

INDEX